Modern Country Cooking

MODERN COUNTRY COOKING

Kitchen Skills and Seasonal Recipes
from Salt Water Farm

ANNEMARIE AHEARN

PHOTOGRAPHS BY KRISTIN TEIG

To my husband, Nathan, who keeps things steady, and our infant daughter, Ana Maeve, who laughs like a drunken sailor.

CONTENTS

As I near forty with the publishing of this book, I am grateful for so much. My cooking school, which is now a decade old and at full enrollment, encompasses so much of what I love and live for in this world. Waking up each morning to the sound of the ocean waves, walking through our vegetable gardens to monitor their growth, harvesting ingredients for the day's recipes, and then collectively cooking and eating with a roomful of students is nothing short of a dream. What started out as a few cooking classes for the local community has become a full-fledged business with more than eighty class offerings a year and an annual student body of about five hundred cooks from across the globe. Over the years, our mission at the school has evolved to meet the needs of its guests in ways that only time and experience can offer. Our focus is empowering our students to cook instinctively and resourcefully and, above all, to have a light heart in the kitchen.

I truly believe that we all have an inherent ability to cook, an instinct that we were born with as human beings. There was a time when, in order to survive, we had to scavenge for food and light a fire to make a meal. I realize that we have evolved since then, and that cooked food is now readily available. But it's important that we trust our instincts, our ability to be resourceful, and in each of our senses. These are the tools of a good home cook. When I look across the kitchen island at the faces of a fresh batch of cooking-school students, I sense their apprehension. Their expression says, "Can I do this? Do I know enough? Will she put me on the spot? What if she finds out that I don't make my own stocks or that I've never made a loaf of bread before?"

It's hard to gauge our skill in the kitchen in a day and age when we are surrounded by media experts telling us or showing us how to do something the "right" way. I do not believe that there is a right way in the kitchen. There is usually an easier way or simply another way of doing something, but never one way. When a student asks me how much buttermilk to add to a biscuit dough, I ask them, what is the desired consistency? When they ask whether an herb is edible, I tell them to take a small bite and tell me what they think of its flavor. When they ask me how long a fresh-made pasta or a piece of fish takes to cook, the answer is always the same: "Until it's done. Touch it, taste it, and you tell me!" It's important to have an intimacy with food. If a cook does not taste food throughout the cooking process, how can they be sure that it is a success? The best home cooks do everything by hand and never send out a dish until they are happy with its texture and flavor.

Cooking in this way requires curiosity and some persistence. A question that I often get at the school is "How did you know you wanted to be a cook?" In my college years, I spent more time preparing for dinner parties than I did studying. After graduation, I moved straight to New York City and got a job fact-checking at *Saveur* magazine. It was there that I realized how much more there was to learn about food. I enrolled in the professional culinary arts program at a New York City culinary school and immediately recognized that working with food was my calling. I also came to understand that becoming a line cook was not my objective. Hours spent perfectly dicing potatoes, peeling roots down to nubs, and setting gelatins into terrines didn't satisfy my appetite for learning new skills. It wasn't fine dining that intrigued me so much as country-cooking skills. Boning a leg of lamb or properly roasting a whole chicken seemed to be a more important and practical skill. In city kitchens, I worked a sous vide machine and made hundreds, maybe thousands of tiny ravioli, but I didn't understand the bigger picture. How do we feed ourselves well at home? There were so many basic cooking skills that I didn't acquire in my years working in the food industry in New York City. It was time to deepen my knowledge of country cooking.

When I moved to Maine, I began to truly understand what it means to be a country cook. First, it means growing some, not necessarily all, of your own food, establishing a deeper connection with the earth and sea that provide us with nutrients. Much of this depends on the seasons and the food that is available. In Maine, much is preserved in the summer and fall to get through the barren months of winter. Second, it means revisiting the basics of food production: making bread, butter, yogurt, stocks, pickles, preserves, pies; cleaning and storing vegetables and herbs from the garden; cleaning mushrooms, filleting fish, butchering poultry; and much more. And then there are what I like to call the country-cooking basics: cooking in and caring for cast iron, reaching for a mortar and pestle rather than a food processor, correctly sharpening and using a knife, and cooking over fire. There is something empowering in understanding and appreciating these skills, feeling a sense of usefulness once they are acquired.

One of my greatest pleasures since moving to coastal Maine is the changing seasons. A day in late April is spent in the greenhouse, wearing a T-shirt and

overalls, my hands in potting soil. In August, I fill a basket with our first harvest of nectarines, eating a few while I pick, the juice running down my chin. In October, my father and I are basting a leg of lamb on a spit that hangs over the coals of a fire, lit hours before. And in January, I'm kneading bread dough and watching a red cardinal nibble on the birdseed that hangs in a feeder attached to the kitchen window. Each of these narratives is distinctly different in feeling, and as the seasons change, so do I. There is renewal in the spring, work in the summer, reflection in the fall, and rest in the winter. Despite being highly evolved creatures in this world, there is something so fundamental, so basic about living in tune with nature, and it makes me feel connected to something much greater than myself. It also reminds me that there is still harmony in this world despite the morning news reports.

Our days and diets are determined by the seasons. In the winter and early spring, my family of three (my husband, Nathan, our daughter, Ana Maeve, and I) live in a restored farmhouse in Camden, Maine. There, I spend much of my days testing recipes, documenting my efforts, and reading the culinary works of others. In the summer and fall months, we move onto my family farm and live in a barn apartment above the cooking school. We wake up to the farm chores and begin preparing for the day's classes. After the cooking school gets out, we often have impromptu barbeques for friends and family and watch as the sunset casts a pink light over the islands in the bay. Much of what we eat in the summer and fall months are leftovers from the cooking school, a sort of cleaning of house. In the evening hours, there's always a fire in the pit surrounded by a few lit faces, taking in the summer air along with a cold beer.

It is these twin aspects of cooking that I share in this book: rustic country-

cooking skills paired with seasonal living and eating. Like my first book, *Full Moon Suppers at Salt Water Farm*, the chapters of this book are divided into months of the year from January through December. As someone who lives in a part of the country where so much in the kitchen is determined by the season at hand, I find that the best way to organize my thoughts is by time of year. Each chapter opens with a portrait of the month, followed by an offering of simple, seasonal recipes (many of which are staples of the Salt Water Farm curriculum). My goal with this book is for you to be inspired by a moment in time—the chill of an October morning, an apple tree heavy with fruit, or a garden bed offering vegetables at their peak—and head straight to the kitchen to celebrate that moment. A country-cooking approach is typically void of recipes. It's an instinct, a gathering of thoughts and resources, rather than the execution of a list of tasks. I encourage you to use these recipes as a loose guide. If you don't have a certain ingredient at your local shop or growing in your garden, there are surely substitutions to be made. There is no such thing as failure in the kitchen if you have faith that there are many paths to success. And if you don't believe me, come cook with us at Salt Water Farm and I'll prove it to you!

In addition to helping you learn more about a country-cooking approach, this book is about pleasing the cook first and the audience second. I find that if the cook is happy, nourished, and inspired by the food in front of her, so are the people that she is feeding. In trying to please the guest first, we naturally make sacrifices that inhibit our ultimate vision in the kitchen. For example, rather than thinking about who's coming to dinner and what they like or don't like, consider first what shines in the market or in your garden that will please everyone. Choose ingredients that are not substitutes for something else but, rather, something worth celebrating that gets you, the cook, excited to roll up your sleeves and start chopping. If a dish calls for something that is not readily available in your region, don't be discouraged; instead, go to your local market with an open mind and a sense of anticipation about what will be freshest, most bountiful, and enticing to you and those consuming the meal. There is no need for discouragement or disappointment in a home kitchen. There is always another path to feeling satisfied and accomplished with the meal you lay down on the table. Indulge your sense of culinary exploration and find comfort in the forgiving nature of home cooking.

AN INTRODUCTION TO MODERN COUNTRY COOKING

If you were to take a cooking class at Salt Water Farm, you would likely hear me say much of what you are about to read. We always start with the basics: my approach to cooking, knife skills, basic techniques, and an overview of the tools necessary to complete the day's tasks. Then, we review each of the recipes and their components, harvest any required herbs or vegetables, and roll up our sleeves to begin cooking. Think of the first section of this book as the introduction to a Salt Water Farm cooking class—a briefing on our mission in the kitchen and helpful tips to successfully execute the recipes here.

THE FUNDAMENTALS

When you tie on an apron and begin meal preparation, use the following section as your metaphorical tool kit, a practical and enjoyable approach to making any meal. Cooking should always be fun, even it's a weeknight and you're simply throwing together a salad. As a general rule of thumb, if you're meeting resistance in the kitchen (whether it's a missing ingredient or a shortage of time), alter your approach and adapt the recipe to suit your needs.

A Country-Cooking Manifesto

The following principles are what define country cooking. They are as relevant today as they have been for hundreds of years. Simplicity, resourcefulness, economy, and instinct are the pillars of good home cooking and are second nature to any seasoned home cook. If you are new to country cooking (as I was ten years ago), stick to these imperatives and you will find satisfaction in the comfort of your own kitchen.

Keep It Simple

It's easy to overdo it in the kitchen. And most of the time, you are better off keeping things simple. This applies both to creating a menu for a full meal and to an individual dish. Rather than spending hours laying out the perfect menu, it's best to develop a general sense of what you'd like to cook and then let availability and the quality of ingredients be your guide. Seasonality plays a large part in quality cooking. Always choose dishes that are seasonally appropriate. If you are married to a particular dish or ingredient and it's not what shines at the market or your local shop, then be flexible and reshape the meal. Let the ingredients speak for themselves and let their flavors guide the dishes they are in. As cooks, we have a misguided impulse to dress up simple foods with extra steps, flavors, and presentations. This often compromises the virtues of the dish. For this reason, I often lean on traditional European preparations, trusting that if people have relied on a recipe for decades, it's doing justice to the individual components of the dish. There is a reason that good-quality fish needs little more than butter and herbs, and a perfectly ripe tomato needs little more than a shake of sea salt, olive oil, and a basil leaf. You will also find that once you've internalized the "simpler is better" mantra, cooking becomes an even greater joy and a far less daunting proposition.

Be Resourceful

It breaks my heart when I see a totally capable cook deflated because they are missing something on the ingredient list of a recipe. A recipe is simply a guide, a printed list of suggestions to aid in the construction of a meal. It's your experience, your love of cooking, and whatever presides on the shelves of your pantry and in the drawers of your refrigerator that make a good meal. Don't let a missing ingredient throw you off. Something so trivial should never stop you in your tracks. Tailor the dish to what you have on hand. And use up the odds and ends from your inventory, if they are appropriate in application. For example, a ¼ cup of leftover sliced almonds can add a nice textural flourish to a green bean salad, some leftover parsley or cilantro can almost always find a home in a salsa verde, and a lonely cup of farro can bulk up some roasted vegetables.

In the same vein, with all the kitchen gadgets available to us these days, it's easy to abandon a recipe because you simply do not have the tools. Generally speaking, we can make do with the tools that we have. The most important kitchen tools are the human senses: sight, smell, taste, sound, and touch. Trust in those and you will make delicious, balanced, and respectable food.

Employ Economy in the Kitchen

In a sense, resourcefulness and economy are one and the same. They both affect your pocketbook and require old-fashioned common sense, born of necessity. Here are a few tips to avoid doling out a significant portion of your paycheck for sustenance. Plan out three meals at a time. Consider how investing in one ingredient (a whole chicken is the best example of this) can aid in the assembly of a number of dishes. Cook grains, beans, and root vegetables in bulk and scatter them in a handful of dishes. This saves you money and time. Choose meals that lend themselves to substitutes. Buy what you can afford. If a recipe calls for halibut steaks but you have sticker shock at the price of halibut, buy haddock instead at generally half to one-third of the price. Learn how to portion and resist the urge to overfeed yourself and others, especially when it comes to protein. A little protein goes a long way. Economy can also mean making a dish with the intention of having leftovers. Again, keep it simple. Sometimes the best meal is a simply cooked protein, a well-dressed salad, and a warm loaf of bread. If you buy something special, such as a nice piece of cheese, cured meat, or chocolate, make it last and store it properly. It is possible to eat extremely well every day and be a frugal cook. It simply takes planning and good common sense.

Trust Your Senses

This is quite a literal directive. For some reason, we don't trust our own natural abilities to smell, taste, touch, and listen to food. Instead, we Google it, ask a pro, or shy away from the process of culinary discovery in defeat. These natural gifts, the senses, are precisely what enable us to measure progress and success in the kitchen. The smell of something burning tells us to turn the heat down or add water to the pan. If a salad dressing tastes flat, it likely needs more acid or salt. If cooked pasta feels or looks dry, it probably just needs a splash of starchy pasta water. And the sizzling sound of meat hitting a hot pan assures us that it will develop a crispy exterior if left alone for a few minutes. These are all sensory assessments of food and, frankly, what draw many of us to the kitchen. Trust that if something looks dry, it is. Or if it tastes like it needs salt, it does. Or if the meat doesn't sizzle in the pan, turn up the heat! Your instincts are your single best set of tools, enabling you to grow as a cook.

Country-Cooking Tools

My favorite food writer of all time, Nigel Slater, emphasizes throughout his writing that a good home cook needs only a few tools to make great meals. He leans heavily on a carbon chef knife, a trusted wok, and just a few other items that he customarily reaches for as mealtime nears. I share this perspective with the one caveat. Having attended culinary school, I noticed that there are few professional tools that would do well by a home cook. Here are what I consider to be the basics.

KNIVES Knives are a very personal tool. I never recommend a particular brand, make, or model because I believe that the best knife for any chef is the one that feels the most natural, almost like an extension of your own body. A good chef's knife is the one that you instinctively reach for every time you make a meal, the one that you learn how to sharpen because it needs it desperately from use. It ought to be the right size for your hand, as we all come in different sizes. It should be cleaned only by hand and thoroughly dried. (While the dishwasher gets it clean, it will not properly dry the knife, and standing water can shorten the knife's life span.) Other than a good, trustworthy, and sharp chef's knife, you really only need a paring knife and a serrated bread knife. That's not to say that other knives (a boning knife or a cleaver, for example) don't have functionality in the kitchen. But you can certainly do without them.

HOW TO HOLD AND USE A KNIFE

Most of us hold a knife incorrectly, about 80 percent of us, in fact. There is a strong tendency to rest your index finger on the top of the blade of the knife, as if pointing at what you are about to cut. Unfortunately, this is not the best or most stable way to hold a knife. The correct way to hold a knife is with your thumb and pointer finger on either side of the blade or by holding the whole handle with your thumb around one side and your remaining four fingers around the other. As home cooks, we have a bad habit of chopping up and down, using the same middle section of blade over and over again, thereby dulling the center of the blade while the top and bottom remain nice and sharp. Knives were intended to be used with longer strokes, applying the full (or nearly full) length of the blade to make cuts. Rock the knife back and forth, moving away from and toward your body. Proper knife skills require a bit of focus and commitment in the beginning. I always say that using a knife correctly is like learning a new language. You have to force yourself to do it in the beginning, even if it doesn't come naturally, but over time you will become a much better cook.

SHARPENING KNIVES In several of our classes, my father demonstrates how to sharpen a knife on a Japanese whetstone. While many of the students carefully observe as he draws the blade across the stone at a very precise angle, I wonder how many of them will go home and attempt to do the same. It is true that a whetstone is the best and most effective way to sharpen a knife at home, but there is a fair bit of skill involved and lots of practice required to hone that skill. As an alternative, you can bring your knives to be professionally sharpened at the local knife store. Generally speaking, mechanical knife sharpeners will do more damage than good by taking more steel off the blade than is necessary. And if you're wondering what that long slender device is that comes in your knife block, it's used for honing the blade, or bringing the edge back to center, rather than sharpening it. Honing is incredibly useful in restoring a well-used knife, but it cannot sharpen a dull blade. As for the serrated blades, they must be sent back to the manufacturer to be properly sharpened.

COOKING IN CAST IRON For those of you who are not comfortable cooking in cast iron, it's time to take the leap. Cast iron is essentially nonstick, it's a wonderful conductor of heat, it will last a lifetime (if properly conditioned . . . we'll get to that in a moment), and it's even good for those with low iron in their blood (according to my doctor). At Salt Water Farm, and in my home kitchen, we cook just about everything in cast iron, and I have made many a convert. In the morning, I fry eggs in a little butter in cast iron, letting the whites develop a golden-brown crust before I flip them with ease. For lunch, I'll fry up some seasonal vegetables such as asparagus or sliced zucchini on high heat in a touch of olive oil, almost as if I were grilling them. Because cast iron can take the heat, it allows them to get some nice color on the outside without overcooking in the middle. On quiet afternoons, I use a cast-iron Dutch oven to make a loaf of bread, the perfect vessel to encourage a good rise and a thick and flavorful crust. And in the evening, I'll sear some pork chops along with rosemary and garlic, making sure to turn the chops at every angle with a set of tongs and hold them to the heat of the cast-iron pan to get nice, crispy fat around the edges. Then the pan goes straight into the oven. As you can see, cast iron has a rightful place in my kitchen, and I'd be a bit lost without it.

To care for it, you must wash it with mild soap and a soft sponge. To dry cast iron, you must place it over the burner until it is bone dry. Moisture will cause rust and shorten the life of your pan. When there is grit and grime, simply add a pinch of kosher salt and some olive oil and rub the salt and oil into the pan with a paper towel. Wipe out the salt and give it a quick rinse. Then cure the pan by placing it on the stove top just until it begins to smoke. Turn off the heat and you're all set until the next meal.

MORTAR AND PESTLE In every class at Salt Water Farm, there is a heavy-duty English-made Milton Brook mortar and pestle on the countertop. We use it for a great deal of things but primarily for grinding up fresh garlic with salt to form the base of salad dressings, marinades, and aiolis. What a mortar and pestle does that a blender cannot is grind garlic into a homogenized paste so that the fairly intense raw flavor of

the garlic is evenly dispersed in the sauce. A blender simply grinds the garlic up into one hundred or so pieces and does not infuse the dressing in the same way. A sauce made in a mortar and pestle has a balanced, nuanced flavor, whereas a sauce made in a blender is a bit less even and lacks the same harmony. We also use a mortar and pestle for building sauces and grinding spices. An aioli or homemade mayonnaise is prepared in the bowl of a mortar, the pestle moving around in quick circles to incorporate a slow and steady stream of olive oil. Many of our rubs for meat are built in a mortar, which allows us to grind up spices, such as whole cumin seed, peppercorns, or caraway, with the force of the pestle before adding in olive oil for lubricant. A fresh herb rub can be ground in a mortar, such as a garlic, sage, and rosemary rub for an autumn pork roast. We also, on occasion, will make a true Italian pesto in a mortar and pestle (where do you think the name *pestle* came from?), grinding the garlic, pine nuts, salt, and basil leaves by hand before introducing the olive oil and Parmesan. And on a less functional note, a mortar makes for a very serious and rustic presentation of a sauce, the implication being that whatever's in the bowl was lovingly ground by hand.

MANDOLINE It took me a few years to realize the potential of this now-essential kitchen tool. Perhaps the tales of shaved fingers and blood-stained cutting boards dissuaded me from adopting a mandoline as a necessary piece of equipment at a cooking school. But its utility outweighed its inherent risk. When presented with the challenging task of an extremely thin cut, I simply did the best I could using a knife. But the results were never uniform or thin enough. It took the right mandoline and lots of practice for me to feel confident in its use. At the cooking school, we have a fairly shredded oven mitt that I offer to students who are afraid to use the mandoline barehanded. They hold the vegetable in their hand with the mitt so that they can slice with less trepidation. The benefits of the mandoline are greater than just a thin and even cut. It opens the door to many more recipes. Even the toughest of vegetables can be eaten raw when sliced thin enough. The perfect example is the Carrot and Beet Salad, which can be found in the August chapter of this book (see page 172). My preferred mandoline is the cheapest variety, purchased at a commercial kitchen store, plastic, and usually a pastel color. They are thirty dollars. The more expensive variety is bulky and cumbersome, and the guard destroys the vegetable it is meant to elegantly slice with its teeth. I find that our tattered oven mitt is a fine safety guard.

A SET OF TONGS While many home cooks employ tongs on occasion, they do not use them nearly enough. In culinary school, we used them for just about everything but stirring (which is generally done with a well-worn wooden spoon). They are used the way hands are used—to pick things up and move them around—and to handle items that are too hot to touch. Tongs are wonderful because, similar to chopsticks, they are gentle on food and hold it together by applying even pressure on both sides. Always keep a set of tongs nearby and form a new habit of reaching for them 90 percent of the time. Anyone in the business will think you are a pro.

CHINOIS AND CAMBRO There are some tools that are commonly found in professional kitchens but seldom found in the home kitchen. I have a short list of professional tools that I think every home cook should have. A chinois is one of them. It's a conical fine-mesh sieve that's used to strain stocks in restaurant kitchens. With a little elbow grease, it allows you to make soups velvety in texture. A chinois adds a bit more work, but it's absolutely worth the effort. The second extremely useful tool is a cambro, which is a large, heavy-gauge plastic container that can take high heat. It is wonderful for holding and cooling large amounts of liquid, whether it be a soup or a stock. Cambros come with well-fitting tops for storage, a must for soup production.

Handling the Heat

While I don't exactly love the quaintness of an oven mitt (its sole purpose is to hold hot things and therefore it deteriorates over time), I am nothing without my fire gloves. These were initially purchased for cooking in our wood-fired oven and open hearth. Their long sleeves shield your forearms from extreme heat, and the gloves can protect your hands from an 800°F pot or a blazing hot oven door that needs to be regularly removed and put back in place. I find myself reaching for them even when I'm removing an item from our regular oven at a mere 350°F. They are more expensive than oven mitts but have the life span of ten of them put together, legitimizing the cost. Another pro tip: when something is hot out of the oven, drape a kitchen towel over the corner of the vessel, letting those in the kitchen know that it's dangerously hot. We find this to be very useful at the cooking school, ensuring that no one gets burned.

Essential Ingredients

As someone who shops for food nearly every day, I keep very little on hand in the kitchen. The following few items are just the bare essentials (salt, olive oil, butter, stock), but understanding their correct applications is fundamental.

SALT I use kosher salt (Morton's) for cooking and flaky sea salt (Maldon) for finishing food. You can throw out your table salts and iodized salts, as they are a thing of the past and do very little for flavor. I actually find that they have a slightly chemical taste to them. Kosher salt is coarse, and if you cook with any regularity, you will know just how much you are holding in your hand or between your fingers before you throw it in the pot. This is a critical skill. There is no need to measure salt. In fact, I'd even go so far as to say that no chef is "worth their salt" if they can't master seasoning. Wink wink.

Now, sea salt or any high-quality salt is not intended for cooking. Its lovely crystallized structure and profound taste of whatever sea left it behind are things to cherish as is, not to alter with heat. Use sea salt on the flesh of a tomato, the yolk of an egg, or the fruit of a melon both to bring out the flavor of these exquisite foods and to add a sharp contrast in texture. I like to keep both kosher salt and sea salt in a little wooden bowl with a cover. This prevents it from dehydrating. But let's be honest—if you cook

as much as I do, between pasta water, salad dressing, and roast chickens, you're going through cups of salt each week, so there is no thought given to its expiration.

SEASON TO TASTE This is arguably the most important skill of all for both professional chefs and home cooks. And often, it is what distinguishes good-tasting food from something that is entirely average. My students are often shocked by the amount of salt that I use when I'm cooking. This doesn't surprise me, as I, like many restaurant chefs, was trained professionally how to use salt to bring out the utmost flavor in food. There is a story that I tell all of my students to best illustrate this point.

When I was in culinary school, our chef instructor asked us to make a very simple pureed vegetable soup. We sweat the onions and garlic and added in some mushrooms, a few squash rounds, and broccoli florets. Then we added enough vegetable stock to cover the vegetables and pureed the contents of the pot with an immersion blender. Each student had a little bowl of salt and was asked to add a pinch of salt and taste the soup. We did, and our instructor said, "Now what do you taste?" We all agreed that we couldn't taste much. So, we continued adding salt until one of the students remarked that they could taste the broccoli. Then another student said, "Now I taste the mushrooms." And sure enough, we all continued to salt our soups until we could taste a true medley of flavors: onions, garlic, squash, mushrooms, and broccoli. The chef said, "Now, add more salt and tell me what you taste." We followed his orders and agreed that all we could taste was salt.

The message here is that there is a point at which salt brings out maximum flavor. Professional chefs know precisely where this threshold exists. It's what makes your burger and fries taste so good, your steak "the best you've ever had," and your pureed summer corn soup sing with flavor. It's also what makes you feel parched when you get home from a fancy restaurant, what makes it hard to sleep comfortably, and what would probably lead to a shorter life if you exclusively ate out at restaurants.

It's important to understand that salt is the key to flavor. The best way to know how much to use in any given dish is to experiment by salting the dish as you go, rather than salting it at the very end. This way, when it comes time to taste a tomato sauce or "season to taste," as they say, you are already 90 percent of the way there. The final pinch is a simple course correction rather than a blind overhaul of flavor. And given that most of you are home cooks, you probably need more salt than you think when you are cooking. So, when I say "a pinch" in this book, I mean half a teaspoon, not a few granules.

OLIVE OIL Many of our students ask what kind of olive oil we use at the cooking school. Each time, I am reminded of Mimma and Franca, guest chefs (and sisters) in their eighties from Tuscany, who came year after year to teach at Salt Water Farm. They would always say, "The olive oil you use in this country is garbage! It doesn't even have an expiration date!" Of course, not everyone is as lucky as they are to have olive trees in their backyards and a press to make fresh oil, but their point remains. Most olive oils we buy at the grocery store lack an expiration date. Lord only knows when they were pressed and how many different olives (and in what condition) were used. They are marketed as "for marinating," "for grilling," or "for salad dressing," but the truth is that most of them, even if they are extra virgin, are of very poor quality. That being said, not everyone can afford to cook with imported olive oils at thirty dollars a bottle. So, we find uses for each.

For cooking, I use the olive oil that my Italian-American mother used, Colavita. It's not because it's the best; it's because it's what I can afford and it's what I'm used to. No doubt, there are better olive oils out there. I also keep a smaller bottle of expensive, imported olive oil for finishing dishes. Another common question is "When do you use a cooking oil and when do you use a finishing oil?" The difference is simple and generally implied in their titles. A cooking oil is a run-of-the-mill oil that is used when heat is applied. A finishing oil is consumed in its raw form, so that you can actually taste it. Once heat is applied to oil, it loses its finer qualities. For instance, you'd never sear a pork chop in finishing oil, and you'd never pour cooking oil over a salad of tomato and basil. Unless, of course, it's all you've got, in which case, go ahead and break the rules. We don't like to get too fussy.

HOMEMADE BUTTER I'm not going to lie, I use a lot of butter in the kitchen. Arguably more than most. And generally speaking, we use Kate's unsalted butter for cooking. It's a local product made in small batches and it tastes wonderfully fresh. It's important to always buy unsalted butter for two reasons: one, you want to control the amount of salt that goes into the food; and two, salt is a preservative and therefore unsalted butter is generally a fresher product. The recipes in this book call for unsalted butter unless specified otherwise.

There is occasion, however, for making butter from scratch. Nothing gives me greater satisfaction as a teacher than watching a grown adult shake cream into butter—that magic moment when the milk solids (butter) separate from the liquids (buttermilk) and the students exclaim, "Look, butter!" with the enthusiasm of a four-year-old child. It really is that simple. Fill a quart-size mason jar with two cups of heavy cream and let it come to room temperature. Secure the lid. Shake, shake, shake until the liquids separate from the solids (it takes about ten minutes). It will look like well-whipped cream just before it splits. You are simply agitating the cream to the point of making butter, mimicking a butter churner. Once the two have spilt, carefully pour the buttermilk into a small jar and reserve for biscuit making or some such project. Then tilt the butter into your hand and gently squeeze the remaining liquid from the butter. I like to do this under cold running water, so that the heat of my hands doesn't start to melt the butter. Now slide the fresh butter into a small crock and sprinkle with sea salt. There is no better compliment to bread, fresh out of the oven.

HOMEMADE STOCKS Despite my insistence that all of my students make stock from scratch, there was a time, in my days as a personal chef in New York City, when I would buy boxed stock. Yes, I admit it, I used the boxed stuff. (This is possibly one of the best examples of how my style of cooking has changed since leaving the city and moving to the country.) Having homemade stock on hand opens two doors for a home cook: infinite possibility in terms of weekly meal preparation, and better-quality of food. A quart of chicken stock or vegetable stock in the refrigerator or the freezer encourages meals such as Braised Chicken Thighs with Leeks and Cream (page 120) or Congee with Poached Chicken and Ginger (page 66) on a cold winter's day. A box of store-bought stock in the pantry provides far less incentive for making soups, sauces, and stews than homemade stock.

There is simply no comparison between a boxed stock and one made from scratch at home. A simmering stock on the stove smells rich and fulfilling, like medicine for anything from a chill to a full-on cold. Historically, stock was a means of stretching protein and promoting economy in the kitchen. There is no excuse for tossing out a chicken carcass (raw or cooked) when it can go into a pot, alongside vegetable scraps and herbs. A traditional chicken stock begins with one or two onions, two or three carrots, and two or three stalks of celery. Roughly chop the vegetables and toss them into a large pot along with the chicken carcass. A rustic stock will include the skins of the onions, the greens of the carrots (if cleaned), and the leaves of the celery. Add a few sprigs of thyme, rosemary, oregano, parsley, and a bay leaf or two. Drop a dozen peppercorns in the pot and fill the pot with water. How much water, you ask? It depends on the purpose of your stock. If you are making a soup, for instance, you will need about one and a half cups of liquid per portion. If you are making a sauce, you will need far less, only about a half cup of liquid per person. Naturally, less liquid will make for a richer stock. Make sure, however, that you cover the bird with water no matter what the application to promote cooking it completely. You can always reduce it if it's more than you need. Then bring the stock to a boil and skim any foam that rises to the top with a slotted spoon. (These are impurities in the vegetables and chicken; they will not hurt you, but you want a clear stock.) Now reduce the stock to a simmer and let it cook for one hour. Turn off the heat and let the stock cool a bit. Strain it, store in mason jars, and place in the fridge for soup later in the week. You could also freeze it, but I'd suggest you pack it in a cambro or restaurant-grade quart containers rather than glass (see Country-Cooking Tools, page 9).

For years, I told my students to skip the task of making beef stock due to its inefficiencies, while I insisted that no chicken, rabbit, or fish carcass be discarded but rather thrown in a pot with aromatics and

herbs, covered with water, and simmered until deeply flavorful. My memories of making beef stock were in culinary school, when we roasted enormous beef bones in a commercial oven at 500°F, slathered them with tomato paste, and roasted them further, then loaded them into two-foot-tall stockpots to simmer for most of the day. This seemed like an impossible task for a home cook. And then one day, I decided to make a French onion soup and I just couldn't bring myself to buy beef stock in a box. I asked the local butcher for five pounds of beef bones (cut into manageable four- to six-inch lengths) and headed home skeptical that this could possibly be worth it. Well, I was sorely mistaken. The dark brown stock that resulted from just a few hours of roasting and simmering was divine, loaded with flavor from the marrow of the bones, and made for the best French soup I've ever had. If you're still not up for the task, a good butcher will make beef stock that can be found in the freezer. Don't balk at the price; it's worth every penny.

Here's another thing: sometimes just water can be used in place of stock. When you are making a stew, which often involves many of the same ingredients as stock (onions, celery, carrots, herbs, peppercorns), and you've browned the meat in the pan, establishing loads of flavor, there really is no need for stock. Water will do just fine. And from a purist/ethical standpoint, a dish need not be composed of more than one animal (with certain notable exceptions in culinary traditions; see the Tortellini in Brodo recipe, page 238, in the December chapter). As for vegetable stock, say, for instance, you are making a pureed vegetable soup. You can either simply use water or make a stock from one of the by-products of the soup, such as cornstalks, the tops of leeks, or carrot greens.

Stock is something to be made when you have vegetable and meat scraps in the fridge or left over from a meal and you want to put them to use before they wither away. Once strained, stock can live in the refrigerator if you have a plan for it later in the week or in the freezer if you are not quite ready to put it to use. And if a recipe calls for stock, and you have some, then by all means use it. But if you don't, water is a fine substitute for stock, if properly seasoned, and much more economical.

Fundamental Techniques

In culinary school, the following techniques were required skills, and understanding when and how to employ each was mandatory. Sometimes I take this base knowledge for granted, as it is so engrained in my approach to cooking. While country cooking is generally a looser format than professional cooking, acquiring these skills gives any home cook a leg up in the kitchen.

SMALL/MEDIUM/LARGE DICE It is rare that I use traditional French cooking techniques in my lectures at the cooking school, as our ethos embraces more of a rustic, nonfussy approach. But to reject the notion that French cooking technique (and its precision) has its rightful place in the kitchen is to be ignorant to the extreme. (More on that in another book.) And so, I ask for your patience here as I define the difference between small, medium, and large dice. It's helpful as a reference point to understand the difference in size between these cuts, depending on what you are trying to accomplish. Small dice are ¼-inch cubes, medium dice are ½-inch cubes, and large dice are ¾-inch cubes. I'll never forget how many bags of Idaho potatoes we wasted in culinary school in an effort to master our knife skills. While precision isn't necessary for the home cook, it helps to promote dependable results.

SWEATING VS. SAUTÉING Sweating, as it implies, means to draw liquid out of whatever you are cooking and contain that liquid, allowing the ingredients to cook in their own juice. You might sweat onions, for example, in a little fat such as olive oil or butter to start a soup or a sauce. A pinch of salt will help accelerate this process, as it draws liquid out from within the onions. Sweating is typically done over medium-low heat. Sautéing is very similar; however, there is no need for a cover and you let the liquid evaporate once it has been released. If you are sautéing mushrooms, for instance, you would sit them in a little butter in a sauté pan and cook them until they release their liquid. Then that liquid will evaporate, and the mushrooms will take on a bit of color and be soft throughout. This is typically done over medium heat.

BLANCHING Blanching is a technique that is frequently used in restaurants, as it allows chefs to parboil vegetables to perfection, getting them ready for service. It requires a big pot of well-salted boiling water, a set of tongs, a slotted spoon or a spider, and an ice bath. The vegetable is added to the pot of water while at a rolling boil, cooked quickly to perfection, removed the instant that it is tender, and shocked in cold water to prevent additional cooking and often to maintain its original color, so it doesn't gray. If the water is properly salted (again, way more salt than you think), the vegetable will be expertly cooked and flavored, a welcome addition to any dish or served simply. Blanching is a highly effective technique when you are serving large groups and hoping to knock off tasks ahead of time. For efficiency, I'll often blanch vegetables in my pasta water before the noodles go in.

GRILLING Because much of our curriculum takes place during months with warm weather, I try to incorporate a bit of grilling in each class. Out on the patio, we have a monster grill and we use it for everything from smoking meat and fish to grilling up vegetables to charring bread rubbed with oil and garlic. There are a few basic techniques to consider when standing in front of the grill. Number one, be prepared. You should always have a set of tongs and a landing vessel for the finished foods, such as a platter or a sheet pan. Number two, don't crowd the grill. You want its contents to get nice grill marks and cook independently. Number three, resist the urge to touch the food. We have a terrible instinct to peel the food (think burger) off the grill before it is ready. Let it sit until it has formed a crust and then it will release itself from the grill. You should only have to turn it one time. Most items need to be grilled for a slightly longer stretch on the first side than they do on the second. For ribs, for example, you would grill them for ten to fifteen minutes on the first side and then five to ten on the second.

COOKING OVER FIRE There is something primal about cooking over fire. Perhaps it's the knowledge that people have been doing it for millennia and that while we have evolved as a species (and now use gas to cook instead of fire), we can still do as our

ancestors did: light a wood fire and make a meal over it. If cooking over fire is new to you, you'll find that it's quite challenging to manage heat effectively. But once you get the hang of it, the results can be stunning and deeply gratifying. (Think of that fish you caught and fried up over a campfire when you were a child.)

The first step in building a fire is selecting wood. You only want to cook over hardwood. Hardwoods include oak (which takes the longest to cure), ash (which burns the hottest and dries the fastest), birch, and maple. Softwoods, such as pine and spruce, are resinous and should not be used for cooking. Always build a fire from the top down. Let me explain. Have you ever tried to start a fire with a big log and a piece of paper and struggled to get it to take? Wood burns when it gets hot enough to release a gas, which is what actually burns. Because it's so hard to heat up a large block of wood, we use kindling, smaller pieces that heat up more quickly. Most effective is to use shavings, followed by kindling, followed by large pieces of wood. The shavings ignite easily, providing enough heat to cause the kindling to give off gas that will ignite, and the kindling in turn gives off an increasing amount of heat, bringing the logs to a sufficient temperature to release gas. This method is highly effective when starting with a top-down fire: larger pieces on bottom, kindling in the middle, and wood shavings on top.

Managing a wood oven is specific to its design. We will typically make a fire in the front of the oven, just below the flue. Once the fire has a sustaining heat and embers have begun to form, we move the fire to the back of the oven, allowing room for pots, pans, and pizzas in the front. The floor of the oven is often called the deck, and it's important to allow ten minutes after the fire has been moved to use the oven, as the deck can be up to 1,000°F, which is a little too hot for cooking properly. It takes time and patience to develop confidence when cooking over fire. The only way to learn is by burning a thing or two. Water is your friend. It cools a pan that is too hot and slows the cooking process. Steam will cook things very quickly in a closed pot at a high temperature, almost like a pressure cooker. Keep in mind that cast iron is the best material to cook in, as it can handle extremely hot temperatures.

ESTABLISHING A FLAVOR BASE

While working in a basement kitchen in Paris, I learned that the most crucial ingredient in establishing flavor is time. So many of the soups, stews, and sauces were made a day ahead of time so that they could sit overnight, allowing the flavors to meld. I always suggest to my students that they make the base for soups, stews, and sauces early in the day or the day before, so that they can fortify in flavor.

TOASTING SPICES Culinary cultures all over the world are in the habit of toasting spices as a natural step in the cooking process. It brings out the aroma of the spice and better establishes its flavor in the dish. You must be careful, though, as it is very easy to burn spices, which will add an undesirable bitterness to the food. Just as you are beginning to smell the spice open up, either take it off the heat or add liquid to the pan.

TOASTING NUTS There is no room for error in this endeavor. Nuts will burn in a matter of minutes, even seconds. There are two methods for toasting nuts: on a sheet pan in the oven, or in a pan over the stove. I prefer the oven, as I find it more forgiving and more consistent. Set the oven to 350°F. Any higher and the nuts will cook too quickly. Place them on a sheet pan and, most important, set a timer. For most nuts, eight to ten minutes will do. They will likely need another couple of minutes, but it's important to check them in case they are done. When you check them, do not leave the oven's side. Wait patiently, otherwise you will forget them and your precious and generally costly nuts will be suitable only for the compost pile. If you choose to toast the nuts in a pan, use a heavy-bottomed pan such as cast iron and set them over medium-low heat. Move them around constantly with a wooden spoon and never leave them. When nuts are finished toasting, they need to be moved immediately to a cool surface or bowl. If they are left in the pan, they will continue to cook and likely burn.

USING ALCOHOL IN COOKING I will often find use for a splash of wine left over from last night's dinner in meal preparation, or even better, crack open a new bottle "for cooking" and drink the rest. As someone who drinks good but not great wines (I've never had the budget for them), cooking wine and drinking wine are interchangeable. I don't believe that it is necessary to have cheap wine sitting around just for cooking. More to the point, when using alcohol in food, it's critical that you cook off the alcohol itself so that your food does not taste boozy. For example, if you were making a braised chicken dish and the recipe called for one cup of white wine, you would turn off the burner (alcohol will ignite), add the wine, turn the burner back on, and let the white wine cook down for a few minutes before moving on to the next step. If the dish smells of alcohol, it needs to be further cooked down. (You can tell by wafting the steam toward your nose. If the steam makes your nose hairs tingle and feels like you could get drunk just smelling it, it needs more time.) Now, if you are using hard alcohol and wine, such as cognac or Pernod, add the liquor first, let it reduce, then add the wine, let it reduce, and finally add the water or stock. Always cook first with the strongest spirit and then work your way down the line.

MAKING MOTHER SAUCES Rarely do I retrieve a recipe for a French mother sauce from my days as a culinary student, but in some instances, there is simply no substitute. Béchamel is one of the five mother sauces—along with espagnole, velouté, sauce tomate, and hollandaise—and its role is to thicken and add rich flavor to a dish. It starts with a roux: a bit of melted butter in the pan and an equal amount of flour whisked in to form a paste. A roux can be cooked lightly, for just a minute

or two or until golden, even brownish (as is the case in a gumbo, for example). The roux is then thinned out with milk to make a sauce and salted to taste. At this stage, a variety of ingredients can be added to further flavor the sauce, such as thyme, nutmeg, or grated cheese. Béchamel is typically a binding sauce, bringing together the main ingredients of the dish into blissful and decadent harmony.

HOW TO THICKEN SAUCES There are a number of ways to thicken a sauce. If you are applying heat, flour, cornstarch, or arrowroot can be used as thickening agents. Generally speaking, these agents are gradually whisked and dispersed into hot liquid and aid in thickening the sauce, soup, base, or whatever dish needs more viscosity. However, a cold sauce, such as a salsa verde or romesco, employs other types of thickeners such as ground bread, nuts, or even hard-boiled eggs. These ingredients can add a rustic texture to a sauce that would otherwise be too thin to spread. A good-quality nut, roasted and ground, adds a depth of flavor and offers a richness that comes from the oils produced by the nut. Hard-boiled eggs can add a creaminess to a sauce. And a thick slice of bread, fried in olive oil until golden brown and then pulsed through a food processor, brings a toothsome texture to a romesco.

SOURCING AND STORING FOOD

One of my greatest pleasures is shopping for food. I love the ritual of visiting the local specialty shops (the baker, butcher, cheesemaker) and my Saturday morning cruise through the farmer's market in our charming seaside town. We live in a remote area, so I occasionally shop for spices, dried beans, and ethnic ingredients online, as Maine has its limitations in terms of sourcing and there are some wonderful suppliers across the country.

It's true what they say: food is only as good as the ingredients that go into it. There are no shortcuts here. Good ingredients equal good food. There are, however, ways to maintain the quality of those ingredients if you are not cooking them the same day that you are buying them. Here are some helpful tips that will ensure that your groceries are properly stored until mealtime.

How to Shop at the Farmer's Market

When visiting the farmer's market, there are some weekly essentials that always find their way into my deep woven basket. A local sausage and cured-meat maker offers a small selection of products, and after a few samples on an empty stomach, it's easy to come away with something cured and something fresh. When seasonal ingredients are incorporated into the grind, it's fun to build meals around the flavors. For example, a garlic confit sausage finds its way into a cassoulet, or a Moroccan sausage is the inspiration for a fragrant tagine.

The dairy category holds a big place in both my heart and my stomach. On any given trip to the market, I'll head home with a soft and a hard cheese as well as a quart of yogurt. My sister and I always joke that a nice piece of cheese either is reserved for a special occasion or is a personal cheese that no one is to touch without asking. For as long as I can remember, my father kept a sharp cheddar in the fridge and cut off a good hunk about an hour before we ate dinner to hold himself over. This snack was always accompanied by a sipping alcohol: usually tequila. I wish I could say that I don't do the same.

The next stop at the market is the local bread maker. While there is great joy in making loaves at home, it's fun to try a true baker's product, such as a sourdough made with corn stock and corn kernels or a rye made with locally grown wheat. Bakers are passionate folks, up early in the morning, tinkering hydration ratios with a careful eye on "the rise." It's easy to get carried away in a conversation about sourdough with a true enthusiast, and before you know it, you'll have two weeks' worth of bread in your basket, as opposed to the intended one.

In Maine the mushroom table is always something to behold, although the better (and much more economical) source is in the woods, with the aid of a local and well-informed forager. Mushrooms can be expensive, so you need to carefully consider their application. They are as precious as meat, in terms of their value, so make a plan for them before putting them on the scale.

And finally, there are the many bins piled high with vegetables. A good policy is to buy what you can carry, which in my case is quite a bit. You can't buy too many vegetables. And if one of the purveyors makes pickles or jams, give them a try. The ultimate goal of farmer's market shopping is to have a small assortment of items that you can put out for friends before a meal, locally made snacks to nibble on throughout the week, and the components of a few simple meals.

How to Select Fruits and Vegetables

Whether at the farmer's market or the grocery store, shopping is as important a skill as food preparation when it comes to good home cooking. We all need to be educated on how to tell if something is ripe, fresh, or worth buying. For fruits and vegetables, I find as a general rule that the heavier the item is (compared to its lot . . . apples to apples, if you will), the better and fresher it is, simply because it retains more water, which will evaporate over time. A heavy melon, pineapple, apple, or ear of corn is

generally a better one. And of course, with fruit, there is smell and firmness. Your nose tells you if something is ripe, as it will smell sweet and of the fruit. Too sweet means it's about to rot. And if a fruit is hard as a rock, it has been picked too early and will never develop the flavor that nature intended. Of course, there are exceptions, such as apples, which are meant to be firm when harvested.

Storing Fresh Ingredients

If you're going to purchase quality produce, it's critical that your vegetables, greens, and herbs are properly stored. They will be as beautiful midweek as they were at the Saturday farmer's market, and the extra dollars committed to local produce will feel like money well spent. For example, a bunch of crimson beets with dark green and red leaves will last for nearly a week when stored in an airtight ziplock bag with a sheet of paper towel to absorb excess moisture. The greens will not wilt into a sad pile in the refrigerator, no longer useful to a meal. A head of red leaf lettuce needs to be washed in cold water, fully dried, and stored, same as the beets, in a ziplock with a sheet of paper towel, or else the leaves will wilt and make for a disappointing salad. Good cooks make a habit to properly store food when it arrives in the kitchen. Here are some basic guidelines for food storage.

- All greens, herbs, and vegetables must be washed and then stored in an airtight ziplock bag with a sheet or two of paper towel to absorb excess liquid.

- All salad greens must be washed in cold water, dried, and then stored in an airtight ziplock bag with a sheet or two of paper towel to absorb excess liquid. They will last up to three days without suffering.

- Mushrooms must be cleaned with a damp paper towel, then stored in a paper bag in the refrigerator. They should not be submerged in water, as they lose their fragrance.

- Meat should be removed from any plastic, patted dry with paper towels, and placed in a glass vessel. If you are using it that day, it can be covered with a sheet of parchment. If it needs to be stored longer, you can cover it in plastic wrap.

- Fish fillets and whole fish should always receive a cold bath and then be properly dried (ridding them of any bacteria). Cover them in plastic.

- Shellfish will suffocate, die, and begin to decay if it doesn't have access to air. When it makes its way into the kitchen, give it a good cold rinse (do not submerge it in fresh water, as they will drown) and place in a colander in the fridge. It does not need to be covered.

Storing Cured Meat and Soft Cheeses

If you're going to spend a lot of money on well-aged meats and cheeses, it's important that you store them properly. Sliced meats like prosciutto and serrano ham should be sliced within twenty-four to thirty-six hours of consumption and packed airtight, as they tend to dry out in the refrigerator. Cheese is a living, breathing ingredient and does not like to be contained in plastic. It will do much better wrapped in parchment paper and placed in a part of the refrigerator that is not too chilly. Also, when slicing cheese, you always want to get a cross section, if possible, instead of starting at the point and working your way to the rind. This approach offers a better representation of the cheese as a whole, as it tends to age more toward the edge or the rind.

Sourcing Spices

Many of us have spices kicking around in the cupboard that are as old as time. Part of the reason for this is that Western cooking does not use a ton of spice; rather, we reach for spices only when we are making something exotic or a pot of chili. As a result, we use small quantities with little frequency, and because each jar costs a fair amount, we sacrifice their freshness for having them around. But we lose *so* much flavor. Old spices really aren't worth keeping around. Anything older than a year (and ideally six months) should get tossed. It's no wonder they're not top of mind. What can be done about this? Well, it's all about habits. I challenge you to get to know a single spice or a spice mixture. Use it on a variety of things—on yogurt, on your morning eggs, or on a sheet pan of roasted vegetables. Get familiar with its effect on food, on the taste that it leaves on your tongue. If you like it, you are apt to use it in much greater quantities and, consequently, spice up your repertoire a bit. Two great examples are harissa and za'atar—both Middle Eastern spices that I can't help but reach for when I'm roasting a chicken and vegetables or frying up eggs.

Sometimes Sourcing Means Growing

Most of us have the ability to grow herbs, whether it's in a raised bed in the backyard or in a pot on a windowsill. I really encourage my students to do this, because even a few rosemary clippings thrown into a soup pot brings an element of natural cultivation into your life, connecting your spirit to green growth. At Salt Water Farm, we grow about a hundred varieties of fruits, vegetables, and herbs. Through observation and trial and error, I have learned so much about growing food over the past ten years. I feel like there is a lifetime's worth of knowledge in the science and art of gardening. One of the beautiful aspects of growing is how quickly your culinary palate expands. There are so many herbs and edible flowers that we incorporate into dishes at Salt Water Farm that cannot be found at the market or the grocery store. Another point we impress upon our students is the importance of good soil. Our compost at Salt Water Farm

Cooking School promotes rich, nutritious soil for future crops. Finally, the routine harvest of produce in our gardens often offers impetus for cooking projects that would not have otherwise been considered. These are all good reasons to grow some, not necessarily all, of your own food.

Perennial Herbs

Whether you live in the city and have a little window box or in the country with access to an entire garden, perennial herbs are a worthwhile investment. Even a single pot of parsley, sage, rosemary, and thyme will save you countless trips to the grocery store, and no more will you have browned packages of herbs in the drawers of your refrigerator that are no longer of use. In the context of an outdoor garden, most perennials will come back year after year, providing ample kitchen herbs. Just a couple snips will satisfy most recipes, leaving behind a beautiful and fragrant plant.

When you harvest herbs, you want to snip from the top, where the leaves are more tender because they represent newer growth. A plant stores much of its energy in its base: the root system and the lower portion of the plant. Snipping from the top minimally disrupts the plant, allowing it to regenerate growth. In the heat of the summer, herbs tend to flower due to the hot temperatures. If you pinch the tips before this happens, you will lengthen the life cycle of the plant and have more herbs to harvest. Most herbs, such as chives and basil, will continue to grow throughout the season if properly pruned.

Edible Flowers

Many of my students are shocked when I tell them that some varieties of daylilies, sunflowers, and calendulas are edible, and all of them make beautiful garnishes for several of our dishes at Salt Water Farm. In some of our classes, borage flowers (small purple stars) make the sweetest garnish for a green gazpacho or pureed corn soup. Sunflower petals plucked away from their seeded disk add visual appeal to an heirloom tomato salad. Daylily pods (before they bloom) are sautéed in a little butter and finished with sea salt, then tossed into a green bean salad. When a plant is nearing the end of its life cycle, it often puts off a flower, which for some is a sign to pull it from the ground. But I encourage you to taste the flower before moving it to the compost pile. An arugula flower is peppery and bright and adds interest to a salad of greens. A broccoli flower (typically yellow) makes a beautiful addition to a frittata. And even purple thyme flowers scattered across a focaccia, drizzled with oil, and baked result in a crispy herbal topping. There is a world of flavors in our backyards with which we have yet to acquaint ourselves.

Selectively Clearing Out the Garden

Once the cooking school is closed for the season and most of the vegetables have found their way onto a menu, we must put the farm to bed. First, I make a final round, pulling any remaining carrots, beets, and onions out from the soil, cleaning them, and storing them in the refrigerator. There is always kale and Swiss chard that can be harvested, right up until the frost. I pull all of the now fruitless tomato plants, tomatillos, and husk cherries. Broccoli and brussels sprouts are hearty and can be left until November because they can withstand a mild frost. We typically do not till and turn the beds until the spring. Garlic must be planted before the ground freezes; we plant a German hard-neck variety. The compost pile is finished off with the remains of the garden and left to decompose until the spring, when it is distributed among the beds. It's a full circle, my friends.

Making Compost

We compost everything from meat to shells to vegetable scraps to paper towels at Salt Water Farm. Are there critters late at night, predictably fighting over the scraps? Absolutely! But thankfully, the compost pile is far enough away from the house that it doesn't seem to bother us. I love that we have so little garbage as a result. Between recycling and composting, there is next to nothing in the pail. Throughout our garden are lovely oyster, clam, and mussel shells, which will eventually break down and offer lots of minerals to our soil. Compost should be equal parts nitrogen (wet material) and carbon (dry material). If it's too heavy in nitrogen, it gets stinky and too hot. If it's too heavy in carbon, it doesn't get hot enough. A good mix of the two should break down in about a year in Maine (less than that in warmer climates), making fantastic, nutritious soil for all of our vegetable beds. After all, your food is only as good as the soil in which it grows.

ON FOWL, MEAT, AND SEAFOOD

The art of whole animal butchery is in large part a lost practice in this country as is the skill of filleting whole fish. Seek out butcher shops and fishmongers that receive whole animals and butcher them from head to tail. This process encourages the butcher or fishmonger to make the most of the animal, selling not just traditional cuts but also off cuts and by-products such as ground meat, bacon, brined meat, and lard, and in the case of whole fish, racks (heads and vertebrae) for making stock, cheeks, and roe. There is substantial knowledge and skill in good butchery, whether it be a whole halibut or half a pig. Ethically raised meat is worth the additional cost. And to justify that cost, a cook must know how to employ certain cuts of meat through proper cooking technique. I tell my students that we should be paying twice as much for half as much meat. Not only would this help to solve health issues in the United States among the human population, it would significantly reduce our carbon footprint. Likewise, find a local fisherman or fishmonger who not only will have the freshest catch but can also advise you on the sustainability and health of local fisheries.

Chicken and Duck

Did you know that most butcher shops that provide local meats hardly mark up organic chickens because their margins are so thin? As a meat supplier, they are expected to have whole, locally sourced poultry, but there is very little money in carrying them. The general public still thinks that a chicken over fifteen dollars is a rip-off. On a Monday afternoon, I get a text from my husband (who's generously running errands for me) that reads, "Still want me to buy a whole chicken . . . it's 30 dollars?!?!" Yes! I reply, I will make three meals out of that bird and feed a dozen people, bringing the per person cost down to three dollars at most. And sure enough, I did. Here's how.

Monday, I butchered the bird, made a stock with the bones, and poached the legs, thighs, and breasts in half of the stock. That evening, I invited over ten of my girlfriends and made a big, beautiful salad of spinach, apples, walnuts, feta, and thinly sliced chicken breast (I used only one of the two breasts for this meal). I served it with a homemade lemon and herb focaccia, which was plenty of food, even after several stiff little Manhattans. Tuesday, I made coconut congee with the other breast and a dozen cups of stock for my husband and me. Wednesday, I sautéed some leeks and mushrooms and added the remainder of the stock and the dark meat and slowly simmered it until the chicken was so tender, it literally fell off the bone. We ate it with beluga lentils, and spooned the sauce over the top for a fairly extravagant lunch. So, it seems I've made a case for the thirty-dollar chicken, with no further evidence needed. Not to mention, the bird was raised on a farm just

a few miles from the butcher shop by folks who take excellent care of their flock.

I am a *huge* proponent of buying a whole bird rather than its parts. This does require the basic knowledge of butchery, which I lay out for you in the next tip. It also promotes an old-fashioned sense of economy in the kitchen. Typically, the various applications for the bird lend themselves to a number of meals, as I describe above. Buying the whole bird also exposes you to a wider range of dishes and flavors. For instance, if you buy a whole duck when the recipe calls for legs, you widen your array of possibilities. From this duck, you will procure dark meat, ideally braised in its own fat and served with tender beans; breast meat, which can be sliced thinly and served over greens for a decadent lunch; duck stock, which is perfect for a rich soup or sauce to be served over leftovers; and finally, duck fat, which can be used to cook eggs for breakfast, to spread on toast with a bit of salt and chopped rosemary, or to start your next soup or stew. To buy just a leg or just a breast would be depriving yourself of an abundance of additional culinary opportunities and future endeavors in the kitchen. Not to mention a number of very delicious meals.

HOW TO CUT UP A CHICKEN There is a true art to butchery, one that relies heavily on observation rather than brute force. A chicken is the perfect example of this, as you don't need to cut through a single bone in order to break it down into pieces. It's important that, as you make your cuts, you separate and pull apart the legs from the breasts and the wings from the shoulder bones to see where the joints come together and will more easily come apart. There are natural separations that need only the tip of

the knife to release. Do the animal justice: study its anatomy before each cut. Try not to leave too much meat behind, paying careful attention to where the meat meets the bone. Follow the natural lines of the anatomy; they will guide you.

Sit the bird, breast side up and neck at 12 o'clock, on a clean cutting board. Sharpen a boning knife or simply use your favorite sharpened chef's knife. Stretch the skin across the breast; you want to maintain the skin's position on the meat, as you will likely sear it for ultimate crispness. Pull the leg away from the breast and make a long cut between the leg and the breast, through the skin. Turn the bird upside down, hold it by the leg, and dislocate the hip bone, revealing the ball of the socket. Cut along the spine on the backside of the chicken and wiggle your knife along the interior of the hip bone. Detach the leg and set aside. Do the same on the other side. If you so choose, you can separate the thigh from the drumstick. Place the leg skin side down and make a cut at the joint to reveal the connection. There is a fatty line that delineates the natural separation between the drumstick and thigh. Follow this line with your knife, cutting between the two.

Reset the chicken, breast side up, and feel around the base of the wing bone. Cut through the skin around the base of the wing, full circle, to see how it is connected, and carefully move the tip of your knife between the wing and the shoulder bones. Remove the wing and set it aside. Do the same on the other side.

Reset the chicken, breast side up. Stretch the skin once more over the breasts. Feel along the breast bone to locate it. Make one long decisive cut straight down, through the skin and along one side of the breast bone, all the way to the tail of the bird. With your fingers, pull the meat away from the ribs and gently make small cuts with the tip of the knife, pulling the breast meat off the rib cage. Be mindful of the wishbone at the head end of the bird, under which a good amount of meat is hiding. Once detached, set the breast aside. Do the same on the other side. Save the carcass for stock! There is still lots of meat, fat, and flavor in the carcass.

Of course, there are variations on this. Some like to keep the wing attached to the breast. This can be done by separating the wing from the wishbone and the neck,

but not the rib cage. Other ways to butcher a chicken include spatchcocking, which essentially means removing the spine with a pair of cutting shears and flattening the bird. It's a far less elegant way of butchering a bird, but it is a practical skill for grilling, as it promotes even cooking. I should also mention that in some countries chicken breasts are butchered without removal from the rib cage and are still essentially on the bone. You don't see this very often in the United States, but it's a wonderful approach for slow, low cooking, grilling, or roasting. Meat is always better on the bone. (More on that later.)

Animals with Four Legs

We are lucky in my town to have a wonderful local butcher shop that regularly gets in whole animals. When the time comes for cooking a protein, I will call ahead and ask the butcher what has come in recently and what cut he would advise based on the size of the animal, the number of guests that I'm feeding, and my desired cooking technique. It's always helpful to keep an open mind, because the more flexibility you have as the cook, the more likely you are to get a good product. In this instance, the butcher suggested I get shoulder steaks, which are sizable and cook like a rib eye or a strip steak. There are essentially two ways to cook red meat. If you are dealing with a tougher cut, such as the leg or the neck, you would cook it at a lower temperature for a longer period of time to tenderize the meat. If you have a tender cut, you can cook it at a higher temperature and go for a blush color at the center (pull it out of the oven at about 125°F). Tougher cuts are the harder-working muscles and need a little coaxing to tenderize. That being said, they often have better marbling and more fat, and let's not forget that fat is the broker of flavor. Most serious cooks will always opt for a cut of meat that is well marbled over a cut that is lean and tender. We are one of the only countries that has put such a high price on the tenderloin of a pig, cow, or lamb. Americans love boneless, skinless, fatless meat. Sadly, these are the three greatest virtues of meat from a culinary perspective.

In fact, a great deal of meat in this country is sold cut away from the bone for convenience's sake, but there are so many reasons to keep the bone in. Animal bones contain albumen and collagen, which are converted into gelatin when cooked long and slow, increasing viscosity and trapping molecules in which flavor resides. Whether it's a chicken, a piece of fish, a leg of lamb, or an oxtail, protein always benefits from staying on the bone. Even in quick cooking, such as a pork chop or a rib eye, the meat closest to the bone always has the most flavor. Ribs are perhaps the best example of this.

Seafood

As Americans, we are twice as likely to order fish at a restaurant than we are to cook it at home. Why, you ask? I believe that the answer is twofold. One, we are buying old fish. (More on that in a moment.) Two, we are overcooking it. These two acts in combination result in a lingering fish smell in the house that is generally unpleasant. It doesn't have to be this way, my friends. Here are a few tips on buying fresher fish: understand the industry. There are generally two big fish deliveries a week. Go shopping with an open mind. Instead of asking if something is fresh (naturally, the fishmonger will say yes to that question regardless of the truth), ask which day the halibut or the cod came in, demonstrating that you have reasonable expectations as a customer and that you are informed. The best fish markets have wholesale accounts and are going through a lot of product. If you see chefs from your local restaurants buying fish there, it's a good sign. Buy only what's plentiful. If there are just a few fillets or a half dozen mussels left in the case,

inquire if there is more in the back. If not, they have probably been there for a while. Your nose tells you everything. If something smells fishy, it's old. It's that simple. If it's white fish you are after, buy what's plentiful and fresh looking, even if the recipe calls for a different, less fresh-looking fish. Now, on the subject of cooking fish. I've never cooked any piece of fish for more than ten minutes (at 400°F), not even if I'm feeding twenty people and I have a whole tray of portioned fillets. Fish is extremely delicate and cooks (and overcooks) quickly. The minute you see the fish emit little white flecks of coagulated protein, take the fish out of the oven immediately. Otherwise, you will end up with a tray full of water and overdone fish. The water or liquid on the tray belongs in the fish. I always say, pull the fish a couple minutes before it's done and cover it with foil to allow the residual heat to finish the cooking process. If you have to pop it back in the oven, so be it, but *do not overcook it*. Now that I've said my piece on sourcing and cooking fish, here are a few more specific notes on ingredients that are pertinent to the recipes in this book.

ON THE SUBJECT OF CLAMS Shellfish has the unique ability to hide its freshness, with very few visual indicators as to how long it's been out of water. You can tell when the most recent delivery came in based on the volume of shellfish in the case, as with fish fillets. If all you see are a dozen lonely clams left in the fish tub, inquire whether there are more in the back. If not, choose a different type of shellfish for dinner. What clams can't hide is their smell. If they smell at all off, or fishy, it's a dead giveaway that they aren't fresh. When the fishmonger hands you a bag of mussels or clams, always give them a sniff to be sure it's what you want.

When you get home, clean the clams. This may involve a little scrub brush or simply a cold-water bath depending on how dirty they are. Clams can be quite sandy and there are a number of approaches to ridding them of sand before they go in the pot. Some folks swear by letting them sit in a bath of cold water and cornmeal for twenty to thirty minutes. Others suggest a cold and salty bath. I find that it really depends on the clam; some are sandy and some are not. Usually I'll cook them in a separate pot and leave the sand behind before introducing them to a dish.

ON THE SUBJECT OF MUSSELS

Determining whether or not a mussel is fresh can be easily accomplished with a sniff test. They are not good at concealing age. An old bag of mussels from the grocery store will likely smell fishy and is not worth buying. However, mussels from your local fish shop can be wonderfully fresh and essentially scent free. Another good way to gauge the freshness of a mussel is to see how easily it responds to you. Fresh mussels will be slightly opened when you buy them and bring them home, in an effort to breathe and explore their new environment. If you tap them on a hard surface, such as the countertop, they will close quickly to protect themselves. This is a good sign. I usually tap any slightly open mussel, and if it doesn't close in a matter of seconds, it's not fresh and possibly not alive. Those are to be discarded. Mussels attach themselves to ropes and one another with a wiry net called a beard. Beards need to be removed before the mussels are cooked. Simply pull them from the shells. A really fresh mussel will close and pull back a bit, making it harder to remove the beard. To clean mussels, rinse them in very cold water. Fresh mussels are firm and delicious. Those that have been out of water for more than a few days will stink up a room when cooked. Again, your nose tells you everything you need to know. Don't hesitate to return them or take a hard pass if they don't smell fresh.

ON THE SUBJECT OF SQUID Fishing for squid in Maine is an activity reserved for those in the know. When squid are running, word spreads across town. All of a sudden, the harbor docks are flooded with locals dipping their squid rigs into the salty sea in hopes that a mighty squid will wrap itself around the thorny bait and wriggle about, out of the water, and into the fresh air. Cleaning a squid is not for the faint of heart. First, the beak needs to be removed and the guts pulled out of the body. Then, with a sharp knife, the dark membrane must be pulled from the body; all the while the

ink bleeds onto the dock or cutting board if you've made it into the kitchen. Typically, fish stores will do this for you and sell cleaned bodies and tentacles. Your only job then is to cut the body into ringlets, keeping in mind that the tentacles will shrink the minute that they hit heat.

Now a note on cooking squid. Squid is tender only when cooked very quickly over high heat or for a long time over low heat. For instance, if you are grilling it or frying it in a pan, cook squid over a hot flame for two to three minutes, no more. And do not crowd the pan or the grill. Alternatively, you can cook squid slowly in a sauce or in liquid for two to three hours and it will turn tender over time. Anything in-between will have the texture of a rubber band.

A LESSON ON LOBSTER Some consider the lobster to be a specialty of Maine, summer eating at its finest. Others consider the crustacean to be a bottom-feeding cockroach of the sea. I stand somewhere in the middle. Sitting at a picnic table in the sun, breathing in the salty ocean air while cracking into the brilliant red shell of lobster to devour the sweet and succulent meat dipped in warmed butter is an experience worth the traffic on Route 1 and the twenty-five-dollar cost. But for those of us who live in Maine, lobster is a messy affair, which we inevitably must clean up, and in truth, not all lobsters are tasty. Some of them are too tough or don't have quite enough meat in their shells or are soiled in tamale (the green liver of the lobster, which some consider to be a delicacy and others waste) or roe (the red eggs of the female lobsters). And you never really know what you're going to get until you crack into it. So, again . . . I'm on the fence when it comes to lobster, but for those that aren't, for those who come all the way to the far northern reaches of this country to sink their teeth into a tail or suck the meat from the legs, here are a few tips.

Lobsters are unique in that they are one of the only sea creatures kept alive in tanks until they are purchased. This should make determining whether they are fresh quite easy. When the fishmonger lifts them out of the tank, are they lively and energetic, flapping their tails in protest, their little legs fluttering for something steady to grip? Or are they limp and sluggish, apathetic about their transport? A lively lobster is a fresh lobster. As for storage, they really do need to be eaten the day they are lifted out of the water. A hard-shell will last longer than a soft-shell, but only hours longer, not days. One option is to parboil them right away and then use the meat the following day if you are trying to do your shopping ahead of time. It's also a good excuse to get the mess of shelling lobsters out of the way before you endeavor to make a dish with their meat. Unless, of course, you are simply steaming them, in which case I prefer to do it only in the summer and outdoors. I'll leave that to your discretion though.

Steam them, don't boil them. Steam is hotter than boiling water. It also is a lot faster to boil an inch of water than a whole pot. And don't forget, you need a snug-fitting cover to properly steam anything, and you don't want the lobsters to crawl out!

Salt the water like the sea. If you're beside the ocean, the best water to cook lobsters in is actual salt water, but if that's a tall order (no need to transport seawater more than a hundred feet, folks), just salt the heck out of the water with kosher salt until it literally tastes like the ocean when you dip your finger in it and touch your tongue.

Don't overcook the lobsters. Especially if you are simply trying to get the meat out of the shells for some other culinary application. A soft-shell cooks for about eight minutes and a hard-shell no longer than ten. You will have tough meat if you allow them to cook any longer.

Use the body for stock. There are about two ounces of meat in the body, but breaking into it is messy business. I like to use the bodies to make a stock, rather than tear into them. But I leave this entirely up to you.

Buying Frozen Meat and Fish

So often I am asked if meat and fish are worth buying frozen. Especially local meat and fish, as harvests can be seasonal. The answer is yes, so long as it is properly thawed. And while the temptation is ever so strong to place meat or fish on the countertop to thaw it, as you may have forgotten the day before to take your dinner out of the freezer, the protein will suffer. Meat and fish need to be thawed in the refrigerator. For how long, you ask? It depends on the weight of the protein. A pork shoulder can take two full days to properly thaw; a big chicken, a day and a half; and a pound of fish fillets, eight hours. But what you can't do, under any circumstances, is place a pound of ground meat wrapped in plastic into hot water to hurry things up. And you certainly can't bake a frozen chicken breast at 375°F and expect anything other than a dried-out exterior and a raw interior. Plan ahead and thaw protein in the fridge.

Cooking Meat and Fish

Many of our students are intimidated by cooking meat and fish. This is understandable, as it is easy to overcook protein (such as a pork chop, making it tough) or undercook it (such as a beef stew with cubes of tough chuck). Cooking methods should be determined by the cut. Tough cuts require longer cooking over low heat, and tender cuts, shorter cooking over high heat. There are a number of ways to approach cooking meat and fish, some more forgiving than others. Here are the basic techniques to choose from, some in combination.

SMOKING MEAT AND FISH At Salt Water Farm, we do most of our smoking either on the grill or in a little smokehouse that my sister built down by the water's edge. There are many ways to jury-rig a smoker by building a small wood fire and piping the smoke into a chamber where the meat awaits its fumes. Smoke, like salt and heat, draws the water out of meat and fish, essentially cooking it. Typically we reserve the prunings from our apple trees for this purpose because the smoke from burning applewood lends lovely flavor to food. Our grill has a separate chamber for a wood fire, and when it's closed, the smoke drifts into the main grilling compartment, slowly

smoking whatever we've got going on the grill. It's a really fun way to flavor a fillet of fish or a rack of ribs, but it takes some time. In this instance, we are more or less cold smoking the protein, as there is no direct contact with the heat source. Over time, cold smoking will fully preserve, or remove most of the liquid content of, a fillet of fish or a meat product. When we started experimenting with smoke, we partially cooked the protein over low heat, while simultaneously smoking it. This saved us some time, given that our classes are only four hours in duration. This is considered hot smoking and results in a very different product. Hot smoking is intended for a rack of ribs or a fillet of salmon that you are eating right off the grill.

BRINING MEAT To brine or not to brine? It's a technique that I came around to late as a chef and on a selective basis, as it requires a fair amount of planning. A brine is a salt and water solution that breaks down the proteins in meat over time. It absolutely makes a difference in both tenderizing meat and flavoring it. It is particularly effective for lean cuts of meat, which tend to dry out easily. Corned beef is a fantastic example of a brined meat. It calls for pickling spices such as mustard seeds, allspice, juniper, a cup of salt, and a half cup of sugar, all brought to a boil (so that sugar and salt dissolve) and then cooled. The meat, brisket in this case, is then submerged in the brine for ten days. When the time comes to cook it, the meat is rinsed of the brine and only then does it make its way to the pot. It requires a fair amount of preparation, but the results are stellar. Brining is a useful tool for imparting flavor in all kinds of protein: a garlic and rosemary brine for pork chops, a buttermilk and tarragon brine for chicken breasts, or a lemon zest and bay brine for halibut steaks. It's also a basic skill that we should all have tucked under our belts as competent home cooks.

BROWNING MEAT Whether you are browning meat in a cast-iron pan or on the grill, there are a few rules that enable you to get a nice golden-brown crust. Number one, make sure that your meat is close to room temperature (not cold out of the fridge), which promotes even cooking. Number two, dry it off. You can use a paper towel or a kitchen towel meant soon for the wash. Wet meat

won't brown, it will steam, which is not what we are after here. Next, season your meat just before it goes onto the grill and brush it with a little oil or put a splash of oil in the pan. You want to start with a hot pan or hot grill. When the meat touches the iron, you should hear a good sizzle. Now for the most important part: don't touch it! We have a nervous tendency to try to pick up meat before it's ready for fear that we will burn the meat or that it will stick to the pan or the grill. All protein (and most vegetables for that matter) will form a crust and seal in the juices, after which you can pick them up with ease and flip them with a set of tongs. This usually takes at least five minutes, if not more. There is no need to tear anything off the pan. Patience here is an absolute virtue. Once you've flipped the meat, let it cook on the other side for half the amount of time it cooked on the first side. And finally, let it rest. When you let meat rest, the juices settle, making for the right texture when you cut into it. Otherwise, the texture is a bit off. Also keep in mind that when you take meat off the pan, out of the oven, or off the grill, it will continue to cook from residual heat. So, pull it off of or away from the heat 10 to 15 degrees below what you are ultimately shooting for.

BRAISING MEAT Typically, a braise begins with browning a tough cut of meat, as described above. Browning often does not cook the meat through but rather establishes a crust on the outside. Once browned, the meat is removed from the pan and reserved. Mirepoix is introduced to the pan, releasing the fond, or the flavorful bits left behind from the meat, into the vegetables. The pan is then deglazed with a liquid of some sort, often wine or stock, and then the meat is reintroduced to the pan. As a general rule, more stock is added to the pot, just enough to not quite cover the meat. The braise is then moved into a 325°F oven for at least two and a half hours to tenderize the meat. This process allows the sauce to reduce, the meat to become soft and full of flavor, and the dish to coalesce. But it cannot be rushed! Only braise when you have the time.

POACHING When feeding large groups, I find that cooking your meat in liquid keeps it nice and moist for long periods of time and saves you the stress of carving a roast or checking internal temperatures just as dinner is going down on the table. It also ensures that the protein will not dry out. Poaching is a wonderful technique that gently cooks a chicken breast or a fillet of fish and allows it to stay supremely moist, as it is sitting in liquid. It also gives you the opportunity to infuse flavor such as wine, stock, and herbs as a sort of warm marinade. It's best to portion your meat or fish ahead of time and prepare your poaching liquid. Then turn on your oven to 325°F, submerge the fish or meat into the liquid, and let it poach for just enough time to cook through. It should take no more than twenty minutes for fish and thirty minutes for meat.

Simple Gravies

Gravy is a decadent pan sauce that can be made in less than fifteen minutes. What it requires is good drippings or a deep meaty flavor of some kind. This can be achieved by browning meat, which leaves behind a fond. While it doesn't look like much, fond is where the flavor resides. It's critical that after the meat has been browned, the fond is liberated from the pan by deglazing it. This can be done with a splash of any liquid: sherry, cognac, wine, stock, or water. What you have built is an instant, richly flavored base for a sauce. If making a gravy, the next step is to melt a generous amount of butter in the pan and an equal amount of flour and whisk fervently, to create a roux. Flour toasts quickly when exposed to direct heat, so once the roux is even in texture and begins to take on a little color, it's time to whisk in your liquid to thin it out. Chicken stock is generally great for this purpose. Any good French sauce is finished off with a cold cube of butter to give it a little weight and shine and seasoned to taste with kosher salt and pepper. Often there will already be a touch of salt from the browning of the meat, so just a bit more is needed. You may be thinking along the Thanksgiving lines, "What about the drippings?" If a bird has been roasted in the oven (rather than browned on the stovetop), the drippings from the pan are the fortifier of flavor. You would skip browning meat and begin straightaway with building a roux in the pan and adding the drippings.

COOKING VEGETABLES, BEANS, AND EGGS

Vegetables have taken center stage over the past few years at Salt Water Farm. Not only because we grow them but because I increasingly find that students rely less on meat, fish, and starch for sustenance and more on vegetables—especially when it comes to everyday cooking and cooking for one's own health or that of their family. Local agriculture has come a long way in the past couple of decades, allowing us access to hundreds of varieties of fruits, vegetables, and herbs. A trip to Whole Foods today would have felt like a walk through the Garden of Eden in the 1990s. Each of our classes at the cooking school prepares at least three entirely vegetarian dishes. This is not to appease those who don't eat meat or fish but rather because a balanced meal should be comprised of predominately veggies. And in the wintertime, we find that properly cooked beans make a wonderful addition of protein in just about any meal.

Preparing Seasonal Ingredients

Every ingredient has its own unique figure and form and, therefore, its own little guide on how to source and prepare it. Below are a handful of tips on specific ingredients, all of which you will find in the recipes of this book.

CUTTING AND CLEANING LEEKS

There are a number of varieties of leeks, each with distinct characteristics. Some have very short and stout tender white bases (beside the root) and much of the green is tough and must be removed. Others have longer, tender whites and generate a greater yield. After a leek is harvested and cures, it dries out, making it tougher throughout. To determine where to cut the tender white part of the leek from the tougher green part, simply cut across the leek where the color fades from light green to dark. If you meet significant resistance, slide the knife closer to the root. Eventually, you will find a sweet spot. Sometimes, this sweet spot is surprisingly close to the root, which means the leek has been out of the ground for quite some time. Leeks also tend to accumulate soil in their layers. When you cut a leek into rounds, it is often helpful to completely submerge the chopped leeks in water to rid them of dirt and then strain them before use.

HOW TO TREAT RHUBARB

Those of us who live in northern climates are particularly fond of rhubarb, as it's the first of the northern seasonal pie fillings to make an appearance each year. Rhubarb's tartness can be tamed only with shocking amounts of sugar, which is a late spring treat for some and a recipe for heartburn for others. Some folks like to peel off the outer skin with a knife, exposing the tender stalks. I find that heat breaks down this layer, making peeling unnecessary. That being said, remove the ends if they are dry and the skin only if it looks like it has suffered. Rhubarb can be chopped into any size, as it completely breaks down in the oven.

HOW TO HANDLE ASPARAGUS

You can always tell how fresh asparagus is with a simple snap. When you break an asparagus stalk in two, it will snap at the point of acceptable freshness. If it snaps close to the head, the spear has likely been in storage for some time and begun to dry out. If it snaps close to the base, you have a very fresh stalk of asparagus on your hands. You can also tell how fresh the plant is by examining the heads. If they are tight and intact, they are fresh. If they are frayed, they are likely old. When we harvest asparagus at the farm, they need no snapping, as they are fresh right down to the base. Don't skip this step with store-bought asparagus—the base can often be tough and unappetizing. To properly store asparagus spears, first remove the rubber band that holds them together and sink the base of the spears into a bowl with water. Then find a place for them to stand upright in the refrigerator. They will last quite a bit longer in water than they will out of it.

HANDLING STINGING NETTLES

While many steer clear of stinging nettles (and for good reason), they are a pleasure to eat. Nettles are a vitamin-rich, foraged spring green and can be found at your local farmer's market or in a nearby field. They must be handled carefully with a set of gloves until they are cooked, after which they become docile to the touch. To cook them, simply blanch them quickly in a big pot of well-salted water and then shock them in ice water to retain their beautiful color. Then they can be added to any dish that would call for other spring greens such as arugula, mustard greens, spinach, or Asian greens.

THE LIFE CYCLE OF GARLIC

Every fall we plant garlic at the farm, and it is one of the first green foods to pop through the soil come spring. Garlic is truly the crop that keeps on giving. In the late spring, when the garlic plant is still immature and just before the head splits into cloves, farmers will often thin the crop, producing a small harvest of what is known as green garlic. As it turns out, green garlic has its own unique flavor and can be used in place of garlic in the kitchen. It is a bit milder and less spicy. As you would a leek, you use only the white and light greens of the plant, as the darker green tops can be too tough for cooking. That being said, they add a lovely flavor to stocks. In May we harvest a few bulbs before they form cloves and use them as green garlic to flavor pestos and salsas. The base of the plant has a light green color and a milder flavor. We generally slice it thin, the way you would a scallion. By June the scapes (the top of the plant) begin to curl up and circle round. We harvest them (they store marvelously in a ziplock bag for up to two weeks) and throw a few on the grill with a little olive oil and salt. They make a spectacular garnish for grilled meats and fish. By late July the heads are fully established and can be pulled up for more traditional uses. We often let the whole garlic plant dry in the greenhouse and then lop off the stem once it is cured and ready for storage inside.

HOW TO CUT AN AVOCADO This is a task best left till the last minute. Simply cut around the pit lengthwise. Twist one half away from the pit (if the avocado is ripe, one side will fall off the pit) and with a large knife, whack the blade into the pit. Twist the pit with the knife dug into it and it should release from the flesh, leaving you two pitless avocado halves. With a paring knife, hold the avocado half in the palm on your hand and carefully cut the flesh into long half-inch strips without puncturing the skin of the avocado (and therefore your hand). Make the same cuts perpendicular to the first slices. Use a spoon to release the flesh from the skin and you should have a pile of more or less similarly sized avocado hunks.

CHOPPING CILANTRO THE MEXICAN WAY For years, I gingerly picked the soft cilantro leaves from their stems just before using them as garnish or adding them to a blender to make salsa. Until one day, when a Mexican cook peered over my shoulder and said, "Qué haces?" or "What are you doing?" As it turns out, I had been wasting my time. The upper stems of the cilantro plant are not only edible, they lend their own unique flavor to whatever they go into. (The lower third of the stems can be removed, as they tend to

be tougher and stringier.) Cilantro needs only to be cleaned, dried, and roughly chopped, stem and all.

DRYING FRESH HERBS While this may seem like a skillful project, it's the simplest task in the world. If you have an abundance of herbs in the garden and you know that you are not going to get through them come the first frost, harvest a few handfuls of each, remove the leaves from the stems, and allow them to dry on a large flat rack over a sheet pan. Don't crowd the rack. Once they have fully dried (about one week), pack them up in a labeled mason jar. You can make a mixture of herbs that you regularly reach for or keep them separate. I like to make a savory mix of rosemary, thyme, and oregano, and we also make a za'atar with sumac, oregano, thyme, and salt. We grow lots of lavender on the farm and we always make sure to dry a jar or two, adding a floral summer scent to winter dishes.

INFUSED VINEGARS When we find ourselves with an excess of herbs, we often steep them in vinegar to preserve their flavor. One of my favorite vinegars to make is chive flower vinegar. We pack sterilized mason jars with purple chive flowers and pour apple cider vinegar over them right up to the top. We let the chives macerate in the vinegar for about a week, which lends a wonderful and mild onion flavor, and then strain the vinegar and discard the flowers. It's my preferred vinegar to use in salad dressing throughout the summertime. We do the same with tarragon and rosemary a little later in the season.

ON TOMATOES The first ripe tomato is a true gift—the perfect balance of sweet and acid, juicy and firm. You would think you could eat tomatoes endlessly with nothing more than a knife and pinches of sea salt. But come September, after countless tomato salads, sandwiches, soups, and the like, you are hard-pressed to come up with yet another creative tomato dish. The solution is this: a huge roasting pan (we call them hotel pans in the food biz) full of the remaining tomato harvest, regardless of the variety. It starts with an earnest harvest, every last cherry tomato and all of the big boys. Even if the fruit is a bit bruised, or dare I say a touch nibbled on by some sort of garden critter, the better part can still be used toward making a tomato sauce. Once all of the tomatoes have been collected, they need to be washed and roughly chopped. Then toss them into a very large hotel pan and add a generous amount of salt, maybe a tablespoon, the peeled cloves of one head of garlic, a tablespoon of sugar, a couple fragrant bay leaves, a few shakes of red pepper flakes, and several glugs of olive oil. Now place the pan in an oven set to 325°F for three to four hours. The sauce should reduce and become sticky around the edges. You can even add a cup or two of red wine for a richer flavor. Now you have a tomato sauce that can be frozen, canned, or simply eaten tout de suite with a couple pounds of pasta and a dozen friends.

Alternatively, you can put up tomatoes whole. Bring a large pot of water to a boil. Score the base of each tomato with a little X. Drop the tomatoes in the boiling water for thirty seconds, or until the peel comes off with ease. Once you have peeled all of the tomatoes, fill a tea kettle and bring it to a boil. Add two tablespoons lemon juice to each of the sterilized mason jars that you are using. Then fill with tomatoes right up to the brim of the jar, pushing them down so they are a snug fit. Pour boiling water over the tomatoes, leaving about one inch of head space. Screw on the lid fairly tight. Now process the jars by submerging them in boiling water for fifteen minutes, or until the lid naturally indents. Dry them off. Double-check to make sure all the lids are tightly fastened. Store in a cool, dry place until you are ready to use them.

Usually by about mid-January, I have used up all of my jarred tomatoes and homemade tomato sauce from the previous growing season's harvest. I am reduced to buying canned tomatoes from the store. But not any canned tomato will do. There are a number of brands out there when it comes to canned tomatoes. I can say, unequivocally, that buying imported San Marzano tomatoes is worth the extra couple of bucks. They are sweet (not acid) and soft (not stiff) and make for the best sauces. That being said, if you don't have access to these canned beauties, there are some things you can do to mimic them with domestic varieties. Number one, a teaspoonful of sugar simulates the natural sweetness of the San Marzano. Number two, give them more time in the pan on a slightly lower heat. They

need it to coax flavor. And number three, a bit more salt will fool the palate. One of my favorite things to do in the kitchen is sink my (clean) hands into a glass bowl full of San Marzanos and break them up by squeezing them through my fingers, being careful to keep them fully submerged or else I've ruined my shirt. It also means that I can't be bothered to do anything else . . . similar in nature to peeling beets.

Cooking Vegetables

While there are a million ways to cook vegetables, not all of them have stellar results. It's important that you select the best cooking method for each vegetable in order to set yourself up for success. Some ingredients don't like to be rushed; others like it hot and fast. Understanding when something is done cooking is a critical skill in any kitchen. Use the following tips as a guide for the vegetables that are included in the recipes of this book.

FORK TENDER This is a term that is often referenced when blanching vegetables. The idea is that if you push a fork through a vegetable (a potato, a turnip, a broccoli stem), the fork meets with some resistance and does not go sliding through. At this stage, the vegetables are perfectly cooked for both correct texture and easy digestion and need to be cooled quickly to prevent additional cooking. Knowing precisely when a vegetable is fork tender is a certain sign of a competent home cook. If you are unsure, test for doneness frequently, rather than guessing.

SWEATING ONIONS I can't emphasize enough the importance of this step in the cooking process. Onions and their traditional companions, carrots and celery (traditionally known as mirepoix), are the base of flavor for soups, stocks, sauces, and more. Many home cooks turn up the heat a little too high and cook the onions too quickly, burning the outer edges, while the middle remains raw. When this happens, you have lost the fight in the first round, making whatever you are cooking taste bitter and pungent. Onions need finesse. They are the king of flavor and must be treated as royalty. So, start them in some fat in a cold pan. Add a pinch of salt. Salt pulls the liquid

out of the onion, allowing it to cook gently in its own natural juice. Turn the heat to medium low and cover the pot. Once the fat melts, move the onions around in it, coating them. Now place the cover back on the pot and check the onions every five minutes, pushing them around each time. Once they are translucent (no whites!), you can move on to the next step. This can happen with other vegetables in the pot, but let the onions be your guide.

COOKING MUSHROOMS When presented with a glut of mushrooms, there are a number of ways to handle them. They can be preserved in vinegar and olive oil, or they can be cooked. While there are many ways to cook mushrooms, it's important to understand their basic composition. Mushrooms are made of mostly water. When you cook them, you must choose whether you want the water to remain in the mushroom and for them to stay more or less the same size, or whether you want the mushrooms to release their liquid and shrink in size. A beautiful golden and crisp fried mushroom that retains its original size is achieved in a large frying pan over high heat with a good amount of butter. It's crucial that you don't crowd the pan, or else the mushrooms will steam, release liquid, and shrink. If you're adding mushrooms to a soup or stew, you would take a different approach. Cook the mushrooms over a medium-low heat with a cover on the pan, steaming the mushrooms. They will eventually release their liquid, which will deeply flavor whatever dish they are in. You can further enrich the dish by allowing the mushroom liquid to evaporate, condensing the flavor. Of course, there are other cooking methods, such as grilling or cooking them over wood fire, but those would fall in the "hot and fast" category, leaving the moisture within the mushroom.

ROASTING VEGETABLES I prefer to roast vegetables at a high temperature, 400°F or higher, to establish a nice crisp around the edges. This means watching the oven carefully, giving the tray a good shake from time to time to loosen things up, and occasionally rotating the tray to promote even cooking. It is also very important not to crowd the pan, otherwise its contents will steam. Always make sure to use plenty of olive oil and salt when roasting vegetables. There's a reason the potato chip industry has been so successful.

COOKING WITH GREENS AND GREEN HERBS Most greens need minimal cooking. High heat instantly wilts them, whether in liquid or in a dry, hot pan with a bit of oil. While so much preparation can be done ahead of time, adding greens to a soup or a sauce should always be done at the last minute in order for them to retain their bright color and unique flavor. A handful of baby kale, arugula, or spinach adds a beautiful accent to a simple soup. A pile of roughly chopped parsley and basil tossed into a pasta sauce at the last minute gives it a wonderful lift in terms of visual appeal and flavor.

Come September, greens such as Swiss chard, kale, and collards have matured and have a tougher, more fibrous nature. They can no longer be eaten raw like they can when they are small and tender earlier in the season. As a result, they need to be treated differently. There are a number of approaches. The first is to cook them down, which tenderizes them. A little garlic and olive oil, a few minutes in a cast-iron pan, and kale is delicious and easily digestible. Depending on the level of maturity of Swiss chard, you can cut the ribs out and chop them up along with a small yellow onion and sauté them in a pan before adding the greens, as they take a bit longer to soften. Then add some salt, a small pour of vinegar, and let the greens cook down for no more than five minutes. Collards can handle longer cooking and benefit from some animal fat, perhaps a little bacon and some apple cider vinegar.

The next approach is to break down the greens in their raw form with a pungent acidic dressing. The perfect example of this is a garlic and lemon-based dressing. The acid in the lemon helps to break down the fibrous nature of the kale. Dress the greens about thirty minutes before they are consumed to let the acid do its thing.

The final approach is to massage the greens. The combination of heat and pressure will also break down the toughness in the greens. Again, this works best with kale. Massaging Swiss chard or collards won't have a desirable outcome.

Making Salads Magic

It's not hard to turn a simple salad into a deeply flavorful and gorgeous ensemble of seasonal ingredients, thoughtfully dressed and beautifully plated. It just requires a few extra steps. We should crave a salad with every meal and give it the extra five minutes of attention that it deserves. Here are some notes on how to enhance your salads at home.

SALTING GREENS My students are always a little surprised to see me salting the greens of a salad before dressing it. Which is funny, because I never worked in a professional kitchen where they didn't salt the greens before dressing the salad, as it brings tremendous flavor to lettuces. Conversely, once they are coated in a thin layer of oil, the salt tends not to stick but rather to fall to the bottom of the bowl. *Always* salt your greens before dressing them. Even if it's not lettuce season, your salad will sing with flavor.

SALAD DRESSINGS Building a salad dressing is arguably one of the top-ten most important culinary skills. A good dressing shines a light on lettuces, greens, and crisp vegetables, which we could all use more of in our diets. It starts with a mortar and pestle, at least in the Salt Water Farm kitchen. We smash a clove of garlic with a big pinch of coarse kosher salt and grind it into a paste. Then we add the acid component of the salad dressing, usually the juice and zest of a lemon, a tablespoon of Dijon mustard, and a splash of vinegar. Then we add a spoonful of honey to balance the acidity and double the quantity of dressing with oil. (A good dressing is about 50 percent oil and 50 percent acid base.) After a little more salt and pepper, the dressing is ready for the next important step: resting at room temperature. The flavors need time to meld. I will usually store it in a mason jar and give it a good shake just before it's time to dress the salad.

DRESSING AND PLATING A SALAD There is nothing more tragic than an over- or underdressed salad. Here's the trick: After you've salted the greens, add a few tablespoons of dressing to the salad bowl and gently toss with a set of tongs. Plate the salad with the tongs in a tower, giving height to the greenery. (No one likes a flat salad, as its decidedly less dramatic.) Now use a tablespoon to add an additional spoonful of dressing around the outside of the tower of greens. This allows the person eating the salad to "draw in" additional dressing if desired without the burden of an overly dressed leaf.

What about Beans?

Over the past few years, I have fallen in love with cooking beans. In the wintertime, I cook loads of dried beans, coaxing flavor from them over hours of monitored cooking alongside onions, garlic, and bay. In the summer and fall, we cook with fresh, local beans such as borlotti, favas, and scarlet runner beans, which are the ultimate treat and a sort of agricultural delicacy. Here's a quick guide on cooking dried and fresh beans and where to source them.

SOURCING BEANS For years, I bought dried beans locally from bulk bins or packaged at the grocery store. And then a friend gifted me four beautifully colored bags of dried beans from a now very well-known company called Rancho Gordo, all with fantastic and unfamiliar names like Eye of the Goat and Domingo Rojo. I was instantly made a convert. The quality of the beans from Rancho Gordo was exceptional, almost like another food group. They held their form after hours of cooking and were creamy and full of flavor. They did wonders for just about every dish that I put them in. The difference between the store-bought beans and these was clear: they were much fresher and simply better grown. This is an instance of how, from time to time, sourcing online can improve the quality of your meals.

COOKING DRY BEANS Before dry beans find their way to the pot, they need to be soaked overnight. If you're making a cassoulet, a bean soup, or any dish involving dry beans (which is almost always better than canned beans in texture and taste), you must think to cover them in water the day before. Once they have been properly soaked, drain and rinse them in a colander. Fill a large pot with water, and add the beans and a bay leaf or garlic if you choose. Bring the water to a boil and skim any residue that floats to the top. This is simply impurities (or dirt) that is on the bean shells. Now reduce the water to a simmer, over low heat, and gently cook the beans until they are tender but not overcooked. Most beans take about an hour and a half, but some are stubborn and may take a little while longer. At about one hour into the cook time, introduce a tablespoon of kosher salt per two cups of dry beans. Be patient, tasting them for doneness after an hour or so of cook time. Once they soften up, they can overcook quickly.

COOKING FRESH BEANS Fresh beans are a luxury and fairly uncommon in American cuisine. We are not talking about green beans here; we are talking about fresh shelling beans that need to be removed from a pod. Some of my favorites are fava beans, borlotti beans, and scarlet runner beans, all of which are gently cooked, for about five minutes, in salted water for optimum flavor. A fresh bean has a creamy texture and an earthy flavor and can act as the star of a dish rather than a means of bulking up a meal. Be sure to shock the bean in cool water once it's fully cooked, otherwise it will turn to mush and all that work shelling will no longer seem worth your while. Also, consider holding on to a cup or two of the water in which the beans are cooked, as it is rich in protein and can help lubricate a pasta dish or add richness to a soup.

Egg Cookery

While there are many ways to cook an egg (fried, in a frittata, scrambled, etc.), I find hard- or soft-boiling them and poaching them to be the most common preparations at the cooking school. We use them mostly to bulk up salads and to thicken sauces. Here are some useful tips on both techniques.

HARD- AND SOFT-BOILING EGGS Here's how we do this at Salt Water Farm. I always start the egg in cold water. This prevents the shell from cracking, which often happens when you lower a cold egg into boiling water. Make sure that the egg is completely submerged in water. Once the water is at a boil, allow the egg to cook for two minutes to soft-boil it and five minutes to hard-boil it. Then transfer it to a bowl filled with cold water to stop the cooking process. This ensures a hard yolk that is tender and not dry from overcooking. Now, peel the egg. Not everyone knows that it is nearly impossible to peel a fresh egg. This

is because the membrane between the egg and the shell is virtually nonexistent, as there has been no time for evaporation. As an egg ages, the liquid inside of it slowly evaporates through the shell, widening the gap between the egg and the shell, making it infinitely easier to peel. This is why farmers place their eggs in water to see if they are fresh or have been in the coop too long. A fresh egg will sink, while an old or rotten egg will float. I'm not saying buy old eggs, but if you want to make your life easier, save the fresher eggs for frying and poaching and the slightly older ones for peeling. Oh! And use a spoon to help you peel the egg. Slide it between the thin membrane just under the shell and the flesh of the egg. Pull away the shell with the spoon. You'll be delighted at how much easier it is.

POACHING AN EGG Of the several tricks and techniques for poaching an egg, I prefer the simplest method. In a rondeau, or shallow saucepan, bring three inches of water to a very gentle simmer. Add two tablespoons of distilled white vinegar. Crack your egg (a colder egg will yield a tighter poached egg) into a small, heatproof bowl with gradual sides (Pyrex). Making sure that the water is not too hot to create motion (such as a rolling boil), very slowly pour the egg into the water, touching the bowl to the water's surface so that the egg gently falls into the water. Set a timer for two and a half minutes. Let the white begin to set, keeping close tabs on the heat of the water, making sure that it is not creeping toward a boil, which will disrupt the egg. After two and a half minutes, use a slotted spoon to remove the egg from the water and place it on a resting plate or in a shallow bowl. If the white doesn't look set, let it cook for another thirty seconds. It should be easy to handle without breaking. If you are making multiple poached eggs, you can reserve them on a flat plate once poached until it's time to serve them. Then heat up a pot of water to a gentle simmer and simply dip each already-poached egg into the water for ten seconds with the slotted spoon to reheat them.

WORKING WITH FLOUR

Some of us consider ourselves to be more savory cooks, others partial to baking. Working with flour is daunting to those who like to shoot from the hip in the kitchen. The general consensus is that baking is more of a science and cooking more of an art. I challenge that assumption. While I am trained in the culinary arts (as opposed to the art of pastry), I love making pies, cakes, and other nonfussy desserts. And while I have a basic understanding of how a cake comes together and how to make a light, flaky piecrust, by no means am I laminating dough in my kitchen or piping decorative icing flowers onto cakes. I'm a rustic baker and proud of it. Here is some helpful advice on working with flour. We are grouping pasta in this category, as it necessitates a dough of sorts.

Making Pasta

My husband claims that his "move" to win over the hearts of women (before he met me, of course) was to make pasta from scratch on a first or second date. Thankfully, this act was not limited to his years as a bachelor. To this day, he unclothes down to a white undershirt (almost as if pasta making were a sport) and kneads the dough with force. Flour coats his hands, the countertop, and the side of a glass of red wine that he's working on, surely an important ingredient in the affair. I love to watch him, as my method is far less passionate. Don't get me wrong, I love to make pasta, but Nathan really puts his back into it.

My method: Pour two cups of flour onto a work surface. Sprinkle with ½ teaspoon of salt. Using a ladle, make a well in the center. Crack three eggs into the well. Use a fork to break up the eggs. Gradually incorporate the flour into eggs with the fork until a dough has formed. You may not need all of the flour depending on the size of the eggs. If the eggs run over the wall of flour, it's OK. Knead the dough, bringing in small amounts of the leftover flour on your hands if they are sticking to the dough. You don't want to use more flour than is necessary or the dough will dry out. Knead until the dough is very elastic, so much so that when you press on it, it slowly springs back. Now wrap the dough in plastic wrap and place it in the refrigerator to let rest. Twenty to thirty minutes later, take the dough out of the fridge and remove the plastic. Cut it into two pieces if you're rolling it out by hand and six if you're using a machine. Flour your work surface again and roll out the dough until it's as thin as fettucine, either with a pasta maker or a rolling pin. Using a sharp knife or the pasta-maker attachment, cut the dough into half-inch strips. Make sure the pasta is tossed in a little extra flour so that it doesn't stick. (The flour will fall off into the pasta water when you cook it.) I like to twist my pasta into little floury nests to store it until it's ready to cook. It also allows me to portion it out. You could also do this with a pasta machine, but it would be decidedly less fun. This loose recipe will make enough pasta for four people.

PROPERLY COOKING AND PLATING PASTA There is a distinctly wrong and right way to cook and serve pasta. Without going into too much detail, the wrong way looks something like the spaghetti and red sauce at the lunch bar in the cafeterias of your youth: a bowl of dry, overcooked pasta with a spoonful of viscous sauce on top. The right way starts with a very large pot of well-salted boiling water. It's important that the water is properly salted (two tablespoons kosher salt per gallon of water) and at a rolling boil. Now add the pasta, give it a stir, and cover the pot so that the water resumes a rolling boil. Once it has, remove the lid so that the pasta does not boil over, and give it another stir to prevent sticking. Cook the pasta until it is al dente or just tender but with no bite. With a set of tongs or a spider, bring the pasta to the sauce, dragging salty, starchy water along with it to properly lubricate the pasta dish. Finish cooking the pasta in the sauce for just a minute or two, and for good measure, stir in a little cube of cold butter or a pour of good olive oil and a sprinkle of sea salt. The ratio of pasta to sauce should be 50/50, not the lunch-line 80/20 favoring dry, overcooked pasta. You got this.

The Practice of Bread Baking

For the beginning bread maker, I find that focaccia is a good place to start, mostly because it requires less shaping. While we often use a homemade starter at the school to leaven our bread, there is a world of knowledge and trial and error associated with natural leavens that is better left for another book dedicated solely to authentic sourdough bread (such as Sarah Owens's *Sourdough*). Commercial yeast allows the baker to make delicious, steaming hot, crusty, and flavorful focaccia in about three hours (see Olive, Lemon, and Herb Focaccia on page 60). The process of bread baking is relatively straightforward; it's the tiny nuances that make each loaf distinct. Crucial is the rise, which is what allows the bread to develop its structure. To get this part right, you simply need patience and good observation skills.

Kneading is an activity that centers the soul and cannot be rushed. It is the most physical part of bread making, and while doing it, you must channel all those hands and minds that kneaded bread before you. It is not a task to be executed carelessly but, rather, mindfully. And finally, a hot oven makes for a good dark crust and allows the bread to "spring" up quickly before it settles into its final form. Start with these basic principles, see how your focaccia turns out, and then make it again and again and again. You will learn something new every time, something that only experience can teach you.

STALE BREAD If we are going to take the time to make good bread or spend the money to buy good bread, it needs to be treated like any other high-quality ingredient (think chocolate or heavy cream). We must find applications for every last crumb. The November chapter of this book is full of recipes that use day-old bread as one of their primary ingredients. Bread crumbs are most typically made from stale bread, as they can absorb so much flavor and liquid in whatever dish they are a part of. In my first book, *Full*

Moon Suppers at Salt Water Farm, stale bread is used in a chocolate bread pudding and serves to suck up maple syrup–laced heavy cream to marvelous effect. In a more savory application, day-old bread in this book functions to bulk up and add textural contrast to the Potato Leek Soup with Celery Root Puree (page 216). There are so many applications for stale bread, so it should never be discarded.

QUICK BREADS A quick bread is simply a bread that doesn't use yeast as a leaven but, rather, uses baking powder and/or baking soda. Irish soda bread is a fine example of this, as are corn bread and biscuits. Generally speaking, it also uses fat, whereas yeasted breads generally do not. Having just a few quick bread recipes in your baking repertoire goes a long way toward impressing guests, and as the name implies, they come together rapidly.

BISCUIT DOUGH As a Northerner, I always hesitate to give definitive instruction on what is considered to be a "Southern" specialty. With that disclaimer, I will say this about biscuits: *don't overwork the dough.* Use cold butter, salt the bowl sufficiently, and bring the dough together just enough so that it holds. It's those big butter chucks and cracks in the dough that make each buttery biscuit so divine. Once the dough has been formed, it's important to refrigerate it before it goes in the oven. The butter needs to be cold when it hits the heat of the oven, creating little steam pockets within the biscuit, which is what gives it that wonderful flaky texture. It also allows the biscuits to stand tall and hold their shape and prevents them from falling flat in the oven.

Pie Basics

After ten years of teaching cooking classes, I must have made at least a thousand students come around to making pie dough by hand. Because it really is that easy. And forgiving. But you need to know a few simple tricks to get a consistent product each time.

PIE DOUGH First, be sure to use cold, unsalted butter. You want to control the amount of salt that is used in the pie dough, not to mention that unsalted butter is generally a fresher product than salted butter, as salt is a preservative. You want the butter to be cold, because as it warms, the liquids and solids separate and create a lackluster consistency in your crust. Second, use less water than you think you need. An overly hydrated pie dough will not be flaky and tender; it will be chewy and dense. Remember that there is water suspended in the butter, and with a little elbow grease (which creates heat, so work quickly), you can bring the dough together with no more than two to three tablespoons of water. Third, let the dough rest until it is firm but not hard. This takes about twenty minutes. It's difficult to roll out a rock-hard crust and it will crack. Fourth, roll out your pie dough between two pieces of parchment paper. This allows you to patch it if need be by cutting off stray edges and rolling them back into the dough. It also allows you to move the dough with ease and pop it back into the refrigerator for a minute or two if it's too warm and sticking to the parchment paper. Not to mention, there is no floury mess on your countertop. And finally, colder is better. If the dough is room temperature, pop it in the fridge before it goes into the oven. This will prevent shrinkage.

TYPES OF PIECRUST I first came to understand the difference between a hot crust and a cold crust at the Borough Market in London at a little hand pie shop. I had always insisted in my classes that the butter be as cold as possible to prevent shrinkage in the crust when making any kind of pie, sweet or savory. But as I took a bite out of a beef and stilton hand pie in the market, I recognized a stark difference between my piecrust and the one intended for such a pie. A traditional British meat pie is made with a hot crust, meaning you actually use boiling water and melted butter to make the crust. The difference is this: a hot piecrust is thick and tough and holds in the savory morsels and gravy that fill it. Over time, a hot crust absorbs the contents of the pie, flavoring the crust without losing its tough and glossy exterior. A British meat pie can last a few days out of the fridge, as it has fat (a preservative) in the crust and is structurally sound. You rarely find recipes for a hot crust in the United States. A cold crust relies on cold butter and ice-cold water, and it's much more delicate. We use this crust for a flaky mushroom tart, a berry galette, and an apple pie.

A NOTE ON EGG WASH While there are many varieties of egg wash, I prefer a thicker and more opaque variety that finishes with a rich, robust, and golden crust. This is usually a broken egg whisked with a couple tablespoons of cream and a little melted butter if you're up for it. The butter is optional. It's certainly a rustic approach, especially when brushed on in a thick layer. By contrast, a fine French tart is brushed with a clear egg white to make it shine.

Baking Strategies

From years of conjuring up recipes and watching our students execute them at Salt Water Farm, I have made several observations about baking. Here are a few suggestions that will both add variety to your baking repertoire and ensure a successful finished product.

ALTERNATIVE FLOURS Cooking with alternative flours such as buckwheat, spelt, and amaranth has become more and more popular as gluten-free diets are fairly common these days. My advice to someone experimenting with these flours is to start by cutting all-purpose flour with one of these alternative grains. It's a milder approach that results in something a little more familiar both texturally and in terms of flavor, albeit not gluten-free. A loaf of bread or a pancake made entirely of buckwheat flour, for instance, will surprise any palate with its dense physical form and hearty flavor. Ease into it and you may find that alternative grains bring a point of interest to a simple pancake or the like.

SUBSTITUTING GROUND NUTS FOR ALL-PURPOSE FLOUR If you're looking to make a simple cake a bit more dynamic (and gluten-free), a nut flour is a wonderful substitute for all-purpose flour. The oils in the nuts (especially when roasted) add a deep flavor, and you can alter the texture by grinding the nuts coarse or fine. Walnuts, hazelnuts, chestnuts, and pine nuts all make a wonderful base for cake batter. The texture of the cake will be noticeably different from a traditional all-purpose flour–based cake, the crumb more textural and laced with the oils of the nut. A

cake made with ground nuts always adds a bit of intrigue and has those eating it asking, "What is that delicious flavor?"

THE CUP OF SUGAR RULE If a recipe calls for more than a cup of sugar for a pie, a cake, or the like, it's generally too much. One cup of sugar is really the perfect amount of sweetness in a dessert that serves eight to ten people. The rule with any well-made homemade dessert is that from the time you set down the plate until the time all the plates are clean should not exceed five minutes. Because the dessert is too good to make last. If it's too sweet, some folks will leave a little behind.

LINING A PAN WITH PARCHMENT Having made hundreds of cakes (perhaps over a thousand) at this point in my life, I never make the mistake of forgetting to line the pan with parchment paper. When you've put an hour's worth of work into something, why risk its unmolding? Lining a cake pan is simple: Place the pan on a sheet of parchment paper and trace around the outside of the pan with a pencil. Cut just inside of the line, leaving yourself with the perfect base to protect your cake from sticking. Butter and flour the sides of the pan (no need to butter and flour the bottom) and drop the parchment paper down into the pan. Now you can pour your batter in, without worrying about whether or not it will release from the pan once it's been baked.

PLACING CAKE PANS ON SHEET PANS In an effort to avoid smoking out your kitchen and scraping burnt sugary batter off of the base of your oven or your oven racks, I suggest always placing your cake pans on a sheet pan in the oven. This is a catchall for batter and acts as a sort of insurance against pain-in-the-butt oven cleaning.

PLACING A RACK ABOVE YOUR CAKE Ovens behave differently depending on their make and model. It's important to check their contents frequently (ideally without opening the oven too much but looking through the window), rotating the pan if necessary to promote even cooking. But what happens if your cake is browning too quickly on top and still hasn't set in the middle? This is a common issue, as the sugar in most cakes encourages them to take on color quickly while the center needs time to fully cook. Rather than trying to carefully rest aluminum foil over the cake to shield it from the direct heat above, risking its falling in the cake and destroying the top crumb, simply fix an oven rack on the top setting and slide a sheet pan on top of that. It will deter the cake from continuing to brown while allowing it to cook fully in the middle. I can't tell you how many of my students have indoctrinated this in their own kitchens, saving hundreds of cakes from appearing burnt.

WELCOME THEM IN

When you are entertaining, adding a few simple touches can set the mood for both guest and host. While my first book, *Full Moon Suppers at Salt Water Farm,* goes into much greater detail on the art of hosting, here are just a few informal suggestions that can make a world of difference.

Lighting

This is often overlooked, which is a big mistake. Good lighting is what makes a room feel warm upon entry. An overlit room can be abrasive and set the wrong tone for the evening. It can be tricky at dusk, as the light shifts through a room. Remind yourself to dim the lights as the evening progresses and daylight subsides. Light candles along the dinner table, creating a comfortable glow. I find that a dinner accented with candlelight often results in better conversation.

Putting Out a Little Spread before a Meal

It's always nice to have a small offering when friends arrive, which takes pressure off the host to have the meal on immediately. Get in the habit of doing this. It can be as simple as a bowl of fresh, salty nuts or a bit more involved. I like to put out something salty (cheese, cured meat, nuts or/and olives), something sweet (jams, honey, or fresh fruit), something sour (pickles, mustard), something crunchy (crackers or toasted bread), and some sort of fat (either a bowl of olive oil or salted butter). Of course, these items in combination could constitute a full meal, along with a good bottle of wine.

Flower Arrangements

When assembling a flower arrangement, think outside the box. Sometimes a clutch of field flowers, a small branch from an apple tree with a perfectly ripe apple, a bunch of bolted herbs or vegetable tops make excellent visual material for a bouquet. Let your eye wander as you walk through the yard, along a roadside, or through a meadow. Anyone can assemble a bouquet of precut flowers; it takes vision and creativity to bring together a truly special arrangement. And there's no need for a traditional vase. You likely have a pitcher in the cupboard or a can in the barn that will do just fine. Always give it a go with what you already have, resisting the impulse to buy something new. The eye knows the difference.

Batched Cocktails

There's nothing like a shared drink to get everyone on the same page and in a celebratory mood. Many are daunted by mixing drinks, but this is simpler than that. There's no fancy equipment necessary, just a big pitcher or, even better, a large punch bowl and a handful of small, sweet cocktail glasses. If you come across a punch bowl at an antique market or a collection of small and festive cocktail glasses, don't hesitate to buy them, as a true punch bowl and proper glassware are the mark of a well-seasoned host. Typically, the various ingredients are measured out ahead of time, lemons sliced, and glasses garnished. Always hold off on popping anything carbonated until the last minute. Make sure that you have plenty of ice, as alcohol has a way of making twelve cubes look more like six once they have settled at the bottom of the glass. I find that even those devoted to a certain cocktail (the dirty martini drinkers, the cosmopolitan lovers with a punishing sweet tooth, or the wine-only drinkers) won't turn down a batched welcome cocktail, as it would be an ungrateful act.

JANUARY

On the first day of the year, despite a general groggy state of mind (given the previous evening's festivities), I contemplate the days and months ahead. I find that this cerebral pursuit is best accomplished while making bread. With a fire roaring in the woodstove, as it is sure to be cold enough to warrant one, I dissolve yeast in warm water with a drop of honey and mix in a few cups of flour with a wooden spoon. Then I methodically knead the soft dough gently with the palms of my hands and set it to rest and rise beside the stove, with a damp towel over top. Only after this simple and restorative process can I begin decision-making on such a day.

At a New Year's Eve bash the previous evening, my dear friend (and in many ways, the older sister I never had) gave me this little jewel of advice when I asked what her resolutions for the new year were. With a confident glimmer in her eye and a glass of champagne in her hand, she said, "I never take anything away. I only add to life." What a statement it was, brilliant in its simplicity and certainty. Rather than dwelling on what to forbid, focus your energy on what to embrace. And just like that, I decided to follow suit. After all, there is a great deal to embrace.

In the off-season, we live at our home just outside of town, a classic New England cape built in 1820. What the house lacks in energy efficiency, it makes up for in charm. The original central Russian-style fireplace (still functional) has faces in three rooms. In the living room, an iron door beside the hearth opens to what used to be the primary oven. This was clearly the kitchen before a separate room was put in to serve more modern needs. The ceilings are all under seven feet tall (you can reach up and touch them), and open vents let heat up to the second floor. Original wide-planked floorboards add both character and unevenness to our home, creaking morning, noon, and night. We live across the street from preserved farmland, rolling green hills with the mountains in the near distance. At dusk, the sun sets behind the hills, lighting up the big evening sky and sending a deeply red and orange light through our kitchen windows. A weather vane topped with an iron crow (its wings in flight) sits over our barn, accompanied most days by live seagulls. An old and rather sizable chicken coop has been converted to a little outbuilding, complete with a small bedroom and living room but no plumbing. The property is truly a timepiece.

My husband and I love to entertain in the winter months. We light three fires—one in the chiminea near the entry to our home, one in the woodstove on a cold night, and one in the central fireplace, where guests often migrate for an after-dinner drink or a game. Dinner is served around a narrow, ten-foot-long farmhouse table that sits in a room away from the kitchen. Such a large table is a great excuse to make a big meal. The lights are always dimmed, and candles stretch the length of the table, a soft flickering glow that brings warmth to the faces of our guests. Winter is the perfect time to cook foods that are colorful and exotic. For these winter gatherings, I often cook Asian, Indian, and African dishes, leaning heavily on a big basket of unorganized spices. Turmeric, cumin, coriander, ginger, and saffron loom large in my winter recipes, staining my wooden spoons and cutting boards. Something about having such low ceilings makes the room feel exceedingly cozy and intimate, especially when meals are served family style and passed around the table. My husband is a piano player, a jazz pianist since his youth, and dessert is often consumed while sitting around him, his fingers dancing across the keys. His repertoire has evolved to suit the whims of our friends (think Elton John's "Piano Man"), and now, no winter dinner party feels complete without this musical finishing ceremony.

For me, the winter days are devoted entirely to cooking and documenting my efforts. In my daughter's first year, I would do all the heavy lifting of our kitchen tasks when she napped: searing meat for stews, kneading doughs, chopping onions, and cleaning pots and pans. When she woke, I would fasten her to my chest, facing outward so that she could see all that was at hand, and we would clean spinach, pick parsley, and stir the pot. I made sure she smelled each of the ingredients with high hopes that she wouldn't become a picky eater. When we are cooking for the three of us, comfort foods take center stage, a means of recovery from all the bold flavors of dinner parties (which we host about three times a week). Dishes such as Congee with Poached Chicken and Ginger (page 66), Gnudi with Sage Brown Butter (page 70), and Meatballs in Tomato Sauce on Spinach (page 63) are inexpensive and made in bulk, balancing our rather significant entertaining budget.

If it's not too cold, a little fresh air goes a long way in breaking up the day. After bundling up, the two of us, with her little body tucked into my oversized down coat, walk through the quiet majesty of the day, her big blue eyes taking in the beauty of a Maine winter and the occasional snowflake. The dogs careen through the woods, dipping their nostrils in the fluffy white and coming up looking like arctic wolves, their snouts covered in ice and snow. A day like this almost makes the long winters bearable. After the baby's nose and cheeks turn rosy, we head back home to put the kettle on for a cup of tea. This tiny ritual is ever so important in a cold climate. I fully understand why the British have built their days around teatime. It's a means of welcoming yourself home, recuperating, and warming your body and mind before embarking on the events of the day. One must take care of oneself before others, if they are to take care of others well.

While many folks are dieting or juice cleansing in January, I'm cooking up a storm. On Sundays, after a good long walk in the woods, my husband and I make food for the week. There is always bread or focaccia such as Olive, Lemon, and Herb Focaccia (page 60) hot out of the oven, a chicken stock simmering on the stove top for soups and stews later in the week, and often more ambitious projects such as homemade kimchi. Because lentils are said to be lucky as we enter a new year (symbolic of money and good fortune, apparently), and there always seems to be a bag of red lentils in the cupboard, a pot of bright, colorful, and vegetable-rich dahl is a wonderful dish on a snowy afternoon, garnished with a thick yogurt and a handful of cilantro. Thus, the appropriately named Dahl on a Gray Day is found in this chapter (page 69). January is a time to regroup and ease into the new year. The recipes in this chapter offer comfort in an effort to do just that.

OLIVE, LEMON, AND HERB FOCACCIA

Makes 1 large focaccia

If you're daunted by bread making, this is a wonderful place to start. Focaccia is forgiving by nature, and its easy preparation and simple elegance make it a compelling pursuit. This recipe, inspired by two of my favorite female cooks at the Canal House (a test kitchen in Delaware), has become a staple of the Salt Water Farm curriculum. Many of our students send me photos of their renditions, gloating over their success.

2 cups warm water

2 tablespoons honey

1½ teaspoons baker's yeast

1 cup wheat flour

3 to 4 cups all-purpose white flour, depending on humidity

4 tablespoons extra virgin olive oil, plus 1 tablespoon for greasing the sheet pan

1 teaspoon kosher salt

1 cup pitted mixed olives

1 to 2 lemons, cut into 12 thin rounds and seeded

A few sprigs thyme, leaves removed from stems

A few sprigs rosemary, leaves removed from stems

Sea salt

Preheat the oven to 425°F. In a liquid measuring cup, dissolve the honey into the warm water. Sprinkle the yeast across the surface and swirl to dissolve. Let sit for 5 minutes until the yeast begins to fizz. (Look for bubbles. That means the yeast is active.) Place the wheat flour and 1 cup of the white flour in a large mixing bowl. Whisk to combine. Gradually add the yeasted water, stirring to incorporate, until the mixture resembles mud. Let this rise for 1 hour, covered with a damp cloth. (Ideally in a warm place in your kitchen, between 80°F and 90°F.)

Add 2 tablespoons olive oil and salt around the edges of the bowl. Stir to incorporate. Then add 2 cups all-purpose flour and stir, fully incorporating the flour, until the dough pulls away from the side of the bowl. Add the olives to the dough and gently mix them in. Turn out the dough onto a well-floured surface and knead until it is smooth and not sticky, dusting with flour as needed. Put the dough in a well-oiled bowl and let rise for 1 hour in a warm spot in your kitchen. Line a sheet pan with parchment and coat with a thin layer of olive oil. When the bread dough has doubled in size, pour it onto a sheet pan. Stretch the dough out with your fingers into a rectangle, filling about two-thirds of the sheet pan. Let it rest for 10 minutes. Lay the lemon slices across the top in one layer. Then sprinkle the thyme, rosemary, and sea salt on top of the dough. Drizzle with the remaining 2 tablespoons olive oil. Place it in the oven and cook until golden brown, about 25 to 30 minutes. Remove from oven. Place the bread on a cutting board to let cool. Slice and serve.

POTTED LOBSTER ON SOURDOUGH TOASTS

Makes four 6-ounce ramekins

Historically, what couldn't be eaten or sold from a day's catch was preserved for times when protein was scarce, such as long journeys at sea or Maine's winter months. There are a number of ways to preserve fish (smoke, salt, acid), but one of my favorite ways is in fat—butter, to be precise. It must be clarified, as the milk solids will go bad quicker than the fish that is being preserved. The culinary term for preserving protein in fat is simply "potted," which means that the seafood is generally poached in clarified butter or oil, flavored with herbs and spices, and then sealed with a layer of pure fat to protect the protein from exposure to air. This dish was very popular at my restaurant in its early days, the butter infused with Maine's most famous crustacean and spread on thick-cut, toasted sourdough. Kind of perfect in its simplicity.

Two 1½-pound, hard-shelled lobsters	¼ teaspoon nutmeg
	¼ teaspoon mace
Kosher salt	¼ teaspoon cayenne
2 cups (4 sticks) butter	Zest and juice of 1 lemon
1 bay leaf	8 slices sourdough bread
1 shallot, minced	
1 teaspoon thyme, leaves picked from stems	

Add 4 cups of water to a large pot. Salt to mimic ocean water. Taste if you're not sure. Bring to a boil and add the lobsters. Cover and cook for 6 minutes, then check to make sure that they have turned red. If they have, give them another minute or so to steam and then move them to a bowl of ice water to stop the cooking process. You are parboiling them, not fully cooking them. Remove the claw, knuckle, and tail meat from the shells and cut it into bite-size pieces. Enjoy the legs as a snack.

In a medium saucepan set over medium-low heat, melt the butter and bring it to a low simmer. Skim any foam that rises to the top. Let simmer gently for 10 to 15 minutes or until the milk solids separate from the clarified butter. Pour off the clarified butter into a glass bowl (leaving the solids behind) and add the bay leaf. Set aside.

In the same medium saucepan, add the shallot, a pinch of salt, the thyme, nutmeg, mace, cayenne, and lemon zest and juice. Set it over medium-low heat and cook gently for 2 to 3 minutes. Add two-thirds of the clarified butter back into the pan along with the lobster meat and bring it to a gentle simmer. Turn off the heat. Distribute the contents of the saucepan (lobster, butter, shallots, and herbs) among the ramekins. Pour a thin layer of the reserved clarified butter over the top of each, sealing in the protein. Chill in the refrigerator for 6 hours or up to a week.

To serve, toast the sourdough bread and serve it with the potted lobster. The warmth from the bread will slightly melt the butter and instantly bring out the lobster flavor.

MEATBALLS IN TOMATO SAUCE ON SPINACH

Serves 4 (Makes 12 smallish meatballs)

While some of the greens in the market are quite sad during this time of year, the spinach is always a deep green and has a healthy look to it. A cold-water bath and a few turns in the salad spinner have it gleaming and ready for use. Beyond cooking it down with olive oil and garlic, I often try to find a means of incorporating spinach into dishes that need a little green, both in color and in nutritional value. And, as it turns out, it makes a lovely bed of greens for these slightly sophisticated meatballs.

FOR THE TOMATO SAUCE

1 tablespoon butter

1 tablespoon extra virgin olive oil

1 yellow onion, sliced

Kosher salt

6 cloves garlic, peeled and minced

One 28-ounce can San Marzano tomatoes, broken up with your hands

1 bay leaf

1 pinch red pepper flakes

Kosher salt

Fresh ground pepper

FOR THE MEATBALLS

1 tablespoon extra virgin olive oil, plus more for frying

½ yellow onion, small dice

2 carrots, small dice

2 stalks celery, small dice

2 cloves garlic, peeled and minced

1 tablespoon sherry

¼ cup currants

1 sprig rosemary, leaves removed from stems and finely chopped

2 sprigs thyme, leaves removed from stems

1 pound ground beef (85% lean and locally raised)

1 egg

⅛ teaspoon nutmeg

8 sprigs parsley, washed and leaves removed from stems

½ cup bread crumbs

½ cup finely grated Parmesan

1 pinch red pepper flakes

Kosher salt

Fresh ground pepper

TO SERVE

1 big bunch spinach, cleaned and torn into bite-size pieces

Parmesan

Loaf of crusty bread

(recipe continues)

To make the tomato sauce: In a large, heavy-bottomed pot (the meatballs will eventually go into this), warm the butter and olive oil over medium-low heat. Add the onions and a pinch of salt and sweat with the cover on for 15 minutes, stirring every couple of minutes. Add the garlic and sweat for an additional 5 minutes. Add the tomatoes, bay leaf, and red pepper flakes. Let simmer for 25 to 30 minutes. Season to taste with salt and pepper. Turn off the heat and set the pot aside.

To make the meatballs: In a heavy-bottomed pot, warm the olive oil over medium-low heat. Add the onion, carrot, celery, and a pinch of salt. Cover and cook for 10 minutes, stirring every couple of minutes. Once the onions are translucent, add the garlic and continue to cook for 5 minutes with the cover on. Remove the cover and add the sherry and currants. (You may want to turn off the flame first and then turn it back on after you add the booze so it doesn't ignite.) Add the rosemary and thyme and let cook for 2 to 3 minutes, moving the vegetables around in the sherry. Turn off the heat and reserve.

In a medium mixing bowl, combine the ground beef, cooled vegetables, egg, nutmeg, parsley, bread crumbs, Parmesan, red pepper flakes, and salt and pepper. Mix well. Shape the meatballs into portions the size of a golf ball.

Preheat the oven to 375°F. In a cast-iron frying pan, add olive oil for frying, generously coating the pan. Warm the pan and oil over medium heat. Brown the meatballs in two batches, being careful not to crowd the pan. You want them to have a nice golden brown on each side. Once they have been browned, move them to a plate to rest (they should still be undercooked at the center).

Turn the heat under the tomato sauce to medium-low. Once it is simmering, add in the meatballs, stirring them to coat with sauce. Place the pot into the oven and let them cook for 10 minutes or until you cut into a meatball and it is fully cooked. You don't want to overcook them. Remove from oven.

To serve, place a nest of cleaned spinach in each serving bowl. Spoon the meatballs and sauce on top and then add a little finely grated Parmesan. Serve with a crusty loaf of bread for sopping up sauce.

CONGEE

WITH POACHED CHICKEN AND GINGER

Serves 6 (with leftovers)

If I'm being honest, this recipe was a mistake. I planned to make a meal for my parents in return for babysitting, and the rice went into the pot too early in the day. Once the rice was perfectly cooked, I turned off the heat thinking that the soup would be just right when my folks warmed it up a couple of hours later. Instead, the grains absorbed more of the chicken stock, began to swell, overcooked, and fell apart. And then it became something else entirely, a dish that is the comfort food of so many Asian children: congee. As my father was suffering from a sensitive stomach, it was the perfect dish to calm his digestion.

1 tablespoon peanut oil

1 yellow onion, small dice

4 medium carrots, small dice

1 leek, cut in half lengthwise and thinly sliced

Kosher salt

4 cloves garlic, peeled and minced

1 tablespoon fresh minced ginger

12 cups homemade chicken stock

2 raw chicken breasts, chopped into bite-size pieces

2 cups short-grain rice

2 cups green beans, stemmed and cut into 1-inch lengths

One 13½-ounce can full-fat coconut milk

1 bunch cilantro, roughly chopped, including stems

1 lime, cut into 6 pieces

In a medium, heavy-bottomed pot, warm the peanut oil over medium-low heat. Add the onion, carrot, leek, and a pinch of salt. Sweat, covered for 10 minutes, stirring every couple of minutes. Add the garlic and ginger and continue sweating for an additional 10 minutes. Add the chicken stock and bring to a boil. Reduce to a simmer over medium-low heat. Add the chicken and gently cook through for about 10 minutes. Add the rice, stir, and continue cooking with the lid on partially for 20 minutes.

To blanch the beans, fill a medium pot with water. Salt generously and bring to a boil. Prepare an ice bath in the sink. Add the beans to the boiling water. Let them cook for 3 to 4 minutes and then test them for doneness. Once they are tender but not at all soft, remove them with a slotted spoon to the ice bath to stop the cooking process and maintain their green color. Drain and set aside.

Add coconut milk to the congee and stir thoroughly. Continue to cook for 5 minutes. Season to taste with kosher salt. Add the green beans at the last minute. To serve, ladle congee into bowls and garnish with cilantro and a squeeze of lime.

PEELING GINGER This is just a little trick, but revelatory if you like to cook with fresh ginger. Instead of awkwardly using a vegetable peeler to rid gingerroot of its skin, use the tip of a spoon instead, which allows you to get into all of the nooks and crannies. You will lose a lot less of the ginger this way.

DAHL ON A GRAY DAY

Serves 4

While scrolling Instagram on a gray day, I saw a sweet and comforting little bowl of brilliantly colored red lentil stew in a beautiful ceramic bowl and felt that, despite never having made dahl, it would be supremely comforting. The scent of the spices toasting in the pan and fresh garlic and ginger warming the cold air of my kitchen certainly improved the mood of the day.

2 tablespoons extra virgin olive oil

1 large yellow onion, small dice

Kosher salt

4 cloves garlic, peeled and minced

1 tablespoon fresh minced ginger

1 teaspoon ground cumin

1 teaspoon ground turmeric

1 teaspoon ground ginger

¼ teaspoon cinnamon

¼ teaspoon cardamom

1 tablespoon tomato paste

2 tomatoes, diced

8 cups vegetable stock or water

1 cup red lentils

2 medium sweet potatoes, peeled and diced

1 bunch cilantro, roughly chopped

Lime juice, to finish

1 spicy pepper (such as serrano or jalapeño)

Whole-milk Greek-style yogurt, to serve (optional)

In a heavy-bottomed, medium to large pot, warm the olive oil over medium-low heat. Add the onion and a pinch of salt. Sweat the onion with the lid on for 10 minutes, stirring every couple of minutes. Then add the garlic and ginger and cook for an additional 5 minutes. Add the cumin, turmeric, ground ginger, cinnamon, and cardamom and stir well into the aromatics, toasting the spices in the pan for 1 to 2 minutes. Then using a wooden spoon, massage the tomato paste into the onion and spice mixture and let toast in the pan for a couple of minutes until you can smell the spices and tomatoes cooking. Add the diced tomatoes and a pinch more salt and let cook for 5 to 10 minutes or until they soften.

Add the stock or water. Bring to a boil and add the lentils and sweet potatoes. Reduce to a simmer and let cook for 30 minutes. Test the lentils and sweet potatoes for doneness. They should have some texture to them and not be mush. They may need another 5 minutes. Season the dahl to taste with salt. Ladle into deep bowls and garnish heavily with chopped cilantro and a squeeze of lime. Add a little thinly sliced pepper and a spoonful of yogurt if you like a tart contrast in flavor.

GNUDI

WITH SAGE BROWN BUTTER

Serves 4

Made famous in the United States by the British chef April Bloomfield (despite its Italian origin), gnudi is a humble yet decadent pillowy pasta reminiscent of gnocchi. After forming the pasta and letting it rest overnight, then boiling it and sliding it into a little brown butter sauce flavored with sage, I understood the obsession. It's the buttered pasta of your childhood dreams: soft and rich and simple.

1 pound ricotta

1 egg, beaten with a fork

¼ teaspoon nutmeg

1 cup semolina flour, plus more for storage

1 teaspoon kosher salt

½ cup grated Parmesan

8 tablespoons (1 stick) unsalted butter

6 sprigs sage, piled up and thinly sliced

Sea salt

Fresh ground pepper

In a medium bowl, combine the ricotta, egg, nutmeg, flour, salt, and ¼ cup of the Parmesan. Mix thoroughly until a dough is formed. On a floured surface, gently knead the dough and then split it in two. Shape each piece of dough into a fat tube and then gently roll each out into about 16-inch lengths. Try to keep them as even as possible in width. Cut the tubes every inch or so, into little pillow-shaped squares. Flour a sheet tray and place the dough squares on it, rolling them in the flour so that they don't stick together. Cover with plastic and place in the refrigerator overnight. This helps them to dry out a bit so that they don't fall apart in the water.

Bring a large pot of water to a boil. Salt it generously. Simultaneously, melt the butter in a large sauté pan over medium heat. Once the butter is melted and starts to foam, add the sage and let it cook until butter is golden, about 4 minutes. Turn off the heat. Drop the gnudi into the boiling water. Let cook for 4 to 5 minutes or until cooked through. You can test them by simply cutting into one of them. You will be able to see if they are cooked through. Now turn the butter pan back on over medium heat. Once the gnudi are just cooked through, with a slotted spoon, move them into the sage butter and sauté them in the butter sauce for a couple of minutes. Slide them into bowls (there should be about eight per bowl) and sprinkle the remaining Parmesan on top. Season with sea salt and a little fresh ground pepper.

PISTACHIO CAKE

Serves 8

This cake was discovered during a search for the perfect dessert for a French Provincial cooking class, on the third day of our French Regional Cuisine Workshop. You know that a recipe is a success when after the first bite, nobody speaks for a few seconds, takes a second bite, and then simply grunts. Make sure you are using fresh and flavorful pistachios and you will not be disappointed. A tender crumb, a rich nutty aroma, and a shade of green make this cake a memorable one.

FOR THE CAKE

1 cup unsalted shelled pistachios

1 cup all-purpose flour

2 teaspoons baking powder

½ teaspoon ground cardamom

¼ teaspoon salt

8 tablespoons (1 stick) unsalted butter, softened

1 cup sugar

3 large eggs

½ teaspoon pure vanilla extract

½ cup heavy cream

Zest of 1 orange

FOR THE WHIPPED CREAM

2 cups heavy cream, chilled

½ teaspoon vanilla extract

1 tablespoon sugar

Preheat the oven to 350°F. Butter and flour a 9-inch-round springform pan and line the base with parchment paper.

Pulse the pistachios in a food processor until finely ground. (Do not overprocess, or the mixture will become paste.) In a mixing bowl, combine the ground pistachios, flour, baking powder, cardamom, and salt and whisk to incorporate.

In the bowl of a stand mixer, beat the butter and sugar with the whisk attachment until light and fluffy. Add eggs one at a time, beating well after each addition and scraping the sides of the bowl to achieve an even batter. Add the vanilla extract and mix in. Reduce the speed to low and alternate adding the flour mixture and cream one-third at a time, mixing for 20 seconds after each addition. Add the orange zest and mix to combine.

Pour the batter into the prepared cake pan. Tap on the counter to get rid of any air bubbles. Place on a sheet tray and set in the middle of the oven. Cook for 50 minutes. To make sure that the cake is done, insert a toothpick and if it comes out clean, it's done!

Whip the cream, vanilla extract, and sugar in the bowl of a stand mixer until soft peaks form. Store it in the refrigerator until ready to serve.

WHIPPING CREAM Whipped cream is so simple but can so easily be screwed up. Follow these rules and every batch will be sublime. One, whip it to soft peaks. Don't overwhip the cream, as it will become heavy and blocklike. You want a smooth, sexy pillow of white that gently falls off the spoon. Two, add a little sugar. About 2 teaspoons will make it delightfully sweet. Three, a little extract goes a long way. A couple shakes of vanilla, almond, or hazelnut extract will lace your cream with a lovely flavor, which usually enhances the whole dessert.

FEBRUARY

In early February, the blue jays nibble seeds from the bird feeder outside of the kitchen window. Their bright blue feathers are reminiscent of the shade of blue paint used to color the facades of the buildings in Oaxaca, Mexico, our home away from home. Each winter, I head south with my family to Mexico, a country that has held a special place in my heart since I was a child. My parents lived in Mexico City just before I was born, and their tales of dinner parties that lasted well past midnight and demonstrations in the streets suggested a vitality that was lacking in our midwestern suburb. Once a year, my family would travel to Mexico, usually to the Pacific coast, where my sister and I would do cartwheels in the break of the ocean waves, our skin more than kissed by the sun. As we passed through the markets, women in layered skirts, their hair braided down their backs, sold woven rugs, leather huaraches, and cotton dresses in shades of blue, green, red, yellow, orange, and purple. We sat at plastic tables in the sand eating grilled meat and fish covered in red and green salsas alongside a stack of warm tortillas. As far as I was concerned, there was no need to go to Disney World. Mexico had it all.

Fast-forward a few decades, and I find myself continuing with this annual tradition. My husband and I have explored the Yucatán, the Federal District, the western coast, and the southern region of Chiapas. But the place that has its grip on us is a mountain town called Oaxaca City. I am routinely asked by Americans why I am so fond of a Mexican town that is not on the beach. The answer is simple. Never before have I seen so much life and culture celebrated publicly in the streets in such magnificent display. It's hard to pass through the town without sighting a celebration of some kind: a bride and groom emerging from the glorious Santo Domingo Church with a well-dressed wedding party in tow; a culinary festival complete with horns, drums, and women in traditional Oaxacan costumes, their skirts twirling in a rainbow of color; adolescents in an organized salsa dance resetting the boom box to start from the top; a familial gang of motorcyclists showing off their steely bikes as if unfurling a plume of peacock feathers; or clusters of children roller-skating through the park and licking goat's-milk caramel-flavored ice cream under the palms. It is a sweet respite from the bone-chilling winter winds of Maine.

In my carry-on are photocopied recipes from Diana Kennedy's books to use as my guide once we've reached our rented apartment or house. I always make sure that there is a well-appointed kitchen before booking. The markets are the place where I feel the most fluent, with a better grasp on words for food than on verb conjugations. Before shopping, I'll sit to enjoy a bubbling breakfast of chilaquiles smothered in salsa or a quesadilla pressed with queso Oaxaca (Oaxacan string cheese) and *flor de calabaza* (squash blossoms) or *huitlacoche* (corn fungus). A steaming bowl of cinnamon hot chocolate is a must and provides a zip for an ambitious shopping list. I am also drawn to the piles of bright yellow chickens (their skin colored by the corn and marigolds upon which they feed), their feet facing out. I watch the women wielding cleavers behind the counter, butchering them in a way I would never think to, effortlessly and on the bone.

It's taken years to familiarize myself with all the varieties of dried chilies, piled high in burlap sacks, in assorted shades of red. At the produce stands, there are fresh shelled green peas, fava beans, and lima beans, all ready for the pot. Piles of herbs such as epazote, *herba santa*, *herba buena*, *chipilin*, and many other fragrant greens unique to this region beg for culinary exploration. Handmade tortillas in white, yellow, and blue are stacked, still warm from the comal, their vendors pulling from a sticky pile of masa dough and shaping balls for the press with only muscle memory. A group of elderly women sit low to the floor with bowls of *chapulines*, chili and lime–treated grasshoppers, a popular snack in Oaxaca. Butcher counters line the periphery of the market, with marinated pork, fat little links of chorizo, a thinly cut and air-dried beef called *tesajo*, and piles of shoulder and rump meat for *estofado*, or the many local stews.

Oaxacan food is known throughout the world for its heritage and integrity. As the region is made up of a wide variety of landscapes and climates, its recipes vary depending on where you are, but the basic components of the cuisine are unique to the region. And they have little to nothing in common with what is perceived by Americans as Mexican food. Much of the cuisine is dry roasted and ground, then cooked in fat or nestled into masa. Fire is key in almost all of the recipes, as so much of the food is still cooked over an open flame. Chilies and spices play a huge role in flavoring the various soups, stews, and sauces of Oaxacan food, and while proteins and vegetables are abundant in the dishes, it is the base that gives a dish its character. And I hate to say it, but while Oaxacan food can absolutely be re-created outside of Mexico (thanks to online Mexican food shops), certain ingredients such as fresh Mexican herbs, tortillas, and particular cuts of meat are hard to come by in the United States. Hopefully, before long, I'll be teaching classes in Oaxaca and we can have this experience together.

Since this book is not solely about Mexico (although that is where my mind and body reside for most of the month of February), let's get back to the country cooking of Maine. As it's a quiet time of year, I tend to linger at the butcher shop and the fish market, passing town gossip back and forth over the counter about which businesses will make it through the winter and which will close their doors. This is a common annual refrain in a small, seasonal town. With no line at the register, I am afforded the opportunity to try different local and imported cheeses, ask the butcher what he's working on behind the counter, and wait a few minutes for the sourdough to come hot out of the oven. There is joy in having the time to converse with my local food professionals, because come Memorial Day, there will be no time for such conversations.

In an effort to expel the winter blues, my kitchen is often an explosion of color and scent—African and Asian spices staining my wooden cutting boards, tropical fruit stewing alongside meat on the stovetop, and hot chili seeds finding their way between the cracks in our countertop. But on the off night where my husband and I need a break from my around-the-world food experiments (and their leftovers), we make a simple meal, something that resets the clock, so to speak. In this chapter, there are a couple examples of this: Mushroom, Fennel, and Leek Galette (page 89), filled with items from the drawers of my refrigerator; and Ditalini with Sardines, Fennel, and Bread Crumbs (page 81), a simple pantry pasta dish that actually has its origins in Sardinia but still feels basic and restorative.

There are a number of ingredients worth celebrating, some local, some not, even in the winter months in Maine. Scallop season begins in January, and there is nothing more luxurious than a super-fresh and simply prepared winter scallop. This chapter includes a recipe for Scallop Aguachile (page 78), with a bit of acid in the form of lime juice and a few thin slices of habanero (yes, another nod to Mexico). Any supremely fresh fish could receive a similar treatment, whether it's halibut in June or mackerel in July.

Citrus is a category that should not be overlooked during this time of year, their firm, juicy varieties aplenty at the grocery store. I can't help but fill my cart with blood oranges, Cara Cara oranges, grapefruits, and limes, knowing that this is the only time of year we can get citrus of such exceptional quality. A drawer full of colorful orbs in the refrigerator challenges the cook to incorporate citrus into salads, stews, and desserts, such as the Lemony Ice Cream (page 91) that finishes this chapter.

A traditional Sardinian pasta dish in this chapter features tinned fish. Not all tinned fish is the Bumblebee canned tuna of your youth (sadly, the most commonly consumed fish in the United States). There is a wonderful variety of preserved fishes. For instance, a high-quality tuna, caught and canned at peak freshness and exported from places such as Italy, Spain, and Norway, is worth building a meal around, not tossed into a bowl with mayonnaise and bits of celery. Whether it's tuna, sardines, kippers, mussels, or octopus, never judge a tin of fish. The tradition of preserving fish goes back hundreds of years, and often a forkful of canned tuna, preserved in good olive oil or brine, is far superior to seared tuna steak that has been out of water for some time.

Many of the recipes in this chapter are a means of escaping the frigid winter days: Tortilla Soup with Dried Chilies and Jacob's Cattle Beans, with notes of smoke and spice (page 84); Mexican Chicken Stew with Fruit (page 87), bright as the sun, made sweet with tropical fruit; Scallop Aguachile, pristine raw fish marinated in acid and herbs; Minted Hummus with Celery Leaves, Feta, and Radishes (page 82), a crunchy salad atop a minted dip; and a cheerful Lemony Ice Cream to make your mouth pucker. The winters are long here in Maine, so a little escapism in the month of February is permitted.

SCALLOP AGUACHILE

Serves 4

A trip to Mexico City is not complete without a reservation at Contramar, a bustling lunch spot in Colonia Roma where you'll find diners wearing everything from sneakers and sweats to haute couture. The waiters are of the old guard sort: all men over fifty with long, white aprons moving effortlessly through the crowded restaurant and upselling every table. They are the definition of professional. The menu is almost entirely seafood, with a special section devoted to aguachile, a wonderful dish with lime and chili marinade for supremely fresh fish.

FOR THE SCALLOPS

8 ounces super-fresh scallops

½ cup lime juice

¼ cup orange juice

¼ small habanero, seeded and thinly sliced

FOR THE AGUACHILE SAUCE

1 clove garlic

Kosher salt

1 cup chopped cucumber, peeled and seeded

½ cup cilantro, upper stems and leaves, roughly chopped

¼ cup mint leaves

½ grapefruit, segmented

½ Cara Cara orange, segmented

¼ cup minced red onion

1 avocado, roughly chopped

Sea salt

Extra virgin olive oil

1 stack tostadas (fried tortillas)

To marinate the scallops: Remove the scallops from the refrigerator. (You only want to work with seafood when it's cold.) Remove the tough little muscle from each scallop. Cut them horizontally into thin slices with a mandoline, about 3 to 4 slices per scallop. In a medium glass bowl, combine the lime and orange juice with the habanero. Submerge the scallops in the citrus juice. Cover with plastic and let sit in the fridge for 30 minutes or until opaque.

To make the aguachile: In a small food processor, grind up the garlic with a pinch of salt. Add the cucumber, cilantro, and mint and grind until coarse. Move to a mixing bowl.

To serve: Remove the scallops from the fridge. Pour off the lime and orange juice. Combine the aguachile (cucumber mixture), citrus segments, and the scallops in a mixing bowl. Fold in the onions. Move to a shallow bowl and garnish with avocado. Finish with a little sea salt and a small pour of olive oil. Serve with a stack of tostadas to use as a vehicle to eat the dish.

COOKING FISH IN ACID I remember the first time I watched my dad make ceviche, the acid in the citrus slowly denaturing the proteins in the fish, turning the fillets from glossy to opaque. It seemed like a bold move, given that we lived in the Midwest and it was hard to say how far the fish had traveled to get to our kitchen. Not to mention, I had never eaten raw fish before. But my dad explained that it was in fact cooked, just by different means. Cooking, by definition, is removing the liquid from food and does not necessarily require heat. Acid functions in this way, as does salt and smoke. It is important that the fish does not spend too much time in its acid brine; otherwise you begin to lose the delicate texture of the protein. (No more than one hour.) You want a little tension in each bite.

DITALINI

WITH SARDINES, FENNEL, AND BREAD CRUMBS

Serves 4

This is a simple country dish from Sardinia, where fennel grows wild along the hillsides and day-old bread is seasoned and repurposed in pasta, along with tinned fish, demonstrating economy and resourcefulness in the kitchen. Help yourself to a glass of vermouth on ice with a slice of orange while you wait for the pasta to cook.

3 thick slices day-old sourdough bread

6 tablespoons extra virgin olive oil

Kosher salt

Fresh ground pepper

Zest of 1 lemon

1 bulb fennel and ½ cup picked fronds

One 4-ounce tin sardines marinated in oil

4 cloves garlic, peeled and minced

¼ cup vermouth

1 bay leaf

1 large pinch red pepper flakes

Good-quality chili oil

1 pound ditalini pasta

8 sprigs Italian flat-leaf parsley, leaves removed from stems

Tear up the sourdough and place it in a food processor. Pulse until the bread is coarsely ground. Add 2 tablespoons of olive oil to a cast-iron frying pan and warm over medium heat. Add the bread crumbs and salt and pepper to taste. Move the bread around in the pan until it is nice and toasted, even a little crunchy. Add the lemon zest, mix it in, and turn off the heat. Move the bread crumbs to a bowl and reserve.

Thinly slice the fennel bulb—very thin—ideally on a mandoline. Open the tin of sardines. Pour off the oil into a large, heavy-bottomed sauté pan or frying pan. Add 2 additional tablespoons of olive oil. Set the pan over medium heat. Add the fennel and a pinch of salt. Cook for 10 to 15 minutes, then add the garlic. Cook for an additional 5 to 10 minutes or until the fennel begins to caramelize. Deglaze with the vermouth and let cook for 2 to 3 minutes. Then add the bay leaf and red pepper flakes to the pan. Season to taste with salt and fresh ground pepper. Add an additional 2 tablespoons olive oil. Break up the sardines and add them to the pasta sauce. Cook for 2 to 3 minutes and turn off the heat.

Fill a large pot with water and salt generously. Bring it to a boil. Add the ditalini and cook, stirring every couple of minutes to prevent sticking. Roughly chop the parsley. Strain the pasta when it's al dente, reserving about 1 cup of pasta water. Turn the sauce over medium heat. Add the pasta and ½ of the reserved pasta water to the sauce. Mix with a set of tongs. Add the parsley and mix to combine. Use the remaining pasta water to loosen the sauce if necessary. Set out four bowls. Spoon the pasta into bowls. Spoon extra sauce on top. Garnish with bread crumbs and picked fennel fronds.

MINTED HUMMUS
WITH CELERY LEAVES, FETA, AND RADISHES

Serves 4 to 6

There are a host of vegetables that hold up well in the wintertime and provide a welcome crunch and much-needed color in a fairly drab month. Celery and its leaves, and radishes seem to shine beside the limp heads of lettuce and lackluster bunches of herbs. I often employ them in salads to follow a rich or fragrant stew, a sort of palate cleanser. Here, they are plated up with a wonderful hummus, which makes for a great first course at a dinner party or a lunch for two.

FOR THE HUMMUS

2 cloves garlic

Kosher salt

One 15-ounce can good-quality (organic) garbanzo beans

6 sprigs mint, leaves picked from stems

Zest and juice of 2 small lemons or 1 large lemon

½ cup extra virgin olive oil

1 large pinch red pepper flakes

2 tablespoons tahini

FOR THE SALAD

6 ounces fresh feta cheese, broken up into bite-size pieces

1 cup thinly sliced celery, cut on a slight diagonal (ideally on a mandoline)

4 radishes, sliced in half

1 cup cleaned celery leaves

8 sprigs parsley, leaves picked from stems

¼ red onion, small dice

Kosher salt

Fresh ground pepper

FOR THE DRESSING

1 tablespoon lemon juice

1 tablespoon sherry vinegar

2 tablespoons extra virgin olive oil

TO FINISH

Chili oil or additional extra virgin olive oil

Sea salt

To make the hummus: In a food processor, grind up the garlic with a pinch of salt. Add the garbanzo beans, mint, lemon zest and juice, olive oil, red pepper flakes, and the tahini. Grind until smooth (this could take a few minutes) and season to taste. Use more olive oil to thin the hummus if necessary. You want it to hold its shape without being stiff.

Place all the salad ingredients in a bowl. Season to taste with salt and pepper. Dress with lemon juice, sherry vinegar, and olive oil. Toss.

To plate, cover the base of a large, shallow serving bowl with ½ inch of the hummus. Reserve the rest for the week to come. Pile the salad up on top, showing the hummus around the edges. Drizzle with a bit of chili oil or additional olive oil and sprinkle with sea salt.

TORTILLA SOUP

WITH DRIED CHILIES AND JACOB'S CATTLE BEANS

Serves 6

One of our dearest friends is vegetarian and her presence at our table gives me a good opportunity to make a meatless meal. I will admit that in the house I grew up in, a meal was not a meal without meat of some kind, so while it goes against my instincts to cook without meat, it is good practice. I would typically make this soup with chicken stock and pulled chicken, but I must say that it was even more delicious without the poultry flavor. You could really taste the beans and chilies, as they become the focus of the dish.

2 cups dried Jacob's Cattle Beans, kidney beans, or Romano beans, soaked overnight

Kosher salt

8 dried chipotle peppers (or 2 chipotle peppers in adobo sauce)

2 white onions, peeled and quartered

4 cloves garlic, peeled

5 vine-ripened tomatoes

1 to 2 tablespoons adobo sauce (optional, to spice it up)

10 cups homemade vegetable stock

6 small to medium flour tortillas

Vegetable oil for frying (start with 2 tablespoons and add as needed)

3 ears corn, husked and kernels removed from cob

1 cup crumbled or shredded cheese (cotija or pepper jack)

½ bunch cilantro, roughly chopped

2 limes

We recently acquired a device called an Instapot at my house, which miraculously cooks dry beans in under 30 minutes. But you don't need a fancy pot to cook beans; you simply need time. First, rinse your beans in a mesh strainer. Then place them in a large pot and cover them with plenty of water. Do not salt the water as it will toughen the beans. Bring the pot to a boil, skim any scum that rises to the top (this is simply impurities on the bean shells), and reduce the pot to a simmer. Cook the beans until they are tender without losing their shape, typically about 1½ hours. Once they are al dente, you can salt them (heavily if you want them to have a nice flavor) and finish the cooking, about 10 minutes or so. Strain them so as not to overcook them in the residual heat of the cooking liquid. (You may want to keep 1 cup of liquid to enrich the soup base.)

To make the soup base: Seed and devein the dried chilies (with plastic gloves), if using. Place a cast-iron frying pan over medium heat. Blister the peppers and reserve (see page 86). Fill a tea kettle and bring it to a boil. Cover the chilies in boiling water and let them sit for 15 to 20 minutes to rehydrate. Strain and reserve the chilies.

Use the same frying pan to dry cook the onions and garlic until they are softened and slightly blackened. You can also do this under the broiler in the oven, with a careful eye. The onions will take about 10 to 15 minutes; the garlic, 5 to 10 minutes. Blacken the tomatoes by placing them on a sheet pan and under the broiler for 10 to 15 minutes or until soft and slightly blackened. In batches, blend the onions, garlic, tomatoes, and chilies, seasoning to taste as you go. You

(recipe continues)

are looking for a coarse puree. Add a little stock to each batch to get things moving if they're stuck. Now add the tomato mixture to a large, heavy pot and cook over medium heat for 20 minutes, slightly reducing and condensing the flavors. Season to taste and add some adobo sauce for a little extra spice and sweetness if you like. Add the vegetable stock and cook for an additional 15 minutes, allowing all of the flavors to meld. Then add the beans and bean cooking liquid, and cook for 5 minutes more.

In a large frying pan, heat the oil. Add one tortilla at a time, allowing a minute or so on each side to turn golden and get crisp. Move to a paper towel–lined sheet pan to cool. Season with a pinch of salt. Once they have cooled, place them on a cutting board and cut them in half and then into thin strips. Use the remining oil to cook the corn with a big pinch of salt over medium heat for about 5 minutes or until it has softened and begins to gain a bit of color. Add the corn to the soup.

Set out six soup bowls. Place a handful of tortilla strips and a heavy sprinkle of grated cheese in each bowl. Ladle soup over each bowl and garnish with cilantro and a heavy squeeze of lime.

COOKING WITH DRIED CHILIES AND HOW TO BLISTER THEM A distinct memory of blistering chilies in a cooking class in Oaxaca always gives my husband and me a chuckle. The instructor, Nora, guided us first through the market and then back to her home, where we made a spectacular multicourse meal, which included a squash vine soup and black Oaxacan mole. When it came time to toast the chilies on the comal, she said repeatedly to make sure that the skin of the chilies had "blipsters." Consequently, my husband and I have forever called blisters "blipsters." What Nora was demonstrating is that in order to liberate the essence of the chili, you must first release the oils in its skin by warming it to the point of blistering. You literally press the skin directly against the dry comal (or cast-iron pan) until the skin blisters, or blipsters. You must be careful because the skin can go from blistering to blackening very quickly, which will make the sauce bitter. Only after blistering the chilies can you rehydrate them. Skipping this step robs the sauce of a critical flavor.

MEXICAN CHICKEN STEW

WITH FRUIT

Serves 4 to 6

What struck me about this dish and several others that I made during a visit to Mexico City is that the sauce is built almost entirely in a blender. Only then is it cooked in the fat of the pan, along with the browned meat. The marriage of sweet tropical fruit with the sourness of mustard and fruit vinegar, warming spices such as cloves and allspice, and the spice of the peppers makes an irresistible flavor that lights up the palate. Make sure you heat up plenty of tortillas to sop up all the delicious sauce. And a pot of white rice bulks up the dish nicely.

8 guajillo peppers, seeded and deveined

2 chipotle peppers in adobo sauce

1 white onion, peeled, root removed, and quartered

6 cloves garlic, peeled

4 vine-ripened tomatoes, cored and diced

1 fresh bay leaf

⅛ teaspoon ground allspice

⅛ teaspoon ground cloves

One 1-inch piece Mexican cinnamon stick

1 tablespoon Dijon mustard

6 tablespoons fruit vinegar (apple, raspberry, pineapple, or quince)

1 teaspoon Mexican oregano

½ teaspoon kosher salt

1 cup tropical fruit juice (mango, guava, or pineapple)

1 apple, peeled, cored, and diced

2 tablespoons vegetable oil

1 whole chicken, cut into 12 pieces

1 cup chicken stock

18 corn tortillas

Warm a cast-iron pan over medium heat. Blister the guajillo peppers (see page 86). Preheat the oven to 325°F. Fill your tea kettle and bring it to a boil. Soak the guajillo peppers in boiling water for 10 to 15 minutes. In a blender, in two batches, combine the strained guajillo peppers, chipotle peppers, white onion, garlic, tomatoes, bay leaf, allspice, cloves, cinnamon stick, Dijon mustard, fruit vinegar, Mexican oregano, kosher salt, fruit juice, and diced apple. Blend well.

In a large, heavy pot heat the vegetable oil over medium-high heat. Lay the chicken pieces out on a cutting board and salt to taste. In two batches, sear the chicken pieces over medium heat, skin side down, until golden brown. They will release themselves from the pan once they are finished browning, about 10 minutes on the first side and 5 on the second. Move the chicken to a plate to rest and turn the heat down to medium.

Add the contents of the blender (both batches) to the pan and mix in with the oil. Be careful, as the sauce will spit and splatter, so have the lid handy to protect yourself and the stovetop. Add the chicken stock to the blender and swish it around to get the dregs of the sauce. Pour it into the pot. Now sink the chicken into the sauce in one layer. Place the lid on the pot, leaving it open a bit for air to escape. Place it in the oven for 2½ hours. When the stew is done, the meat should be falling off the bone.

Heat the tortillas by sitting them directly on top of the open flame of your stovetop for 30 seconds. They will begin to blacken around

(recipe continues)

the edges quickly. Flip them with a set of tongs and let them blacken on the other side for 20 seconds or so. Wrap them in a clean dish towel to keep them warm as they come off the flame. If you do not have a stovetop with an open flame, you can do this in a cast-iron frying pan as well. They will not blacken but they will warm thoroughly and take on some flavor from the pan.

BUILDING FLAVOR THE MEXICAN WAY Dry heat is a common method of cooking in Mexico, typically over a comal, which is a stone or cast-iron flat top under which a fire is built. One of the characteristic flavors of Oaxacan food is the char from the slightly blackened skin on tomatoes and tomatillos, peppers, onions, garlic, and more. Even tortillas are best heated up over an open flame so that they get a little black around the edges. Once the ingredient is soft throughout and charred around the edges, it is typically ready for the next step, which is usually, you guessed it, grinding it up. Think of this step (charring) as the equivalent of sautéing an onion or a carrot in a little olive oil or butter. It's similarly ubiquitous in the cooking process but with a totally different result.

WHY EVERY MEXICAN RECIPE CALLS FOR A BLENDER One can't help but notice that every Mexican kitchen (and nearly every recipe for that matter) includes a blender. Entire dishes are built in the blender in batches and then moved to the pot for cooking. It is a fundamentally different approach to much of the American and European cooking I've done. I found it incumbent upon myself to get a better blender. Grinding foods together is an age-old tradition in Mexico, one that typically takes place in a communal *molino*, where commercially powered mills can be rented to grind up large quantities of food. Families bring a multitude of ingredients to be ground into a paste and kept in the pantry for cooking throughout the year. Mole is the most common example of this.

MUSHROOM, FENNEL, AND LEEK GALETTE

Serves 4 to 6

This recipe was born out of the task of cleaning out the refrigerator. Perhaps that doesn't sound so appealing, but let me tell you, our impromptu dinner guests had to fight us for the last piece of pie. This galette includes my standard butter crust and is loaded high with sautéed vegetables deglazed with white wine. Serve it alongside a crisp salad and the rest of the bottle of white.

FOR THE PASTRY

1¾ cups all-purpose flour

½ teaspoon kosher salt

12 tablespoons cold unsalted butter

2 to 3 tablespoons ice-cold water

FOR THE FILLING

4 tablespoons butter

2 cups sliced button or cremini mushrooms

Kosher salt

2 cloves garlic, peeled and minced

2 sprigs thyme, leaves removed from stems

½ cup white wine

1 bulb fennel, thinly sliced

3 leeks, white and light greens thinly sliced

1 cup Castelvetrano olives, pitted and roughly chopped

½ cup finely grated Parmesan

FOR THE EGG WASH

1 egg

2 tablespoons heavy cream

To make the pastry: Preheat the oven to 375°F. Combine the flour and salt in a mixing bowl. Cut the butter into 12 pieces and then quarter each piece. Cut the butter into the flour with a pastry cutter or crumble with your hands. Once the butter is broken up so that no piece is bigger than the size of a pea, add the cold water and pack the dough into a ball as quickly as you can. Once fairly consistent in texture, wrap in plastic and place in the refrigerator for 20 minutes or until firm but not hard.

To make the filling: In a frying pan, melt 2 tablespoons butter over high heat. Add the mushrooms and a pinch of salt. Cook, without moving the mushrooms around in the pan, until they begin to brown on one side, about 5 minutes. Flip them with a flick of the wrist (or a spatula if that's a tall order) and let them begin to brown on the other side, about 3 minutes. Add the garlic and thyme and give the pan a little shake. Let cook for another minute or two and then deglaze with ¼ cup of the white wine, turning the heat off when you add the wine so as not to ignite the wine. Let cook down until wine is almost evaporated and then move the mushrooms and garlic to a plate to rest.

Add the remaining 2 tablespoons of butter to the pan and place over medium-high heat. Add the fennel, leeks, and a pinch of salt to the pan. Sauté for 10 to 15 minutes or until the vegetables are soft but not falling apart. It's OK if they get a little color. Deglaze with the remaining wine, turn the heat up to high, and let reduce for a minute or two. Move to a large mixing bowl and let cool for a few minutes. Add the olives and the mushrooms.

(recipe continues)

Roll out the pastry into a circle between two pieces of parchment paper to meet the top and bottom edges of a sheet pan. Peel off the top layer of the parchment. Spoon the filling in an even layer onto the pastry, leaving at least a 1½-inch border. Sprinkle the Parmesan on top of the filling. Use the parchment to pull the pastry up over the sides of the filling, folding it over itself as you go around the galette and pressing down to seal.

For the egg wash: In a small bowl, whisk an egg and the heavy cream. Generously brush the egg wash over the pastry, making sure to cover all exposed dough. Place in the oven for 35 to 40 minutes or until the crust is a nice golden brown. Slice and serve warm, beside a little pile of greens with shaved fennel.

LEMONY ICE CREAM

Makes 1 quart

With all the beautiful citrus available in the winter months and my ice cream addiction, it seems only natural to combine the two. I reserve ice cream making for stress-free days, when I have both hands free (aka, my daughter is at daycare) and there are no more pressing tasks. Making a custard is a simple and cathartic act, but it requires 100 percent of your attention.

2 cups heavy cream

1 cup half-and-half

1 heaping cup sugar

2 tablespoons lemon zest

1 teaspoon vanilla extract

¼ teaspoon kosher salt

6 egg yolks

½ cup lemon juice

Combine the heavy cream, half-and-half, sugar, lemon zest, vanilla extract, and salt in a heavy-bottomed medium-size saucepan. Place over medium heat and warm until the sugar dissolves. Turn off the heat and cover, letting the flavors steep a bit. Using a whisk, break up the egg yolks in a medium stainless-steel or glass bowl. Turn the heat back on to medium-low under the pot with the cream. Let it warm for a minute or two and slowly ladle the warm cream mixture into the egg yolks, whisking to combine. Move about half of the cream mixture to the egg yolks, whisking constantly, and then slowly whisk the combined yolks and cream back into the pot with the cream. Carefully watch the heat and turn it down if the custard is putting off too much steam. You don't want the egg yolks to scramble. Set a timer and rid yourself of all distraction. Stir the pot slowly with a wooden spoon for 6 to 8 minutes or until the custard coats the back of the spoon. Turn off the heat and remove the pot from the stove. Immediately strain the custard through a fine-mesh strainer into a glass bowl. Continue to stir, cooling the custard down as quickly as possible. Move it to a quart container once at room temperature, then cover and place in the refrigerator overnight. The next day, stir in the lemon juice and churn in an ice cream maker. Once spun to your desired consistency, move it back to a quart container and place in the freezer. Let freeze for a couple of hours to firm up before serving.

ICE CREAM AND CITRUS As you may already know, citrus tends to curdle milk. To combat this reaction, a higher fat content is needed in the dairy. A combination of heavy cream and half-and-half will offer ample fat, along with the rich proteins of the egg yolks, to result in a smooth, creamy, and flavorful citrus ice cream.

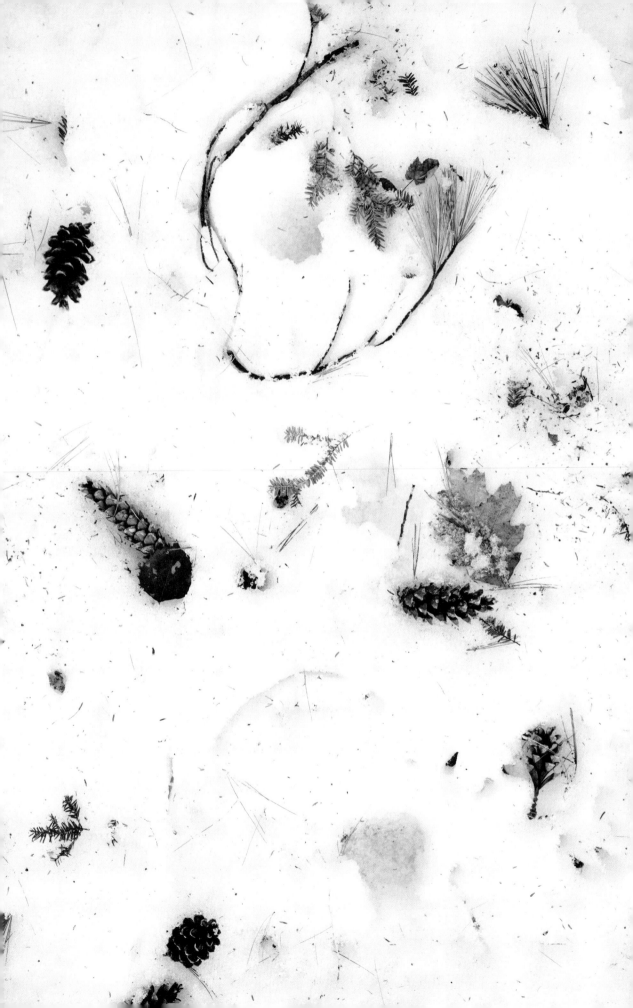

MARCH

March is not-so-fondly referred to as "mud season" in Maine. As the snow melts with the help of the rain, what's left is lots and lots of mud. A few years into living in an old farmhouse, we added on a mudroom as a buffer between the outdoors and the inside of our home. While it alleviates the problem of tracking in mud from our boots, the dogs still find a way to coat their bellies in earth, fall asleep on the kitchen floor, and leave about two cups of dry dirt behind when they get up. Some problems are unsolvable. While I've painted a rather grim image of this month, the upside is that daylight savings rolls around and our days notably lengthen. It's a sweet reminder that summer isn't so far away and we can all legitimately start talking about swimming in the lake and sailing on the bay. The birds come out in March, and you can hear their young chirping for food in the trees. The earth begins to soften, and while there is still no green to speak of, you can smell the thaw. Soon it will be time to start seedlings in the greenhouse and prepare the garden beds for planting.

Branches, and in some cases whole tree limbs, litter the yard, remnants of a battering of winter storms. Once the ragged tree debris has been dragged into a consolidated pile, we assess other winter damages. Fences must be mended, barn windows replaced, and the burrows and droppings of the animals that took shelter in our barn must be swept up and cleaned out. A true spring cleaning! Indoors, there is also work to be done. A box of frozen blueberries from the previous year's harvest must be put to good use, a slab of frozen pork fat can be baked off into biscuits, and the smoked fish tucked into the side door of the freezer shall find its way into a savory pie of sorts. March is a month of finishing off and clearing out to make room for spring's fresh start.

On our morning walk along the lake, most of the ice has thawed and opened up large patches of water. The streams are swollen with the melted snow, and the riverbeds are doing their best to contain the overflow. Up in the mountains, just minutes from the coast, blue lines run through the forests connecting the taps in maple trees, managing a steady flow of maple water. On the third Sunday of the month, Maine Maple Sunday, families across the state visit their local sugar shacks to watch as wood fires heat up huge tanks of maple water and boil it down to syrup, the steam and smoke billowing out of the top of these little log houses. Syrup is sold by the case to families who will commit to making weekend pancakes and waffles as a vehicle to sop up the liquid gold.

March is a wonderful time for baking, filling the cold, dry air with the smell of buttery biscuits and sweetbreads studded with fruit in the oven. These are shorter-term baking projects that require only a minor commitment but offer a significant reward. Similar to traditional bread baking, I find the act of cutting cold butter into flour and packing it into a dough a satisfying routine, one that gives shape to an otherwise quiet afternoon. A cup of milky black tea pairs ever so sweetly with a slice of Skillet Irish Soda Bread (page 103) smothered in honey butter. Predictably, I find both dogs at my feet when I eat anything with butter baked into it. I suppose they share my weakness.

It does not escape me that this is the final stretch of quiet, the earth still too hard for planting projects and the evening lows too cold to sustain growth in the greenhouse. It is the perfect excuse for late mornings in bed and big breakfasts of Blueberry Buckwheat Pancakes with Maple Syrup (page 96) and

Bangers and Mash with Fried Onion Gravy (page 99). Although it feels slightly indulgent, almost like a vacation at home, soon the tables will turn and there will hardly be time for a bowl of cereal before the morning farm routine calls. I particularly enjoy entertaining in the morning hours for our friends, dressed in comfy sweats and oversized sweaters, their hair still matted with sleep. It's commonplace to travel with your slippers in Maine and leave your snow boots at the door. Over the years, some of my fondest memories are of Sunday breakfasts in March with the woodstove roaring. The resident chef serves up steaming cups of coffee and encourages everyone to help themselves to forkfuls of crispy potatoes, thick-cut bacon, and fried eggs moved from cast-iron skillets onto warm ceramic platters. I've always enjoyed making conversation in the morning hours, as there is something more personal about it, as if a veil has been lifted.

Cliché as it may be, I love to cook Irish food in March, as Saint Paddy's Day marks the middle of the month. It's the last stretch of the cold season, where you can get away with eating comfort food three nights a week. (I've also noticed that I am at my heaviest in March each year—no coincidence there, I suppose.) Corned Beef and Cabbage in Broth with Carrots (page 105), Smoked Haddock Pie with Dill Biscuits (page 100), bangers and mash, and soda bread always find their way onto our table in March. These recipes are all fairly traditional and match the mood of the month. As the growing season is around the corner, soon young tender greens and vegetables will take center stage. March is the final opportunity to put a forkful of buttery mashed potatoes into your mouth without making any apology. Cheaper proteins find good purpose in this type of cooking, such as ground meat, brisket, sausages, and smoked fish. And quick breads such as biscuits and soda bread make wonderful vehicles for mopping up gravies and sauces. So, make no grievances about the caloric intake of this chapter. Light one last fire in the woodstove and cozy up to the table with a knife, fork, and spoon because the ground has not quite thawed and patches of snow still linger throughout the landscape. The vestiges of winter are nearly gone.

BLUEBERRY BUCKWHEAT PANCAKES

WITH MAPLE SYRUP

Makes 10 pancakes

The motivating factor for this recipe was a big box of wild Maine blueberries from the previous year's harvest that needed eating. But there were other incentives. "Ployes" are a dish native to Maine and New Brunswick. They are similar to a crepe or a pancake but made with heartier ingredients. This recipe calls for buckwheat flour as a sort of nod to the historic ployes while also calling upon the March maple syrup harvest.

1 cup all-purpose flour

1 cup buckwheat flour

1½ teaspoons baking powder

1 teaspoon baking soda

2 tablespoons sugar

⅛ teaspoon cinnamon

½ teaspoon kosher salt

3 eggs

Zest of 1 lemon

1 cup milk

1 teaspoon vanilla

2 tablespoons unsalted butter, melted, plus more for cooking pancakes

1½ cups blueberries

Powdered sugar

Lots of maple syrup

Salted butter, for serving

In a medium mixing bowl, combine the all-purpose flour, buckwheat flour, baking powder, baking soda, sugar, cinnamon, and salt. Whisk to combine. In another medium mixing bowl, combine the eggs, lemon zest, milk, vanilla, and melted butter. Whisk to combine. Make a well in the center of the bowl with the dry ingredients and pour the wet ingredients into it. Using a wooden spoon, stir to combine without overmixing. A few lumps will only make your pancakes better.

Preheat the oven to 200°F. Heat up a cast-iron frying pan or griddle over medium-low heat. Add 2 tablespoons of butter and let melt. Place ¼ cup of the batter onto the griddle and drop a few blueberries on top. Let cook for 2 to 3 minutes. Once bubbles start to form, flip the pancake and cook for another minute or two. As each pancake is finished, move it to a heatproof serving platter or plate and place in the oven to keep warm.

Meanwhile pour some syrup in a little saucepan and place over low heat to warm. Once you've got ten pancakes, place a few on each plate with a dusting of powdered sugar and a heavy serving of maple syrup. Serve with a crock of room-temperature salted butter.

BANGERS AND MASH

WITH FRIED ONION GRAVY AND A CHARRED TOMATO

Serves 4

A British friend of mine gave birth to a little girl just a couple weeks after I gave birth to my daughter. After a few sleepless months of new parenting, she and her husband invited us over for a "boozy brunch," which sounded divine. The girls slept peacefully in their car seats, side by side on the dining room table, while we drank Bloody Marys and devoured fried sausages with onion gravy on a soft bed of mashed potatoes. It was the perfect daytime indulgence to remedy our general state of exhaustion.

FOR THE BANGERS

3 tablespoons unsalted butter

4 high-quality sausages (such as bratwursts)

2 yellow onions, peeled and thinly sliced

Kosher salt

Fresh ground pepper

2 tablespoons all-purpose flour

1 cup red wine

2 cups rich chicken stock

FOR THE MASH

3 Idaho potatoes, peeled and cut into sixths

2 teaspoons kosher salt

4 tablespoons unsalted butter

1 cup heavy cream

Fresh ground pepper

1 tablespoon extra virgin olive oil

2 vine-ripened tomatoes

6 sprigs parsley, leaves picked from stems and roughly chopped (optional)

Melt 1 tablespoon butter in a large cast-iron frying pan over medium-low heat. Add 1 cup of water and the sausages. Turn up the heat and bring the water to a boil. Once the water has fully evaporated, let the sausages brown in the butter. Flip them and add another ½ cup of water. Let the water reduce again until fully evaporated and brown the sausages on the other side. Remove the sausages and reserve. Turn the heat down to medium and add the remaining 2 tablespoons of butter, onions, and a pinch of salt. Once the onions are nicely cooked down, translucent, and beginning to caramelize (about 10 to 12 minutes), sprinkle the flour over the top and mix into the onions. Push the onions around, allowing the flour to toast for a minute or two. Add the wine to deglaze the pan. Let cook for 2 to 3 minutes. Slowly add the stock, stirring to combine. Let cook for 15 to 20 minutes over medium heat.

Place the potatoes in a medium stock pot and cover with cold water. Add the kosher salt. Bring to a boil, reduce to a simmer, and cook the potatoes until they are tender, 20 to 25 minutes. Drain the potatoes, leaving about ½ cup of liquid behind to mash into the spuds. Add the butter and cream to the pot and mash. Season to taste with salt and pepper. Cover to keep warm until ready to serve.

Cut each tomato in half widthwise. Place a cast-iron pan over high heat. Add 1 tablespoon of olive oil and then the tomato, flesh side down. Let cook until the bottom side is slightly blackened and the tomato is soft throughout, about 6 minutes.

Divide the potatoes, sausage, gravy, and tomatoes between four shallow bowls and serve warm. Garnish with chopped parsley.

SMOKED HADDOCK PIE

WITH DILL BISCUITS

Serves 4

There are sure to be a few late-season snowstorms in March, just when you think spring is around the corner. Rather than stew in sadness, take to the stove and make a dish that combats the cold. A smoked fish pie (this one with a dill-flavored biscuit crust) will keep you company until the snow has melted and the perennials have pushed through the earth, showing the promise of green.

FOR THE FISH

1 pound smoked haddock fillets

2 cups milk

1 bay leaf

FOR THE BISCUITS

2 cups all-purpose flour

2 tablespoons baking powder

2 tablespoons chopped dill

½ teaspoon kosher salt

4 tablespoons cold butter

1 cup heavy cream

FOR THE EGG WASH

1 egg, whisked

FOR THE FILLING

2 tablespoons butter

4 leeks, white and light green parts thinly sliced

3 carrots, small dice

3 stalks celery, small dice

Kosher salt

2 tablespoons all-purpose flour

3 Yukon gold potatoes, small dice

2 cups fish stock

6 sprigs Italian flat-leaf parsley, leaves picked from stems and roughly chopped

½ cup heavy cream

1 cup fresh or frozen green peas

To prepare the fish: Place the fillets in a large rondeau pan, cover with the milk, and add the bay leaf. Place the pot over medium heat. Cook for 10 minutes. Now pour off the milk and flake the fish into small pieces, discarding the skin and any tough bits. Set aside.

To make the biscuits: Preheat the oven to 425°F. Combine the flour, baking powder, dill, and salt in a medium mixing bowl. Cut the butter into small pieces and cut into the flour with either a pastry cutter or your fingers. Once no piece of butter is bigger than a pea, add the cream. Bring the dough together without overworking it. Turn it onto a floured surface and form it into a disk. Move it to a sheet pan lined with parchment paper and place in the refrigerator for 10 minutes. Once the biscuit dough is chilled, roll it out to 1-inch height. Use a knife or a biscuit cutter to shape them into four disks. Place them evenly spaced apart on the sheet pan. Brush each biscuit with the egg wash. Place in the oven for 25 minutes or until the biscuits are golden and set. Let cool for 5 minutes.

For the filling: Preheat the oven to 350°F. In a large sauté pan, melt 2 tablespoons of butter over medium heat. Add the leeks, carrots, celery, and a pinch of salt. Cook for 10 to 12 minutes, stirring occasionally. Sprinkle the vegetables with the flour, moving it around in the pan to disperse. Add the potatoes, the fish, and the fish stock and let cook for about 10 minutes or until the potatoes are just tender. Stir in the cream and let cook for an additional 3 to 4 minutes. Stir in the peas and parsley. Move to a square baking dish and place in the oven for 15 to 20 minutes. Top with biscuits.

SKILLET IRISH SODA BREAD

WITH HONEY BUTTER

Serves 8

While I love the concept of Irish soda bread, I always found it to be a little bit dry. Here, we've solved that problem with a slather of honey butter, which I'm sure even a soda bread purist would not protest. Soda bread is best served alongside a stew of some sort for general sopping up of sauce and juices. You will need a stand mixer for the honey butter.

FOR THE HONEY BUTTER

1 cup (2 sticks) unsalted butter, softened

4 tablespoons honey

½ teaspoon sea salt

FOR THE BREAD

2 cups all-purpose flour

½ cup rye flour

2 teaspoons baking powder

1 teaspoon baking soda

½ teaspoon kosher salt

1 tablespoon sugar

4 tablespoons unsalted butter

1 cup buttermilk

⅔ cup currants

1 egg, beaten

In the bowl of a stand mixer, combine the butter, honey, and sea salt. Whip until well combined. Use a spatula to move it to a crock and set aside.

Preheat the oven to 425°F. In a medium mixing bowl, combine the all-purpose flour, rye flour, baking powder, baking soda, salt, and sugar. Whisk thoroughly. Cut the cold butter into four pieces and then quarter each piece. Work the butter into the flour mixture with your fingers until it's well broken up and no piece of butter is bigger than a pea. Add the buttermilk and the currants and bring together into a dough. Shape the dough into a ball, dusting with additional flour if too sticky to work with. Line a sheet pan with parchment paper. Place the dough on the parchment and flatten slightly. Cut an *X* across the top with a sharp knife, just ¼ inch deep. Brush with the beaten egg. Place the soda bread in the oven for 30 minutes. Remove and let cool for 5 minutes. Eat warm with honey butter.

WATERCRESS, PEARS, AND IRISH BLUE

Serves 4

Comfort food needs a bright companion as a point of contrast to lighten the wintery mood. This peppery little salad with a ripened pear and hunks of creamy blue cheese will do just that, offering a little acid punch and pep. Let the cheese come to room temperature and the pear ripen just enough to have both texture and flavor.

Place the shallot, lemon, mustard, honey, red wine vinegar, and olive oil in a blender. Blend until smooth in texture. Season to taste and blend again. Move to small bowl.

Cut the leaves from the stems of the watercress, leaving about half of the stems attached. Then cut the bunch in half again, so that the cress is bite-size. Place in a bowl and season with sea salt. Toss with two tablespoons of dressing. Slice the pear thinly around the core and toss with 1 tablespoon of dressing. Divide the watercress, pears slices, and broken-up blue cheese among four small salad plates and dress each with an additional spoonful of dressing.

FOR THE DRESSING	FOR THE SALAD
1 shallot	1 bunch watercress
Juice of 1 lemon	Sea salt
1 teaspoon Dijon mustard	¼ pound Irish or English blue cheese, broken into pieces
1 teaspoon honey	
1 tablespoon red wine vinegar	1 ripe Bartlett pear, sliced
3 tablespoons extra virgin olive oil	
Kosher salt	
Fresh ground pepper	

CORNED BEEF AND CABBAGE

WITH CARROTS IN BROTH

Serves up to 10

This is a "Sunday supper" kind of meal, one that requires a bit of preparation and forethought. It's an economic dish for a large group, and you can feel righteous when you tell everyone that you corned the beef yourself. Or, if you're looking for greater efficiency, a good butcher will take care of this step for you.

FOR THE CORNED BEEF

2 quarts water

2 yellow onions, quartered

3 carrots, roughly chopped

3 stalks celery, roughly chopped

1 cup kosher salt

½ cup sugar

1 teaspoon whole peppercorns

8 teaspoons whole allspice

8 teaspoons whole juniper berries

8 cloves

1 inch gingerroot, chopped into ¼-inch slices

1 cinnamon stick

1 fresh bay leaf or 2 dry bay leaves

One 4- to 5-pound brisket

FOR THE VEGETABLES

2 tablespoons unsalted butter

1 yellow onion, thinly sliced

1½ teaspoons kosher salt

1 small green cabbage, root removed and cabbage thinly sliced

2 cups white wine

2 quarts good beef broth (ideally from a butcher shop)

12 small yellow potatoes

6 carrots, peeled and chopped into 1½-inch pieces on a diagonal

6 sprigs Italian flat leaf parsley, leaves picked from stems

To make the brisket: Combine the water, onions, carrots, celery, salt, sugar, peppercorns, allspice, juniper berries, cloves, gingerroot, cinnamon stick, and bay leaf in a large pot and place over medium-high heat. Bring to a boil and give it a stir. Take the pot off the stove and let it cool completely. Once the brine has cooled fully, add the brisket, completely submerging it, and place in the fridge, covered. This can also be done in a large plastic bag. Let the meat brine for a minimum of three days and as many as ten.

When ready to cook, remove the meat from the brine and rinse it off. Fill a large pot with water and add the corned beef. Bring to a boil, reduce to a simmer, and let cook for 2½ to 3 hours with the cover on partway, making sure that the meat is fully submerged in water.

To prepare the vegetables: In a medium, heavy-bottomed soup pot, melt the butter. Add the onion and a pinch of salt and sauté over medium heat for 10 minutes. Add the cabbage, white wine, and 1 teaspoon of salt, and let cook for 15 to 20 minutes or until the cabbage has softened but still has some texture to it.

In a medium pot, add the beef broth. Bring it to a boil over medium heat and add the potatoes and ½ teaspoon of salt. Cook for 10 minutes and then add the carrots. Cook until the carrots are just tender, another 5 minutes.

Remove the brisket from the water and place it on a cutting board with a well. Cut it into thin slices, against the grain. Ladle beef broth, potatoes, and carrots into individual bowls, filling them about a third of the way. Then add a spoonful of cabbage to each bowl and a few slices of brisket on top. Garnish with a sprinkle of parsley.

HOMEMADE IRISH CREAM

Serves 6 to 8, depending on the pour

Homemade Irish cream is a simple finish to a supper, one that few would protest. It's sweet, a touch boozy, laden with cream, and offers a shot of espresso to help your guests up from the table at the end of the meal.

1 cup Irish whiskey (preferably Jameson or Wild Turkey)

One 14-ounce can sweetened condensed milk

1 tablespoon cocoa powder

1 cup heavy cream

½ teaspoon vanilla extract

2 ounces brewed and chilled espresso

Combine all the ingredients in a blender and blend on high for 30 seconds. Pour over ice and serve in good company for dessert.

APRIL

April in Maine is a month that taunts us with suggestions of spring, interrupted by rude certainties that winter is not yet over. Doves coo, perched in the budding apple tree outside of the kitchen window, which faces north and has a thin layer of frost from the previous evening's chill. Skunk cabbages poke their red and green tips up through the wet, muddy soil along the roads that are still being plowed of a late-season snowfall. Heating pads hold seedlings in the greenhouse, protecting their fragile newness from the lingering cold snaps. Tight-headed crocuses show their bright colors against the gray tone of garden beds, while tulips and daffodils show only signs of greenery. The expression "April showers bring May flowers" holds true to form in Maine's lagging springtime.

Snow melts on the mountains, channeling ice-cold water into the streams and out to sea. Cormorants perch on river rocks and branches that hang over the riverbeds, waiting patiently for the alewives to run. When they finally do, the rivers swell with fish, or so the legend has it. A walk through the Maine woods on a cool April morning smells and sounds of rebirth. Peepers fill the wetlands with song and the damp forest floor is lush with new moss. Ferns rule over the nascent growth, establishing themselves in an erotic display. A careful observer may even witness the spring mating dance of the woodcock, a lustful game of cat and mouse.

At home, we alternate between brothy meals of beans and greens and big bowls of crisp, hearty leaves, sprouts, and early perennial herbs. At the local shops, I buy every new, green, fresh thing I can get my hands on: containers of microgreens from nearby greenhouses, bags of spinach and arugula, even fresh-dug parsnips that have been preserved and sweetened in the earth throughout the entire winter. The savory smell of chicken stock with fresh bay is ever so familiar in our home during mud season, a sort of mood-boosting potpourri.

While I do not celebrate Easter for its religious significance, it's a fine excuse for a feast. A dear friend in Hope, Maine, invites a group of us over for an Easter Sunday supper and an egg hunt for the girls. (A pervasive female gene leaves us all with daughters and no sons.) Their home is perched high on a hillside, overlooking Maine's rolling landscape. When we arrive, the host has three grills going on a cool and windy April afternoon with three paella pans in action. I am duly impressed by the ambitious culinary theater of three variations on a Catalan classic. After a heroic effort to finish every last grain of Arborio rice, piles of wonderfully salty shellfish, and an assortment of juicy sausages and chicken thighs, we bundle up over our Easter dresses and walk up the dirt road that crests the hill. On top, we reach a hundred acres of blueberry fields, stained red from their state of hibernation and big, open blue sky. The girls run through the fields with the wind, and we marvel at the sheer beauty of the place in which we live.

At the farm, we survey the snow damages and build lists of spring cleanup. Vegetable beds need rebuilding, perennials need mulching, compost needs spreading, and wood needs splitting and stacking. The time has come to catalogue all of the seeds that were ordered in January from our local seed company. After a proper assessment of the "days to harvest" for each plant and a cross-reference with my grocery lists for each cooking class, I am able (approximately) to plan what needs planting and when. This is a knowledge that has taken me ten years to refine and one that I am quite proud of. There is something therapeutic about laying out all the seed trays and filling them with potting soil. It represents the start of yet another year at Salt Water Farm and a major shift in daily activity from the wintertime. It's also a quiet time to mentally prepare for the work ahead, which is inherently social and dynamic.

While there is little action in the gardens, chives, which seem to thrive in the cool, salty ocean air, are ready for their first harvest by the binful. Lovage and sorrel offer tender leaves for soups and salads, and dandelions begin to proliferate, calling for our full attention by the month's end before they turn bitter. While we are not yet serving the public, these small green offerings find their way into morning omelets and family lunches and the excess is sold to our local farm shops. The crocuses offer little pops of pink, purple, and yellow across the farm, an assurance that spring is on its way. As we prepare for our move back to the farm for the season, I am humbled by the ocean views that will soon greet us each morning with the rising sun.

The food of this chapter is meant to spark a seasonal appetite with young and tender green leaves and delicate sprouts, overwintered parsnips, the first asparagus harvest, and a few clippings of new spring herbs. Dishes like Maine Coast Paella (page 119) and Flounder with Lemon Caper Butter (page 116) showcase local and economical fish made exquisite with exotic saffron and picante capers, both with a heavy squeeze of lemon. A basic recipe for Braised Chicken Thighs with Leeks and Cream (page 120) finds its place in the stars with a splash of heavy cream and precious morel mushrooms. April's recipes lift us out of the winter fog by bringing simple spring meals to the table.

CHICKEN SOUP

WITH NAVY BEANS AND SPRING GREENS

Serves 8

This dish, a chicken broth laden with spring greens and softly cooked white beans, eases the transition from winter to spring. It's a nod to health, nascent growth, and sustenance. Use whatever spring herbs and greens you can find to bring it to life. In our case, many of them came from our greenhouse, which, by the end of April, is a full-fledged plant nursery.

FOR THE STOCK

1 yellow onion, peeled and roughly chopped

2 carrots with greens, cleaned and roughly chopped

2 stalks celery with greens, cleaned and roughly chopped

1 whole, locally sourced 3- to 4-pound chicken

1 herb bundle (2 sprigs thyme, 2 sprigs rosemary, 2 sprigs parsley, 1 bay leaf, 12 peppercorns)

FOR THE SOUP

1 bunch Japanese-style white turnips (such as hakurei), with greens

2 yellow onions, peeled and medium diced

2 leeks, thinly sliced

3 big carrots, peeled and thinly sliced

2 cloves garlic, peeled and minced

12 cups homemade chicken stock (see stock recipe above)

Picked meat from half a chicken (see stock recipe above)

2 cups cooked navy beans (see page 43)

Kosher salt

Fresh ground pepper

Red pepper flakes, to taste (optional)

TO SERVE

2 cups mixed spring herbs and greens (such as dill, basil, parsley, arugula, spinach, nasturtium greens, baby beet greens, kale, turnip greens)

Chive flowers, for garnish (optional)

To make the stock: In a large stock pot, sweat the onions, carrots, and celery over medium-low heat, covered, with a touch of salt until vegetables are softened, about 10 minutes. Place the chicken in the pot and just cover with water. Add the herb bundle and bring the water to a boil and then reduce to a simmer. With a slotted spoon, remove any foam that rises to the top. Let simmer for 1 hour. Remove the chicken and let cool enough to handle. Strain the stock through a fine-mesh sieve, pushing some of the juice out of the vegetables with a wooden spoon. Pick the chicken meat off the bones and reserve the meat. You can use the stock for the week or freeze for up to six months for later use.

To make the soup: Remove the greens from the turnips. Chop the greens and reserve them for the soup. Cut the turnips in half. In a large soup pot, sweat the onions, leeks, carrots, and garlic for 15 minutes or until the onions are translucent. Add the strained stock and half of the chicken meat. (Reserve the remainder of the chicken meat for another use.) Let simmer for 15 minutes. Add the cooked beans and the turnips and cook for 3 minutes more or until the beans are heated through and turnips are tender. Season to taste with kosher salt, fresh ground pepper, and red pepper flakes, if you are using. A couple minutes before serving, add the greens, stir, and serve immediately, garnished with chive flowers, if using.

FARRO, ASPARAGUS, AND ARUGULA SALAD

WITH HERBED BUTTERMILK DRESSING

Serves 4

This simple meal of grains, greens, and vegetables is dressed in a bright and brilliant buttermilk dressing, making each spoonful a pleasure. It's the type of dish that will sit comfortably in the fridge until the next day, and even the day after that, asking only for a little more dressing, a sprinkle of sea salt, and a handful of fresh arugula with each new serving. While you could riff on this dish with a number of spring vegetables, greens, and alternative grains, this combination is pretty stellar.

Bring a large pot of salted water to a boil. Add the farro and cook until al dente according to the package instructions, anywhere from 25 to 40 minutes. Strain, dress with a little olive oil, toss, and reserve.

Snap the ends off the asparagus. Then cut the asparagus into ½-inch pieces. In a cast-iron pan, add 1 tablespoon olive oil and warm over high heat. Add the asparagus and a pinch of salt and cook until it turns green and just begins to soften, about 4 to 5 minutes. Move to a plate and let cool. (Do not overcook.)

To make the dressing: Place the garlic in a blender with a pinch of salt. Buzz until it's completely broken up. Now add the buttermilk, crème fraîche, lemon zest and juice, parsley, chives, tarragon, and olive oil. Blend until the dressing is an even consistency. Add salt, pepper, and red pepper flakes, to taste.

In a large wooden bowl, toss the arugula, farro, asparagus, and 4 tablespoons of dressing. Now add the sprouts and give a final toss. Taste to see if the salad needs more dressing. Serve at room temperature.

FOR THE SALAD

1 cup farro

2 tablespoons extra virgin olive oil

1 bunch asparagus

Kosher salt

1 bunch arugula

1 cup sprouts or shoots

FOR THE DRESSING

2 cloves garlic, peeled

1 cup buttermilk

2 tablespoons crème fraîche

Zest and juice of 1 lemon

8 sprigs parsley, leaves picked from stems

1 small bunch chives, roughly chopped

6 sprigs tarragon, leaves picked from stems

2 tablespoons extra virgin olive oil

Sea salt

Fresh ground pepper

1 pinch red pepper flakes

ALTERNATIVE GRAINS A well-stocked pantry isn't complete without a few mason jars full of hearty grains such as wheat berries, farro, freekeh, and bulgar. Experiment with these grains by filling a pot with salted water and adding a cup or two of the complex grain. Follow the cook time on the package and taste the grain throughout to get a sense of the doneness. Complex grains tend to fill our bellies quicker than processed grains, so we need less of them to complete a meal. I often find use for a cup of cooked grains in a salad or in a soup.

FLOUNDER
WITH LEMON CAPER BUTTER

Serves 4

Flounder is a familiar fish in Maine, one that has been dredged in flour and fried in butter for generations. It's a mild-flavored fish, fairly delicate in structure, and quick-cooking due to its flat figure. It's inexpensive and always in season. This basic preparation doesn't stray far from its traditional butter and flour treatment. I've added capers, lemon, and parsley to pique your interest.

8 fillets flounder (about 2 to 4 ounces a piece), or haddock is a good substitute

Kosher salt

All-purpose flour, for dredging

6 tablespoons unsalted butter, plus more as needed for frying

3 tablespoons capers

Juice of 1 lemon

1 cup Italian flat-leaf parsley leaves

½ cup dill leaves

Preheat oven to 200°F. Prepare a sheet tray lined with foil as a landing zone for the fish. Rinse the flounder in cold water and pat dry. Lay the fish out on a cutting board and season both sides with salt. In a large, nonstick frying pan, melt 2 tablespoons butter over medium-high heat. Dredge two fillets in the flour on both sides and tap off any excess. Fry the fish in butter until just golden brown, about 4 minutes on the first side and 3 minutes on the second, using a fish spatula to flip the fillets when ready. Move them to the sheet tray. Fry the remaining fillets in batches, adding butter to the pan as needed and moving to the platter when finished. Place the sheet pan in the oven while you make the sauce.

Scrape any burnt bits from the pan with a wooden spoon and remove, leaving the browned butter in the pan. Add 4 tablespoons of butter and let melt. Add the capers, lemon, parsley, and dill and let sizzle in the pan for a minute or so. Move the fish to a warmed platter. Pour sauce across the fish and serve hot.

MAINE COAST PAELLA

Serves 8

One of our more popular classes at Salt Water Farm is a Catalan cuisine course, in which wood-fired paella is the featured dish. The students always marvel at how the whole dish, from start to finish, can be cooked over an open flame. Historically, this dish was made over a campfire in a farmer's fields with spare vegetables and proteins from the field (hare and yard birds). It wasn't until much later that it became a coastal dish, showcasing fish and shellfish from the Mediterranean.

4 tablespoons extra virgin olive oil

4 links sausage (andouille or chorizo)

2 pounds shell-on shrimp (optional)

2 yellow onions, minced

6 cloves garlic, peeled and diced

4 vine-ripened tomatoes, stems cut out and roughly chopped

½ teaspoon saffron

1 cup white wine (preferably Albariño, also good for drinking)

2½ cups Arborio rice

1 teaspoon kosher salt

8 cups chicken stock

12 littleneck clams, soaked in salt water for 2 hours

12 mussels, cleaned and debearded

1 pound squid (mixture of tentacles and bodies cut into rounds)

1 cup cooked fresh or frozen peas

½ bunch parsley, leaves picked from stems

6 lemon wedges

Heat 2 tablespoons of olive oil in the paella pan over medium/high heat. Brown the sausages on both sides, about 5 minutes per side. Remove them from the pan and set aside. If using, add the shrimp to the pan. Cook until the shells turn pink, flavoring the base of the pan, and then remove and reserve. Once the sausages cool, cut them into 1½-inch pieces and reserve. Add the onions and garlic to the pan with a pinch of salt and cook over medium heat until soft and translucent, about 10 minutes. Add the tomatoes and saffron and continue to cook for another 10 minutes, until slightly reduced. Add the white wine and cook down slightly, about 5 minutes. Add the rice, salt, and 4 cups of stock and give it a quick stir. Bring to a boil, then simmer on low heat for 10 to 15 minutes. You don't want to move the rice around the pan at this point. You simply add a little stock as the rice cooks and absorbs the liquid.

Over the course of 25 minutes, slowly add an additional 5 cups of liquid (as needed), making sure that the rice is cooking without burning or drowning in liquid. About 15 minutes before the paella is fully cooked, disperse the clams and sausage over the top. (The clams take the longest to cook and the sausage should still be raw at the center.) About 10 minutes before the paella is finished, add the mussels, squid, shrimp, and peas. The heat will cook the clams and mussels to the point of opening and warm the already cooked peas. If the shellfish do not open, give them another couple of minutes, and if they still don't open, discard them. At this point, the rice should be fully cooked and developing a crust on the bottom of the pan. No more liquid is necessary. Once the seafood and rice are fully cooked, garnish the paella with parsley and lemon wedges. Serve with a big wooden spoon.

BRAISED CHICKEN THIGHS
WITH LEEKS AND CREAM

Serves 4

This frugal braised chicken dish falls squarely in the easy-and-delicious weekday-dinner category. While the recipe calls for low heat and long cooking, you could easily bump up the heat to 375°F and cook the dish in 30 minutes, adding the cream for the last 10 minutes in the oven. If you can get your hands on morel mushrooms, the dish becomes elegant and worth pairing with an exceptional white wine, served to worthy company. Everyone will clean their plate, I promise.

2 tablespoons extra virgin olive oil

4 chicken thighs

4 leeks, thinly sliced

3 carrots, peeled and thinly sliced into rounds

6 cloves garlic, peeled and roughly chopped

1 tablespoon all-purpose flour

4 cups water or chicken stock

8 small yellow potatoes, cut in half

1 lemon, cut into 4 thinly sliced rounds

½ cup heavy cream

2 tablespoons unsalted butter

1 bunch asparagus

1 cup cleaned morels (optional)

4 sprigs tarragon, leaves removed from stems and roughly chopped

6 sprigs parsley, leaves removed from stems and roughly chopped

Preheat the oven to 325°F. In a large, heavy-bottomed pan, warm the olive oil over medium/high heat. Pat the chicken thighs dry with a paper towel and season them with kosher salt. Sear them, skin side down, until they are crispy and release from the pan, about 8 minutes. Flip each of them and cook for an additional 4 minutes. Remove the thighs from the pan and move to a resting plate. Turn down the heat to medium-low and add the leeks and a pinch of salt. Cover and cook for 8 to 10 minutes or until the leeks are soft and begin to break down, stirring occasionally. Add the carrots and another pinch of salt and continue to cook until the carrots begin to soften, another 6 to 8 minutes. Add the garlic and cook for another 4 to 5 minutes. All of the vegetables should be nice and tender. Sprinkle flour over the vegetables and stir to incorporate for 1 to 2 minutes, allowing the flour to toast a bit. Add the water or chicken stock and potatoes and bring to a boil. Nestle the chicken thighs back into the pot and top each with a lemon round. Reduce to a simmer and place the pot in the oven for 1 hour or until the thighs are incredibly tender, the meat is falling off the bone, and the stock has reduced by at least half. Stir the cream into the sauce and place back in the oven for 15 minutes.

In a frying pan, melt the butter over medium heat. Add the asparagus and morels (if available) and cook until both are tender, about 6 minutes. Take the chicken out of the oven, and garnish it with asparagus, morels, tarragon, and parsley.

CHICKEN THIGHS Talk about economy in the kitchen. Next to the oyster meat (a pair of tiny meat morsels nestled into the back of a chicken carcass), the thighs are simply the best and most flavorful part of the bird. Of course, they need a little more time in the oven or pan than the breasts do, and a little more liquid to stay moist, but when nicely browned and braised, a chicken thigh is where it's at. When I'm feeling like the grocery budget is spiraling out of control, which is a regular occurrence for me, I always reach for chicken thighs, a sturdy and satisfying source of protein at an accessible price point.

JUST ADD SOME CREAM! For years, my sister was notorious for adding "a little" cream to finish a dish: a pasta sauce, a chicken dish, even a meat sauce for a roast. She wasn't wrong to assume that cream makes everything better, but the persistence of her habit packed pounds onto all of those at her table. Now that she's a little older, and for the sake of her marriage, she's found healthier methods of cooking. But now and again, she just can't help but add a splash of cream at the end of a recipe. When cooking with cream, typically you want to add it toward the end of the cooking process, about 15 minutes before the dish is ready to serve. Cream pairs wonderfully with mushrooms and asparagus; well, actually, it pairs well with most things.

PARSNIP AND ALMOND CAKE

Serves 10

We make a version of this cake with carrots in the summertime, but spring-dug parsnips find a happy home grated and mixed into the batter in the early spring, once the ground has thawed enough to pull them from the earth. You'll find that neither the cake nor the icing are overly sweet. Wash your mind of the dry and sugary carrot cake of your youth and welcome this nutty, spice-scented root-vegetable cake with a tender crumb and a devilishly good frosting.

FOR THE CAKE

1 cup (2 sticks) butter, softened

1 heaping cup light brown sugar

4 eggs, separated

Zest and juice of 1 orange

1 cup all-purpose flour

½ cup almond flour

2 teaspoons baking powder

2 teaspoons baking soda

1 pinch ground cloves

1 pinch ground nutmeg

1 pinch ground cinnamon

½ teaspoon ground ginger

A few drops almond extract

½ teaspoon kosher salt

3 cups grated spring-dug parsnips

FOR THE FROSTING

8 ounces cream cheese (preferably Philadelphia)

8 ounces mascarpone

1 cup confectioners' sugar

¼ cup toasted sliced almonds

Preheat the oven to 350°F. Butter and flour an 8-inch round cake pan and line the base with parchment paper.

Beat the butter and sugar until light and fluffy in the bowl of a stand mixer with a whisk attachment. Add the egg yolks, one at a time, and mix until fully incorporated. Use a spatula to push down the sides of the bowl so that the mixture is even in texture. Add the orange zest and juice and mix. In a medium mixing bowl, combine the all-purpose flour, almond flour, baking powder, baking soda, cloves, nutmeg, cinnamon, ginger, almond extract, and salt and mix to combine. Add to the stand mixer and beat until fully incorporated. Remove the bowl from the mixer along with the whisk and stir the grated parsnips in by hand. Move the contents of the bowl to another mixing bowl. Clean the bowl that fits in the stand mixer and run it under cold water to cool it down. Clean the whisk attachment and fit back into the stand mixer. Whisk the egg whites to stiff peaks. Fold the whites into the parsnip mixture in three parts, making sure to incorporate air so that the batter doesn't deflate. Once the batter is consistent in texture, fill the cake pan with the batter, give it a few knocks on the counter to remove air bubbles, place it on a cookie sheet, and put it into the oven. Cook for 50 minutes or until the cake has set at the center and browned nicely around the edges. Let cool fully.

Whip the cream cheese, mascarpone, and confectioners' sugar until well blended. Spread the frosting across the top and sides of the cake in an even layer. Decorate with sliced almonds, slice, and serve.

MAY

There is an excitement in May that fills the air: the knowledge that summer is on the horizon. The Saturday farmer's market starts up again, with carefully packed bags of tender lettuces, bundles of spring herbs tied with string, tiny turnips and radishes, and crates of eggs in pink, green, purple, brown, and white. If you've ever raised chickens, you know that with longer days come a heavier laying schedule and more eggs than ice cream, omelets, and fresh pasta can satisfy. It's always a pleasure to see the faces of the growers after the long winter break. The warming soil and air keep them busy around the clock, as they take full advantage of the short Maine growing season.

At Salt Water Farm, May is almost entirely devoted to getting the farm ready for the season. My husband and I move into the barn above the cooking school at the beginning of the month so that we can get up with the sun and begin work. Once the garden beds have been tilled, shaped, and topped off with compost, we lay wood chips between the rows made from the chipped trees that fell during the winter storms. Irrigation tubes lay across each row, in preparation for the dry summer stretches. Perennials are trimmed and the soil at their base is weeded and generously mulched to encourage growth. I love watching all of the plants on the farm begin to bud out: sea berries, honey berries, apple trees, pear trees, beach plums, and so many more. The fields that slope down to the sea turn a tender green and begin to rise up like a slow tide. New bird life fills the air: eaglets learn to fly and catch fish from the sea, ducks chase one another through the low brush in a mating dance, and the whip-poor-will sings at night in a less-than-charming chorus.

Flowers begin to bloom in little bursts of color across the landscape. Our quince trees have spectacular pastel blossoms in peach and purple, assuring us that many firm little quince are on the way. The lilacs in pink, purple, and white perfume the sea breeze, inviting our first guests down the grassy path and into the cooking school. A forsythia bush beside our cottage (the original building on the farm) is highlighted in yellow, offering excellent material for early-season floral arrangements. Crocuses and violets are tiny delights that seem to pop up where you least except them.

In the greenhouse, each square inch of tabletop supports seedling trays. The entire farm sits in waiting, germinating in the warmth and stillness of a controlled climate. We gently water all of the seedlings each day, monitoring their growth, and by Memorial Day, when the threat of frost is behind us, we begin the great plant migration into the lovingly prepared beds. Some plants require a "hardening," which simply means that they need to spend a day or two in their trays out of the greenhouse to adapt to the wind and the cold before they are moved directly into the soil. Some of the hot crops, such as tomatoes, peppers, and eggplants, are moved first to bigger pots to spend a little more time in the hothouse. I find that they profit from the warmth of the greenhouse until mid-June, when warmer temperatures are a sure thing.

The prevailing theme of our May farm work is the asparagus harvest. When we started the farm, my father and I spent a cold, wet day digging trenches in the mud to house fifty asparagus plants. We padded their tiny roots with compost and backfilled the trench, and by the end of the day, we both had sore backs and head colds. But, man, was it worth it. Every year, in late April, a few purple and green spears poke through the soil announcing the first harvest. April rains feed the roots and May sun drives their growth. It would not be exaggerating to say that these spears grow three to four inches a day. We harvest a few dozen every morning, and by lunch you can see even more of them reaching into the sky. The difference in taste between a freshly cut asparagus spear and the dehydrated bunches at the store, strangled by a rubber band, is tremendous. In fact, homegrown asparagus can be eaten even raw, one bite at a time. It's that tender and full of moisture. I suppose it goes without saying that asparagus features in every meal from early May through mid-June. You'd think I'd get sick of them, but on the contrary, I'm sad to see the final harvest.

Asparagus is not the only rapid growth in the month of May. Perennial spring herbs quickly transform the dark brown earth into a garden of green, their tender leaves pushing through last year's dead growth and quickly obscuring it. I love to watch this progression from my bedroom window, a visual assurance that the growing season is underway. Lovage fills out, its anise-scented leaves a deep green. Two types of sorrel, green and variegated, spread like wildfire in the herb gardens. Oregano, sage, and thyme are full and healthy in the blink of an eye. Chives grow like weeds, offering their purple flowers for garnish before the season has even begun. With each rain comes more growth. May is the time for salsa verde, green compound butters, and any excuse to incorporate generous amounts of tender herbs into recipes.

May is an excellent time for foragers. A magical walk through the woods and along the riverside reveals ferns of all kinds, including fiddleheads that can be fried up in butter over a hot flame. Watercress collect on the outer edges of natural ponds, peppery and crisp, perfect for salads or beneath slices of grilled steak. Dandelions rule the days of May in their conquest of the lawn. We try to collect them early in their growth, as they tend to get more bitter over time. There is also foraging along the coastline. At low tide, sleek razor clams hide just beneath the sandy shores, sending up little bubbles of air as a hint to their location. Steamers require a rake and a little faith to capture but are well worth the hunt on a warm, sunny day, especially when the day ends with a bucket of clams, a driftwood fire, and friends to share them with.

After long days on the farm, our fingernails caked with dirt, and blackfly bites on the backs of our necks and behind our ears, a hot shower and a cold beer are just what is needed to relax. Most May evenings are spent out on the patio, my husband standing over the grill with a set of tongs as I throw together a simple salad of spring greens. May is the final month to see local friends before the tourist season kicks off and everyone is hard at work. On Memorial Day, we host an annual industry potluck, a big party in honor of all the folks who will devote their summer and early fall to hosting the tourists. As there are so many talented cooks in the community, our farm table is packed with wonderful dishes and never fewer than four rhubarb desserts. At the end of the night, we all wish each other luck and say half-joking, "See you next winter."

ASPARAGUS SOUP

WITH ROCK CRAB AND CHIVE FLOWERS

Serves 4

This is the simplest recipe in the world, celebrating the glut of asparagus on the farm in the month of May. It's important that you don't overcook the asparagus or you'll lose the brilliant green color that makes this such a visual spring gift. A little lump of crab meat makes the soup into a more robust meal.

2 tablespoons butter

1 medium yellow onion, medium dice

Kosher salt

1 cup water or vegetable stock

2 bunches asparagus

1 squeeze lemon

2 tablespoons crème fraîche

8 sprigs parsley, leaves picked from stems

Fresh ground pepper

1 pinch red pepper flakes

One 8-ounce container rock crab, chilled

Sea salt

Chive flowers, for garnish

In a medium saucepan set over low heat, melt the butter. Add the onions and a pinch of salt and cover. Let sweat for 15 minutes, moving them around in the pan every couple of minutes. The onions should be translucent before you move on to the next step. Add the water or stock and bring it to a boil. Turn off the heat.

In a separate medium saucepan, bring 8 cups of water to a boil. Salt generously. Prepare an ice-water bath. Snap the ends off of the asparagus and cut the spears into 1-inch pieces. Blanch the asparagus by dropping them into the boiling water for 2 minutes or until just tender. Lift them out of the water with a slotted spoon and place them into the ice-water bath. This will prevent overcooking and keep them nice and green. Once fully cooled, strain and reserve the asparagus.

In a blender, combine half of the asparagus and half of the onion and stock mixture once room temperature. Add half of the lemon juice, half of the crème fraîche, and half of the parsley. Blend on high until the soup is an even consistency. Season to taste with salt, pepper, and red pepper flakes and blend once more. Move the soup to a serving bowl. Do the same with the other half of the ingredients. Add them to the bowl. Mix the two batches together. If it's too thick, add a touch of water. Serve the soup at room temperature or chilled with a spoonful of crabmeat at the center and sprinkle sea salt and the chive flowers on top.

LITTLENECKS, LEEKS, ROMESCO, AND CRUSTY BREAD

Serves 4 to 6

The star of this dish is the sauce, which requires a fair amount of preparation. While you'll find that it pairs well with salty clams and bread, its versatility makes it a great sauce for just about anything that comes off the grill. You will end up with extra for precisely that purpose.

NOTE: *To purge the clams, place them in cold, heavily salted water for 30 minutes. Then rinse them in a strainer.*

FOR THE ROMESCO

½ cup whole hazelnuts

½ cup whole almonds

4 guajillo peppers, seeded and deveined (using gloves)

2 tablespoons plus 1 cup extra virgin olive oil

1 thick slice sourdough bread

1 cup canned San Marzano tomatoes, broken up with your hands

2 cloves garlic, peeled

Kosher salt

½ cup flat-leaf parsley

Juice of 1 small lemon

A splash sherry vinegar

Kosher salt

1 crusty loaf sourdough

FOR THE CLAMS

2 tablespoons extra virgin olive oil

3 leeks, dark green tops removed

Kosher salt

1 cup sherry fino

30 littleneck clams, purged (see above)

To make the romesco: Preheat the oven to 350°F. Arrange the hazelnuts and almonds on a sheet pan and place in the oven for 8 to 10 minutes, until they begin to release their oils and become fragrant. Be careful not to burn them. (Set a timer if necessary.) Remove the nuts from the oven and move them to a bowl to cool.

Heat up a cast-iron frying pan over medium heat and gently toast the peppers by pressing their skins to the pan with a set of tongs until they are fragrant. Be careful not to burn them. Once toasted, turn off the flame and place the peppers in a heatproof bowl. Fill a kettle with water and bring to a boil. Cover the peppers with boiling water to rehydrate them for 15 minutes.

Pour 2 tablespoons of olive oil into the cast-iron pan and put over medium heat. Fry the slice of bread on both sides until golden brown. Remove the bread and set it aside to cool. Once cool, tear it into small pieces. Add the tomatoes to the pan and cook them down slightly, about 5 minutes over medium heat.

Strain the peppers, discarding the water. In a food processor, add the garlic and a pinch of salt, and blend. Add the nuts and blend. Next, add the torn bread, peppers, tomatoes, parsley, lemon juice, vinegar, and 1 cup of olive oil. Blend the ingredients until you have a coarse puree, adding a few tablespoons of olive oil if the mixture is too thick. Season to taste and blend again. Move it to a bowl or small pitcher and top with a little pour of olive oil to keep it moist, or store it in an airtight vessel for up to a week.

(recipe continues)

To prepare the clams: In a large frying pan with a lid, warm 2 tablespoons of olive oil over medium heat. Add the leeks and a pinch of salt and cook slowly until softened, stirring occasionally, about 10 minutes. Turn off the heat. Add the sherry and the clams and turn the heat on high. Be careful, as the sherry could ignite. Cover the pan and let it cook until the clams are opened. If the pan dries up before the clams have opened, add a little more sherry. Move the romesco into a crock, mortar, or small serving bowl.

Place the loaf of bread in the oven for 10 minutes or until warmed throughout. On a large platter, pour out the cooked clams. Place the romesco on the platter. Tear the bread into big pieces and place them around the edges of the platter. Eat the clams with a fork, dipped in a little romesco, and use the bread to sop up the remainder of the sauce.

HOW TO SKIN HAZELNUTS The skins of hazelnuts can contribute bitterness to the overall flavor of a finished dish, so most recipes call to remove them. Here's how to do it: Once you've roasted the hazelnuts in the oven for 8 to 10 minutes, pour them onto a clean, dry kitchen towel and close up the towel, allowing them to steam for a minute or two. Then use the towel to rub off the skins and discard them. It's a messy job, but it needs to be done. Of course, you can buy them skinned, but often the skin protects them from drying out, so you will be sacrificing a bit of quality.

DANDELION SALAD

WITH RADISHES, BACON, EGG, AND SPRING HERB DRESSING

Serves 4

Many of our students are intimidated by poaching eggs. We use the simplest of techniques that doesn't require any fast-paced swirling of water or special equipment. The poached egg is then placed on a bed of dandelions, which can be picked up at your local market or found in your very own backyard, assuming they are naturally grown.

FOR THE DRESSING

1 clove garlic

Kosher salt

1 teaspoon Dijon mustard

Juice and zest of 1 lemon

1 tablespoon white wine vinegar

1 teaspoon honey

1 cup mixed spring herbs (chopped chives, lovage leaves, sorrel leaves)

Fresh ground pepper

¼ cup olive oil

FOR THE SALAD

6 strips thick-cut bacon

1 large bunch dandelion greens

2 tender spring radishes or turnips

1 bunch scallions

Kosher salt

Fresh black pepper

4 poached eggs (see page 44)

To make the dressing: In a blender, grind the garlic clove with a pinch of salt. Add the Dijon, lemon juice and zest, vinegar, honey, herbs, salt and pepper, and olive oil to taste. Blend until smooth. Move the dressing to a mason jar and let rest for 20 minutes so that the flavors can meld.

To prepare the salad: Lay the bacon across a cutting board and cut it into 1-inch pieces. Place it in a medium frying pan set over medium heat and let the fat render, moving the bacon around so that it doesn't stick. Let the edges crisp up a bit, about 8 to 10 minutes, and then turn off the heat.

Cut the ends off the dandelion greens, lay the greens across a cutting board, and chop them into 1-inch pieces. Submerge the greens in water in a salad spinner, drain, and spin till dry. Place them in a big bowl and set aside.

Using a mandoline, slice the radishes or turnips very thinly. Chop the white and light green parts of the scallions into thin slices on a diagonal. Reserve.

Bring a medium saucepan of water to a simmer. Season the dandelion greens with salt and pepper, then dress them with a few tablespoons of dressing and give them a toss. Distribute the dressed greens among four bowls. Then distribute the bacon, scallions, and radishes or turnips among the bowls. Gently lower the poached eggs into the water to reheat them for 10 to 15 seconds and then place an egg on each salad. Drizzle a spoonful of additional dressing over each salad. Serve.

PORCHETTA
WITH SALSA VERDE

Serves 8 to 10

Porchetta has always intrigued me, as it calls for a nontraditional cut of pork that is very heavy on fat. I've learned that it is a wonderful cut for a large and informal gathering, paired with a bright sauce that cuts through the fat. If you have access to a rotisserie, that's the way to go. Otherwise, an oven-roasted porchetta won't disappoint.

FOR THE PORCHETTA

One 6- to 7-pound pork belly with skin on and center-cut pork loin attached (ask your butcher ahead of time to prepare this for you)

1 head garlic, cloves peeled and minced

6 sprigs rosemary, leaves picked from stems and minced

8 sprigs thyme, leaved picked from stems

1 tablespoon fennel powder, or ground fennel seeds

Zest of 3 lemons

6 tablespoons extra virgin olive oil

2 tablespoons kosher salt

1 teaspoon fresh ground pepper

FOR THE SALSA VERDE

2 tablespoons capers

1 hard-boiled egg, cut in half

1 small bunch Italian flat leaf parsley, leaves picked from stems

1 small bunch chives, minced

1 small bunch tarragon, leaves picked from stems

1 small bunch cilantro, leaves picked from stems

½ teaspoon kosher salt

1 tablespoon Dijon mustard

Juice of 1 lemon

Kosher salt

Fresh ground pepper

1 cup extra virgin olive oil

Toasted bread, to serve

To make the porchetta: Preheat the oven to 450°F. Let me preface this next step by saying that you can have the butcher do the cutting. If you are doing the cutting yourself, first, slice the skin away from the meat and fat in one piece. You will use this to wrap up the whole porchetta later. Now unroll and open up the pork belly by cutting into it to create as much surface area as possible, keeping it in one piece. Lay it flat. (You are more or less butterflying it.) Combine the garlic, rosemary, thyme, fennel, lemon zest, olive oil, salt, and pepper and mix well. Rub down the interior of the porchetta (all of the cut pieces) with the marinade and let sit for an hour. Roll the porchetta up tightly and wrap it with the skin. Tie up the skin (around the outside) tightly with three pieces of kitchen string to hold the whole thing together. Place the porchetta on a rack fitted into a roasting pan and move it to the center of the oven. Cook for 45 minutes or until the skin gets nice and crisp. Reduce the heat to 350°F and cook for an additional 2½ hours. A thermometer inserted into the center of the pork should read 160°F when done.

To make the salsa verde: Place all the salsa verde ingredients into a blender. Blend until smooth. The salsa should be spreadable. Add additional olive oil to thin if it's too thick.

Remove the porchetta from the oven and allow it to rest for 20 minutes so that the juices evenly distribute. Slice the porchetta into ½-inch thick rounds. Serve with salsa verde and some good toasted bread to make simple sandwiches.

PIZZA

Makes 4 pizzas

At our house, pizza is a casual meal, typically eaten standing up and hot out of the oven. I usually put out a little spread of antipasto and batch up a cocktail with Italian bitters (a Negroni is perfect) so that folks can graze while they are waiting for a slice. A simple salad of tossed greens in lemon and oil is always a nice accompaniment.

FOR THE DOUGH

1½ teaspoons rapid-rise yeast

1 cup warm water

2½ cups all-purpose flour

½ teaspoon salt

1 tablespoon honey

1 tablespoon extra virgin olive oil

FOR THE TOPPINGS

2 bunches stinging nettles (or spinach, arugula, mustard greens, or Asian greens)

Kosher salt

2 cups coarsely grated fontina cheese

4 stalks green garlic, tender parts, thinly sliced

Fresh ground pepper

Red pepper flakes, to taste (optional)

FOR THE SET-UP

½ cup all-purpose flour

½ cup cornmeal

Extra virgin olive oil, for brushing

Large, thin cutting board or pizza paddle

Pizza stone

To make the dough: Mix the yeast into the warm water. Let stand for 5 minutes. In a large mixing bowl, combine the flour, salt, honey, and olive oil. Mix to distribute. Add the yeast solution to the flour mixture and stir until it begins to come together. Knead the dough with your hands, adding a little extra flour if necessary, until the dough begins to tighten up and the texture is consistent throughout. Place in an oiled bowl. Let stand for at least 2 hours at room temperature, covered with a damp cloth. You can speed this up by placing the bowl in a warm place (100 to 110°F), which will help the dough to rise faster.

Remove the dough from the bowl. Place a pizza stone on the middle rack of the oven. Turn the oven on to 500°F and let the stone heat along with the oven. You can also turn on an outdoor grill to medium heat.

To prepare the toppings: Using a pair of gloves and scissors, snip off the top two-thirds of the nettles. Prepare an ice bath. Bring a medium pot of water to a boil and salt it generously. Place the nettles in the water and blanch them for 30 seconds. Shock the nettles in the ice bath and drain. Squeeze out additional water. Put the grated cheese and the sliced garlic in small bowls.

To get yourself set up: You'll need a small bowl with the flour, a small bowl with the cornmeal (which acts as a conveyor belt to move the pizza around on the board), a small bowl of olive oil, a brush, salt, pepper, and red pepper flakes, if you want a little heat. Have the other toppings—the nettles, grated cheese, and sliced garlic—at hand.

Remove the dough from the bowl and cut it into quarters with a knife. Using flour to prevent sticking, roll out the dough to your desired size. (I like to use a rolling pin to roll it out to about 8 inches in diameter.) Sprinkle the cutting board or pizza board with a thin layer of cornmeal. Place one rolled-out dough on the cutting board or pizza board. Brush the dough with olive oil, making sure to avoid getting too close to the edges, as you want to keep the board dry. Arrange one-quarter of the cheese, greens, and garlic on the pizza. Drizzle with a little more olive oil and sprinkle with salt, pepper, and red pepper flakes, if using. Give the board a little jiggle to make sure that the pizza is free and moving on top of the cornmeal. Now slide the pizza onto the stone or grill and let cook until the dough bubbles up and cooks through and the cheese has melted, about 10 to 20 minutes, depending on your heat source. You will know it's done when the cheese is melted and the dough is crispy. Once finished, remove the pizza from the oven and move it to a clean cutting board. Slice it into six wedges and serve hot. Repeat this process with the remaining three dough balls. I always ask my guests to watch me do the first one so that they can get their hands dirty with the second, third, and fourth, while I indulge in my hard work.

GETTING COMFORTABLE WITH PIZZA DOUGH While you can always buy pizza dough at the store, a homemade dough is a simple project that yields more interesting results. Store-bought doughs tend to be pretty consistent and sturdy in texture, which is helpful if you're just getting comfortable with dough. When cooked off, they are fairy dense, which helps support an overloaded pizza. Here's my advice: Give homemade dough a try. Roll it out thin and don't overload the pizza. You will end up with a crisp, airy, and multitextured crust that allows the toppings to shine, rather than a dense crust where the toppings are lost in the sheer volume of dough.

RHUBARB AND RYE CAKE

Serves 10

I'm always looking for a great rhubarb recipe, as it is so abundant in the month of May. What makes this cake unique is the interesting combination of the nutty flavor of the rye flour and the tartness from the rhubarb compote: it can't be beat!

FOR THE RHUBARB COMPOTE

3 stalks rhubarb, chopped into ½-inch pieces

¾ cup white wine

½ cup golden raisins

¾ cup sugar

Zest of 1 orange

FOR THE CAKE

1 cup all-purpose flour

1 cup rye flour

2 teaspoons baking powder

1 teaspoon baking soda

1 teaspoon kosher salt

12 tablespoons butter, softened

1 cup light brown sugar

3 eggs

½ teaspoon almond extract

½ cup whole milk

Juice of 1 orange

Confectioners' sugar, for dusting

Preheat the oven to 350°F. Butter and flour a 9-inch springform pan and line the base with parchment paper.

To make the rhubarb compote, place all of the ingredients into a medium saucepan and place over medium-high heat. Bring to a boil, give a stir, and let it cook for about 20 to 25 minutes or until the compote has a jamlike consistency. Let cool.

Combine the flours, baking powder, baking soda, and salt in a medium mixing bowl and whisk to combine. In a stand mixer, beat the butter and sugar until light and fluffy. Add the eggs, one at a time, scraping the sides of the bowl between each addition. Add the almond extract and mix. Combine the milk and the orange juice in a small liquid measuring cup. Add one-third of the dry ingredients and one-third of the milk and orange juice mixture to the butter and sugar. Mix well, scraping the sides of the bowl. Add an additional one-third each of the dry ingredients and the wet ingredients. Mix well, scraping the sides of the bowl. Add the final one-third of the dry and wet ingredients and mix well.

Pour the batter into the springform pan. Now pour the compote on top. Using a spatula, swirl the compote into the batter using a circular motion. Place the cake on a sheet pan and move it into the oven for 45 minutes. Check for color. If the top is browning too quickly and the middle hasn't set, place an oven rack on top of the cake and an additional sheet pan on top of that to prevent it from direct heat. Cook for another 15 minutes or until the cake is completely set. Remove from oven and let cool for 20 minutes. Dust confectioners' sugar over the top. Serve slightly warm for best results.

JUNE

Maine's landscape blooms with color in June. The hillsides are flush with lupine in blush and violet, lilacs perfume the air, and peonies reveal their infinite plumage, like a ball gown released onto a dance floor. The woods are rich with ferns, protecting the forest floor from direct sun and creating shelter for earthly creatures. Rivers traverse the hills, their still-cold water plentiful with springtime fish such as alewives and trout. Life on the bay is something of a dream, cormorants and eagles nesting in the tall oaks waiting for a school of fish to shimmer across the top of the water. Schooners sail by the farm, their sheets full of wind. Gulls survey the harbors for fishermen's bait and the stray French fry from a sympathetic tourist. The squid begin to run and those in the know stand alongside the docks with a rig in hand and a bucket full of these primordial fish.

On the farm, the dogs begin their summer ritual of bathing at high tide and drying out on the deck. The ocean water is just warm enough now for a refreshing dunk but too cold for a leisurely swim. After long days tending to the gardens, we gather with family and friends around the fire and pour glasses of the new season's rosés. The fireflies light up the field below, the purest form of summer entertainment. The sun sets well into the evening, sometimes as late as nine o'clock, forcing those who are early to bed to appreciate the long days up until the last light.

The summer solstice holds special meaning in our family, as it was the day that my mother was born and therefore brings us all together to celebrate the longest day of the year. The poached chicken dish in this chapter was made at my mother's seventieth birthday party, a night we will always remember. My dad gave a memorable speech about the first time he saw my mother, her long dark hair parted in the middle (as was common in the 1960s), her tanned summer skin glowing in her beautiful summer dress. The birthday affair lasted well past sunset and the speeches left the guests with welcome tears and rolling laughter. These are the occasions that mark our time here on earth.

The cooking school starts up in June, and students from across the country (and sometimes farther afield) find their way into our kitchen, eager to learn. Our workshop program focuses on fundamental cooking techniques, such as knife skills, egg cookery, bread baking, and much more. Our first meal with the students really encompasses our mission at the school: resourcefulness and eating from the land. We shake cream into butter, bake a rustic country loaf of bread, whip up a frittata with eggs from the coop and vegetables from the garden, cut salad greens from the raised beds, and make a delightful dressing using a mortar and pestle to build its flavor. For dessert, we bake tender biscuits and spoon fresh local strawberries and whipped cream on top. It's a meal that never tires and that gets the students warmed up for the next few days of class (meat and fish cookery). This chapter shares with you the Cast-Iron Frittata with Farmer's Cheese (page 146) recipe from the egg cookery portion of our workshop—an extremely versatile dish for just about any season.

Another popular subject in June is seafood cookery, a course in which we discuss how to source fresh, sustainable fish and various ways of cooking it. This class showcases the abundance of fish that we have in the Penobscot Bay, featuring a New England–style Maine Coast Bouillabaisse (page 150), brimming with clams, mussels, squid, and halibut and topped with a rouille-smothered toast to deeply flavor the broth. When students ask me what my favorite dish to make is, this bouillabaisse is it, in part because it brings me back to time spent in Southern France on the Mediterranean and in part because it's such an exemplary offering of Maine's fish harvest.

After several years of teaching our basic workshop, it was time to build a curriculum for more accomplished cooks, a sort of graduation to a more challenging daily menu. Our Accomplished Home Cook Workshop, a self-designated enrollment, brings cooks from all regions to our kitchen at Salt Water Farm and the result is outstanding. Not only is the pace of the class quicker, the dishes that these creative and confident minds cook up are astoundingly good. This chapter offers a recipe for Sour Cherry Clafoutis (page 153), a French-style egg-based dessert that makes the most of our little sour cherry tree just outside of the cooking school doors. Thanks to a special request to include a clafoutis on our final day of class, this recipe will have a long life in the Salt Water Farm's repertoire.

On the last day of June, we celebrate my birthday. It's the one day that I do not cook; instead, I invite all my friends to the farm and encourage them to bring a dish to share. As so many of them are excellent cooks, we are never short on delicious and beautifully presented food. My father generously marinates a dozen racks of baby back ribs in a deeply flavorful harissa rub to feed the masses. The guests anxiously wait for the ribs to come off the grill as I marvel at the incredible spread across our outdoor farm table. Strawberry season is in full swing and the small, sweet berries find their way into both sweet and savory dishes. A beautifully lain strawberry tart on puff pastry and a layer of mascarpone is always a favorite. And an imaginative salad of Strawberries, Baby Spinach, Japanese Turnips, and Chive Blossom Vinegar (page 145) makes it onto everyone's plate. After dinner and with the light of the moon as their guide, friends wander down the winding path to the dark sea to check for phosphorescence, which makes a warm summer night feel like a fairy tale.

ORECCHIETTE
WITH GREEN PEAS AND BACON

Serves 4 to 6

When peas are in season, we are always looking to tuck them into dishes whether they are in the recipe or not. They add the most brilliant green to a dish, when properly blanched, and just a little snap when you bite into them. They also pair marvelously with cream and bacon and, in this case, a touch of mint, which adds intrigue to a humble pasta dish.

⅓ pound high-quality bacon, cut into ½-inch strips

1 yellow onion, small dice

Kosher salt

3 cloves garlic, peeled and minced

1 cup shelled green peas, preferably fresh

1 pound orecchiette

½ cup heavy cream

Fresh ground pepper

4 sprigs mint, leaves picked from stems and roughly chopped

Render the bacon in a large frying pan. Once it begins to crisp and the fat has collected in the pan, remove the bacon to a paper towel–lined plate and reserve. Add the onion and a pinch of salt to the bacon fat and let it sauté over medium-low heat for 10 to 12 minutes. Then add the garlic and continue to cook over medium-low heat for 5 minutes.

Bring a large pot of water to a boil and salt generously. Prepare an ice bath. Add the peas to the boiling water. Cook until they are just tender, 3 to 4 minutes, and move them to an ice bath with a spider or a slotted spoon. Once cool, strain and reserve the peas. Add the pasta to the boiling water and cook until al dente, using the box instructions as a guide.

Add the cream to the pan with the onion and garlic. Let it warm. Move the pasta to the saucepan with a spider or a slotted spoon, bringing some pasta water along with it to lubricate the pasta and add starchy water to the sauce. Add the peas and crisped bacon and give a toss. Season with salt, pepper, and a sprinkle of mint. Serve warm.

STRAWBERRIES, BABY SPINACH, JAPANESE TURNIPS, AND CHIVE BLOSSOM VINEGAR

Serves 4

While my first instinct with strawberries is to encase them in pastry dough or cook them down into a jam, the occasional savory strawberry dish has its place in the parade of summer fare. This recipe calls for a homemade chive flower vinegar, which can be substituted with a flavored vinegar of your choosing, or a simple apple cider vinegar will do just fine.

FOR THE DRESSING

1 shallot

1 tablespoon Dijon mustard

2 tablespoons chive vinegar

4 tablespoons extra virgin olive oil

2 tablespoons crème fraîche

2 tablespoons chopped chives

FOR THE SALAD

1 pint strawberries

4 cups baby spinach

4 Japanese-style white turnips (such as hakurei)

⅓ cup slivered almonds

Kosher salt

Fresh ground pepper

⅓ cup chèvre

Place the shallot in a blender and buzz until it's broken up. Add the mustard, vinegar, olive oil, crème fraîche, and chives. Blend until even in texture. Pour into a bowl and reserve.

Clean the strawberries and remove the stems. Cut them in half if they are small or fourths if they are large. Wash the baby spinach if it hasn't been. Place the spinach in a large mixing bowl. Chop the greens and tails off the turnips. Discard the tails. If the greens are healthy looking, chop them up to match the approximate size of the spinach leaves and add them to the bowl with the spinach. Using a mandoline, slice the turnips as thin as two sheets of paper.

Place the almonds in a cast-iron frying pan set over medium heat on the stovetop. Move them around with a spoon for 6 to 8 minutes or until they just begin to gain some color. Remove them from the pan and let cool. Season the greens with salt and pepper. Combine the greens, strawberries, and turnips. Gently toss with 3 tablespoons of dressing. Mound up on a platter. Scatter the almonds on top and place walnut-size pieces of chèvre throughout the salad. Drizzle another couple of tablespoons of dressing over top and serve.

CAST-IRON FRITTATA
WITH FARMER'S CHEESE

Serves 8

This dish is essentially how we welcome students to the school on the first day of our workshop program. It is a testament to the value of employing cast iron in the kitchen, a nod to resourcefulness and versatility in a dish and a recipe that can be easily re-created at home. When I invite a friend over for lunch and don't want to head out to the grocery store, this is my go-to, as there are always eggs, salty cheese, and some vegetable odds and ends in the fridge. You can even add cooked, sliced potatoes to this recipe to really bulk it up! Think Spanish tortilla.

4 kale leaves, any variety

20 spears asparagus

1 tablespoon chives

1 teaspoon thyme, leaves removed from stems

2 tablespoons butter

1 large onion, small dice

12 eggs

½ cup milk

Kosher salt

Fresh ground pepper

½ cup crumbled chèvre

Preheat the oven to 400°F. Remove the stems from the kale and rip or chop each leaf into bite-size pieces. Snap the asparagus and chop it into bite-size pieces. Mince the chives and combine with the thyme leaves, and set aside. Melt the butter in a large cast-iron pan. Sauté the onion with a pinch of salt over medium heat until soft and translucent. Add the asparagus and cook until bright green and just tender. Add the ripped kale and wilt.

Meanwhile, beat the eggs in a medium bowl with a whisk. Whisk fiercely to incorporate air. Add the milk, and salt and pepper to taste. Pour the egg mixture into the sautéing vegetables. On medium heat, let the eggs cook until the outside edges set, about 5 minutes. Do not stir. (You are encouraging a golden-brown crust to form on the bottom.) Sprinkle on chèvre, chives, and thyme. Place the frittata in the oven to bake for 15 to 20 minutes, until it is golden-brown, puffy, and has set in the middle. Remove the frittata from the oven and enjoy it warm or at room temperature.

POACHED CHICKEN
WITH NEW GARLIC, EARLY SUMMER VEGETABLES, AND SPINACH

Serves 4

I have never been a fan of boneless, skinless chicken breasts until I made this dish for my mother's seventieth birthday party. The breasts were unbelievably tender and the presentation was stunning. Not to mention, this is healthy summer cooking at its best. Keep in mind that the beets will turn the poaching liquid red, so omit them if you're going for a clear broth.

1 lemon, cut in half

4 stalks new garlic, tender parts, thinly sliced on a diagonal (or 4 cloves garlic, smashed and removed from their skins)

1 bulb fennel, heart removed and roughly chopped

2 leeks, cut into thin rounds

1 yellow onion, medium dice

3 small beets, peeled and cut in half

4 carrots, cut into 1-inch pieces on a diagonal

Extra virgin olive oil, for coating

Kosher salt

2 cups spinach

8 cups chicken stock

1 cup white wine

4 sprigs tarragon

2 sprigs rosemary

2 sprigs thyme

2 sprigs parsley

1 bay leaf

4 chicken breasts, skins removed

Preheat the oven to 400°F. Coat the lemon, garlic, fennel, leeks, onion, beets, and carrots in plenty of olive oil and salt. Place on two sheet pans lined with aluminum foil or parchment paper. Place in the oven for 30 minutes, moving everything around occasionally so that nothing burns. Once the vegetables are tender and beginning to crisp up around the edges, remove them from the oven and let cool. Toss them with the spinach and set aside.

Turn the oven down to 325°F. Pour the chicken stock and white wine into a baking dish that will just fit the chicken breasts in one layer. Tie up the tarragon, rosemary, thyme, parsley, and bay leaf in cheesecloth with kitchen string. Drop it into the stock. Season the chicken breasts on both sides with salt. Slide them into the liquid, being sure that they are fully immersed. If they are not, add more stock or water. Place the chicken breasts in the oven for 30 minutes. Pile the vegetables on top of the chicken and place it back in the oven for 10 more minutes or until the breasts are just cooked through and the vegetables have been reheated. This dish is best served in bowls. Use a slotted spoon to retrieve the chicken and vegetables and use a little ladle to dress each dish with a couple spoonfuls of poaching liquid.

MAINE COAST BOUILLABAISSE

Serves 8

We have made this dish more than any other at Salt Water Farm, as it showcases the abundance of fish and shellfish in the Penobscot Bay. The stock is made with lobster bodies, giving it a wonderfully flavorful base, accented with Mediterranean staples such as fennel, saffron, and summer tomatoes.

FOR THE BOUILLABAISSE

Three or four 1½-pound soft-shell lobsters

2 tablespoons extra virgin olive oil

4 medium fennel bulbs, chopped

4 celery stalks, chopped

4 leeks, white and pale-green parts only, sliced

1 whole head garlic, roughly chopped

1 bay leaf

Kosher salt

Freshly ground pepper

1 cup dry white wine

½ teaspoon saffron

6 to 8 vine-ripened tomatoes, diced

24 littleneck clams, scrubbed

1 pound squid, mix of tentacles and bodies

24 mussels, scrubbed and debearded

FOR THE ROUILLE (AIOLI WITH PAPRIKA)

2 cloves garlic, peeled

1 pinch kosher salt

2 egg yolks

1 tablespoon mayonnaise

1 cup extra virgin olive oil

½ teaspoon sweet paprika

Squeeze of lemon

TO SERVE

6 sprigs tarragon, leaves picked from stems and roughly chopped

6 sprigs parsley, leaves picked from stems and roughly chopped

1 crusty baguette, sliced and toasted

Fill a large pot with an inch of water. Salt generously to mimic seawater. Bring to a boil with a well-fitting cover. Place the lobsters in the water and cover. Let them steam for 5 to 6 minutes. If the water boils over, turn down the heat and leave the cover slightly open. Once the lobsters are red, let them cook for an additional 2 minutes. Remove the cover and run them under cold water to stop the cooking process. Remove the meat from the shells, including the tail meat, claw meat, and knuckle meat. Rinse out the bodies (legs attached) and reserve for the stock. You can discard the other shells.

Heat the olive oil in a medium heavy-bottomed pot over medium-low. Add the chopped fennel, celery, leeks, garlic, and bay leaf. Season with salt and pepper and cook, stirring occasionally, until the vegetables are soft but have not taken on any color, 10 to 12 minutes.

Once the vegetables are soft, increase the heat to medium and add the wine, lobster bodies, and saffron. Cook, stirring occasionally, about 5 minutes. Add the tomatoes and 10 cups of water. Bring to a boil, then reduce the heat and simmer, uncovered, 60 to 70 minutes, until reduced by about one-third and the flavors have melded. Remove the shells from the broth and discard. Leave the broth over low heat.

Steam the clams in 1 inch of salted boiling water in a medium saucepan with a cover. Once they have opened, turn off the heat and remove the cover.

Slice the squid bodies into ¼-inch thick rings. Add the mussels to the pot with broth and turn up the heat to medium-high. Cook until they just start to open, then reduce the heat to medium-low and add the lobster and squid meat, making sure they're submerged

in the liquid. Add the clams in their shells
and simmer for 5 minutes.

To make the rouille: Grind the garlic and
salt into a paste in a mortar and pestle.
Whisk in the egg yolks thoroughly along
with the mayonnaise. One drop at a time,
add the olive oil while stirring quickly until
you've achieved an emulsification, after
which you can pour a slow, steady stream.

Add the paprika and a squeeze of lemon.
Season to taste and reserve.

Divide the seafood stew between bowls
and scatter tarragon and parsley over top.
Serve with the bread and rouille alongside
for dipping into the broth. It's important to
mix the rouille into the soup with the bread,
which gives the base its traditional flavor.

SOUR CHERRY CLAFOUTIS

Serves 4 to 6

Outside of our cooking school, there's a sour cherry tree that provides partial shade to our perennial herb garden. In June, the first fruit ripens. A migrant bird population knows precisely the moment at which the cherries are sweet enough to eat and can clean a tree in an afternoon if we don't net it. For the past two years, however, the birds have been absent and the cherries have ripened to perfection for human hands to harvest. The crimson fruit makes an elegant addition to a clafoutis, a French, egg-based dessert with a smidgen of cherry brandy, and just enough flour to hold the batter together. Like a soufflé, it will deflate in just minutes. In its first hot and glorious moments out of the oven, it is a thing to behold.

Preheat the oven to 425°F. Combine the milk, sugar, brandy (if using), vanilla, eggs, and salt in a blender and run at low speed for about 20 seconds. Add the flour and let run for another minute or until the ingredients are well combined. Butter a 9-inch cast-iron skillet or a similar size pan that can withstand high heat, such as copper.

Pour the batter into the cast-iron skillet and sprinkle the cherries over the top. Bake for 30 to 35 minutes, until the top is golden brown and the clafoutis has set. Quickly dust with confectioners' sugar, cut into 4 to 6 portions (depending on how hungry you are), and serve while still piping hot.

1¼ cups milk

6 tablespoons sugar

2 tablespoons fruit brandy (optional and very traditional)

1 teaspoon vanilla extract

6 eggs

¼ teaspoon salt

¾ cup all-purpose flour

1 tablespoon unsalted butter, softened

2 cups pitted cherries, sweet or sour

Confectioners' sugar, for dusting

JULY

You know that July has arrived when the nights are too hot to sleep comfortably. As the sun rises over the farm, a warm breeze brings with it cedar waxwings that perch in the branches of our sour cherry tree, eating the last of the now overripe fruit. On our routine morning walk to the water, we take a detour to the raspberry patch, where on occasion, two young fawns are sleeping in but quickly spring up and bound through the field at the sounds of our footsteps. The dogs instinctively inspect the beds the fawns left behind—soft, compressed grass where they leisurely digested a meal's worth of ripe raspberries. The seas shine their brightest in the month of July, with schools of silvery fish teaming on the water's surface. As the dogs plunge into the surf, I wave at the harbormaster who is picking up his morning traps, his day's work well underway.

As we ascend the hill back to the barn, the fields are alive with the sounds of summer. Finches weave through the tall grasses, gulls soar overhead, and chipmunks emerge from the rock walls, identifying their next ripe bite. The greenhouse needs constant watering, as the summer heat makes its contents particularly thirsty. The first of the cherry tomatoes begin to turn red. Just outside the greenhouse, a planting of the "three sisters" (corn, beans, and squash) have truly come in—the vines proliferate with green and yellow squash, and beautiful blossoms open to the morning sun. The scarlet runner beans have outgrown their supports and reach high into the sky with bursts of crimson flowers and brilliant green pods. Our crop of bush beans is the perfect size, tender as can be and ready for picking.

The cooking school is in full swing and students from across the country delight in the ocean views and magnificent herb and vegetable gardens. The scent of lavender is thick in the air, perfect timing for our course on the Cuisine of Provence. Berries feature largely in July, especially in our Cobblers, Buckles, and Grunts class. (These are all funny New England names for desserts that are some combination of berries, sugar, flour, and butter.) Borage, calendula, nasturtiums, squash blossoms, and sunflowers are in bloom and make an exquisite contribution to our Edible Flowers and Herbs class.

July is the start of "shedder" season, when the hard-shell lobsters shed their tough exterior and transform into soft-shells with sweet and succulent meat, perfect for our Consider the Lobster class. This is a popular subject in our corner of the world. For one, those visiting the state of Maine can't leave until they've had a boiled lobster or a lobster roll. And two, it's one of Maine's primary industries, and warming waters threaten its future. At Salt Water Farm, we devote an entire class to lobsters: their history, their anatomy, how to source them, and how to cook them. We even head down to the Lincolnville harbormaster's house, where his wife, Lynn, sells his daily lobster catch, held in saltwater tanks that occupy a barn attached to their house. Lynn has the liveliest lobsters around, which makes a fantastic contribution to our seafood stew back at the cooking school.

July also starts the long-awaited mackerel season. My sister goes down to the docks at high tide with her bait and tackle. Nine times out of ten, she comes home with a cooler full of silvery fish. We clean them by the water's edge, rub them with garden herbs and salt, and throw them on the grill just until the meat separates from the bone. Each night, the dogs find their way over to her house, where the smell of fresh fish on a hot grill lures any hungry belly. Occasionally, she will pull up a few squid or stripers, making dinner a truly special affair.

One of July's ultimate delights is wild Maine blueberries, the smaller and sweeter variety. In the afternoons, we head to the hills, where wild blueberry barrens stretch across the landscape. With rakes and baskets in tow, we collect to our heart's content, the dogs grazing alongside us. A mandatory stop at the lake on the way home cools us down, floating on our backs, our faces full of sun. These are the glorious days of summer.

ISRAELI COUSCOUS
WITH TURMERIC, CURRANTS, MINT, AND LEMON

Serves 4 to 6

When I was child, I distinctly remember watching my father prepare this dish, the smells of the exotic spices toasting in the pan, the brilliant yellow color of the turmeric staining the pasta and anything it touched, and the final addition of mint, almonds, and lemon juice—such an intriguing combination. Making this dish has become a summer ritual, and it pairs so very well with my sister's fresh-caught and grilled mackerel.

4 tablespoons extra virgin olive oil

1 yellow onion, small dice

1 teaspoon kosher salt

1 teaspoon ground cumin

1 teaspoon ground coriander

1½ teaspoon ground turmeric

1 pinch ground cinnamon

½ cup sherry

½ cup dried currants or raisins

2 cups Israeli couscous

½ cup slivered almonds

½ cup chopped fresh mint leaves

2 tablespoons fresh lemon juice

Heat 2 tablespoons of olive oil in a medium saucepan over medium heat. Add the onion and ⅓ teaspoon of salt and cook, stirring occasionally, about 7 minutes, or until the onion is very soft. Add the cumin, coriander, turmeric, and cinnamon, and cook, stirring, for 2 minutes. Stir in the sherry and the currants, increase the heat to high, and bring to a boil. Let it cook on high until the liquid just about evaporates, and turn off the heat.

Bring a large pot of salted water to a boil. Add the couscous and cook for about 10 minutes or until al dente. Strain, return the couscous to the pot, and coat with the remaining 2 tablespoons of olive oil to prevent sticking. In a large mixing bowl, combine the couscous with the onion and spice mixture. Let sit for 10 minutes so that the pasta can take on the color of the spices. Stir occasionally.

Preheat the oven to 350°F. Spread the almonds on a sheet tray and place them in the oven for 8 to 10 minutes, until they begin to gain color and become fragrant. Remove from oven and let cool. Add the mint and lemon juice to the couscous. Taste, and add more lemon juice if needed. Scatter the slivered almonds on top. Serve warm or at room temperature.

SPICY LOBSTER PASTA
WITH CREAM AND CHERRY TOMATOES

Serves 4 to 6

While many folks prefer a classic steamed lobster, I am partial to slightly more elevated lobster dishes, such as this one. It combines many of my favorite things—tomatoes, cream, spice, and the much-revered lobster meat—in a deeply soothing pasta dish. It's always a winner, even on a warm summer day.

Four 1½-pound soft-shell lobsters

3 tablespoons extra virgin olive oil

1 head garlic, cloves removed from skins and minced

2 tablespoons tomato paste

½ teaspoon red pepper flakes

2 tablespoons white wine vinegar

1 cup white wine

6 cups cherry tomatoes

6 sprigs tarragon

3 sprigs thyme

12 sprigs Italian flat-leaf parsley

4 cups heavy cream

Kosher salt

Fresh ground pepper

1 pound fettuccine

Sea salt

In a large pot with a lid, bring 1 inch of water to a boil. Salt generously. (You are mimicking sea water.) Add the lobsters and cook for 6 minutes or until they are red. Turn off the heat and move the pot to the sink. Drain the water. When cool enough to handle, crack open the tails, knuckles, and claws and remove the meat. Devein the tail. Wash the tamale (green stuff) out of the bodies (sorry, tamale lovers, but we don't want a green sauce). Reserve the meat and bodies, with legs still attached.

In a large, heavy-bottomed pot, add the olive oil and lobster bodies. Cook over medium heat for about 5 minutes. Add the garlic and let soften, about 5 minutes. Add the tomato paste and red pepper flakes and swirl around, cooking for another 2 to 3 minutes. Add vinegar and wine and reduce slightly, about 5 minutes. Add the tomatoes and continue to cook for 20 minutes. Add the tarragon, thyme, 6 sprigs of parsley, and the cream and bring to a simmer but do not let boil. Cook over low heat for about 15 minutes, allowing the cream to infuse with the flavors of the herbs. Pick the lobster bodies and whole herbs out of the sauce with a set of tongs and discard. Season the sauce to taste with salt and pepper. Chop the lobster meat into bite-size pieces. Add to the sauce just before you drop the pasta into the water.

Bring a large pot of heavily salted water to a boil. Add the fettucine and give it a stir. Cook until al dente, following the instructions on the box. Pick the leaves from the stems of the remaining 6 sprigs of parsley and give them a rough chop. With a set of tongs, bring the pasta to the saucepan, turning it into the sauce. Serve hot with a sprinkle of parsley and a pinch of sea salt.

GRILLED LAMB STEAKS, EGGPLANTS, AND ZUCCHINI

WITH GREEK YOGURT AND GARDEN ZA'ATAR

Serves 6

At Salt Water Farm we make our very own za'atar with fresh oregano, marjoram, thyme, sumac, and toasted sesame seeds. It makes a wonderful marinade for meat, vegetables, or fish.

FOR THE MARINADE

2 tablespoons chopped fresh oregano

2 tablespoons chopped fresh marjoram

1 tablespoon fresh thyme, leaves pulled from stems

1 teaspoon sumac

1 tablespoon toasted sesame seeds

4 cloves garlic, peeled and finely minced

4 tablespoons extra virgin olive oil

1 teaspoon kosher salt

½ teaspoon fresh ground pepper

FOR THE MEAT AND VEGETABLES

2½ pounds lamb shoulder steaks (or lamb chops brought to room temperature)

2 zucchini (or summer squash)

2 eggplants

FOR THE YOGURT

2 cloves garlic, peeled

1 big pinch kosher salt

2 cups Greek yogurt

2 tablespoons extra virgin olive oil

1 teaspoon sumac

Zest and juice of ½ lemon

TO SERVE

1 bunch flat-leaf parsley, leaves picked from stems

Aleppo pepper (or red pepper flakes)

Sea salt

To make the marinade: Combine all of the marinade ingredients in a mixing bowl and mix well.

To prepare the meat and vegetables: Preheat the grill on high. Slice the zucchini on a diagonal into ½-inch-thick slices and place into a large bowl. Slice the eggplant into ½-inch rounds and place in a second bowl. Rub half the marinade over the lamb steaks and divide the remainder between the zucchini and the eggplant. Using your hands, massage the marinade into the meat and the vegetables.

To make the yogurt: In a mortar and pestle, mash two cloves of garlic into a paste with a big pinch of kosher salt. Add the yogurt, olive oil, sumac, and lemon zest and juice. Set in the fridge.

Place the zucchini and eggplant on the hot grill using tongs. Turn the heat down to medium, close the lid, and sear the vegetables about 5 minutes. When there are decisive grill marks, flip the vegetables. Cover and grill until cooked through, about 5 more minutes. When cooked, place the zucchini and eggplant on a sheet tray.

Lay the lamb steaks down on a hot grill for 6 to 7 minutes or until they have established grill marks. Flip and cook for another 4 to 5 minutes, until the meat is medium rare. Remove from the grill and let them rest on a cutting board.

Spoon the yogurt onto the base of a platter and smear to cover the surface in a thin layer. Lay the vegetables on top. Then slice the lamb and lay it over the vegetables. Sprinkle with parsley, Aleppo pepper, and sea salt.

BLISTERED NARDELLO PEPPERS
WITH OLIVE OIL, SEA SALT, AND NASTURTIUMS

Serves 4

Sometimes the simplest recipes are the best. This dish is a perfect example and relies heavily on the quality of the peppers themselves. They should be fragrant and full of flavor. While we have trouble growing some varieties of peppers in Maine's northern climate, Nardellos seem quite happy in our coastal soil, turning from a deep green to atomic red as they mature. It's nice to get a mix of the two colors for presentation's sake, and best of all, they can be fried up without any doctoring. No need to stem or seed them, as they are tastiest whole. If you're unable to source Nardello peppers, shishito or padron peppers will do, but you'll need twice as many, as they are much smaller.

In a large cast-iron frying pan, warm 2 tablespoons of olive oil over medium-high heat until it shimmers in the pan. Add 6 peppers in an even layer and *don't touch them*! Let them burn and blister, about 5 minutes, and then flip them and let them do the same on the other side, another 3 to 4 minutes. Sprinkle them with sea salt and move them to an attractive medium-size serving bowl. Do the same with the second batch and, once done, place them on top of the first 6 peppers. They will steam a bit in the bowl, softening them. Garnish with the nasturtiums and serve warm as a side dish.

3 tablespoons extra virgin olive oil

12 Nardello peppers

Sea salt

8 nasturtiums

GREEN BEANS
WITH MINTY TAHINI DRESSING

Serves 8

My grandmother always said that if you want to eat fresh beans, you have to bring a pot of boiling water into the garden to harvest them. Each year at Salt Water Farm, we have a marvelous crop of green bush beans called Provider (an apt name). I send students out to lift up the leaves and pluck perfectly tender beans from the plants, which find themselves typically blanched for no more than a few minutes and tossed into a brightly dressed summer salad.

2 pounds green beans, root ends snipped (you can leave the stem end attached)

2 small cloves garlic, peeled

Kosher salt

Juice and zest of 1 lemon

2 tablespoons tahini

1 tablespoon honey

6 sprigs mint, leaves picked from stems and roughly chopped

4 tablespoons extra virgin olive oil

¾ cup walnuts

10 sprigs cilantro, lower stems removed

10 sprigs parsley, lower stems removed

Sea salt

½ teaspoon red pepper flakes

Bring a large pot of salted water to a boil. Prepare an ice bath. Add the green beans to the water and let them cook until they are fork tender, about 4 to 5 minutes. (Young and tender green beans cook much faster than more mature beans.) With a spider or a slotted spoon, move them to the ice bath to chill. Strain and reserve.

In a mortar and pestle, grind the garlic with a big pinch of salt into a paste. Add the lemon juice and zest, tahini, honey, mint, and olive oil. Swirl to combine with the pestle and let sit for 20 minutes so that the flavors can meld.

Preheat the oven to 350°F. Spread the walnuts on a sheet pan. Toast them in the oven for 8 to 10 minutes or until they are fragrant and just start to gain color. Remove from oven. Place the walnuts on a cutting board and roughly chop.

Toss the green beans with half of the dressing. Pile them high on a platter. Sprinkle with walnuts. Clean the herbs and chop each stem into 2-inch pieces. Place them in a mixing bowl and gently toss them with a spoonful of dressing and a pinch of sea salt. Pile the herbs high on top of the green beans and sprinkle the whole dish with the crushed red pepper.

RASPBERRY FOOL
WITH LAVENDER

Serves 6

We came across this dessert on a day that was simply too hot to bake. The original intention was to make a raspberry pie, but a cool raspberry cream seemed to be a better fit for the sweltering heat. There is also a deep satisfaction that comes from folding the deep red syrup into the pure white cream. Make sure you leave plenty of time for the dessert to chill.

3 pints raspberries

½ cup sugar

1 pint heavy cream

½ teaspoon vanilla

1 tablespoon sugar

⅓ cup mascarpone

Lavender flowers, for garnish

Place 2 pints of raspberries in a saucepan with the sugar. Cook over medium heat until the berries soften and reduce by half, about 15 minutes. Remove from heat and pour through a fine-mesh sieve, collecting the syrup. Chill in the refrigerator for 20 minutes.

Whip the cream to soft peaks with the vanilla and sugar. Fold in the mascarpone. Then fold in the chilled, cooked raspberry syrup.

Fill small bowls with the raspberry and cream mixture. Place a big spoonful of fresh raspberries on top and lightly sprinkle with lavender flowers. Serve chilled.

AUGUST

For those from away, August is the jewel of the Maine summer, which is reflected in the rates at bed-and-breakfasts and inns up and down the coast. The days are warm enough for ocean swims, paddles through the Camden Harbor, and sunset cruises out on the bay. The inner harbor is brimming with schooners and day sailors, each of them packed snuggly with wide-eyed tourists capped in visors and sunhats. The outer harbor boasts grand vessels from around the world, their crews washing down the decks in matching polos. Regattas are a daily affair with both winners and runners-up celebrating at the local bars with pints of beer and rum cocktails. It is truly a sight to be seen, whether you are seafaring or simply passing through.

But for locals, August brings its own challenges. The lines in town are uncommonly long, the tourists impatient, and service crews exhausted. There are hiring signs in every window, looking for additional hands to push through the final busy weeks of summer. The local restaurants are booked solid until Labor Day, and asking for a reservation is like asking for the moon. For those of us who live and work here, it's as if we've given over the place for the best month of the year. Of course, this is why everyone is here—August can't be beat. Back at the farm, we take refuge at the cooking school, away from the crowds and the commotion, where there is always a cool breeze, only eight students, and a schooner off in the distance, picking up wind in its sails.

There is no shortage of culinary pursuits in the month of August. As cooks, we strive to stay on top of the harvest and gently coax the flavors out of the garden into easy, delightful meals. In the kitchen, our menus are written a day or two ahead of time, reflecting what's ripe and ready outdoors. As a result, the students develop a keen sense of how and when to harvest, paying careful attention to the growth and integrity of the ingredients. Rather than relying on recipes, we make decisions instinctively, making substitutions when necessary and adding ingredients that have intrigue. For instance, a collection of husk cherries finds its way into a salad of Melon, Husk Cherry, Prosciutto, and Soft Cheese (page 178), or a handful of brightly colored pole beans is fried up and mixed into a succotash. This is what makes summer cooking so much fun: spontaneity!

A walk through the vegetable gardens requires at least two harvesting baskets and, ideally, many hands. Tomatoes ripen by the dozens, turning shades of burgundy, purple, deep red, and striped green. Many varieties of squash in colors green and yellow swell, soon to make their way into fritters, gazpacho, succotash, and sweet breads. Eggplants—purple, green, and white—hang like gifts, ready to be plucked from their stems and made into caponata or ratatouille. Peppers turn from green to red in the hot August sun, eager to hit a hot pan. The basil has finally come into its own, begging to be made into pistou or used as the leafy green in tomato salads.

Our perennial harvest is full-on: high bush blueberries, raspberries, sea berries, honey berries, and elderberries all ripe and ready. Finally, the apricots, peaches, and plums in our adolescent orchard are starting to put on weight and ripen, and visions of pies with warm spices and desserts such as Buttermilk Panna Cotta with Peaches (page 181) enter my mind. Summer food is as simple as it comes.

CARROT AND BEET SALAD

WITH CILANTRO AND FETA

Serves 4

While this salad is extremely simple in its assembly, the bright colors of the raw, thinly sliced beets and rainbow carrots give it an atomic presentation, making it a wonderful addition to a dinner-party menu. The feta adds a softness in texture, and the arugula, a peppery bite. This salad can be made well into the winter months with whatever bright herbs and greens the local market affords.

4 carrots, peeled

1 golden beet, peeled

1 red beet, peeled

1 clove garlic, peeled

Kosher salt

1 inch ginger root, peeled and finely grated

Juice from 1 orange

Juice from 1 lemon

2 tablespoons red wine vinegar

2 tablespoons extra virgin olive oil

Fresh ground pepper

½ bunch cilantro

2 bunches arugula, cleaned

½ cup high-quality feta cheese, cubed

Thinly slice the carrots on a diagonal using a mandoline (about as thick as three sheets of paper). Do the same with the golden beet and the red beet, saving the red beet for last so as not to discolor the other root vegetables. Combine the carrots and beets in a mixing bowl.

In a mortar and pestle, grind the garlic with a pinch of salt into a paste. Push the garlic paste around the inside of the mortar with the pestle. Add the grated ginger, orange juice, lemon juice, red wine vinegar, and olive oil and mix. Add salt and pepper to taste. Pour three tablespoons of the dressing over the carrots and beets and toss to combine. Let it marinate for 20 minutes. When ready to serve, remove the base of the stems and roughly chop the cilantro. Place the cleaned arugula in a large mixing bowl, tearing up the arugula leaves if they are too big to pick up comfortably with a fork. Add the cilantro. Sprinkle a little salt over top of the greens and add a couple spoonfuls of dressing. Toss gently. Move to a platter, plating up the greens as high as possible. Nestle the carrots and beets around the outside of the platter, without weighing down the greens. Sprinkle the feta over the top of the salad. Drizzle with a little extra dressing and serve.

ZUCCHINI GRATIN
WITH TOMATO AND OREGANO

Serves 6

While most gratins are reserved for the wintertime, this one screams of summer. Layers of ripe tomatoes, summer squash, and garden herbs are cooked down until their flavors meld, making a lovely side to a roasted leg of lamb or grilled fish. You could also bring pitted olives into this dish to enhance its Provincial appeal.

4 medium zucchini or summer squash or a mix of the two

8 tablespoons extra virgin olive oil

1 yellow onion, small dice

Kosher salt

2 cloves garlic, peeled and minced

1 fresh bay leaf

3 cups chopped tomatoes

1 tablespoon cold unsalted butter

Fresh ground pepper

Red pepper flakes (optional)

3 sprigs fresh oregano, leaves picked from stems

6 sprigs Italian flat leaf parsley, leaves removed from stems

3 heirloom tomatoes, cut into ¾-inch rounds

1 cup finely grated Parmesan

Preheat the oven to 400°F. Cut the zucchini or summer squash into ½-inch rounds. Heat 3 tablespoons of olive oil in a large frying pan over medium-high heat. Brown the squash in batches, making sure not to crowd the pan or else they will steam and resist gaining color. Add more oil if necessary. Once browned, move them to a sheet pan and reserve.

In a heavy-bottomed pot, warm 2 tablespoons of olive oil over medium-low heat. Add the diced onion and a pinch of salt. Sweat for 10 minutes, with the cover on, moving them around in the pan from time to time. Add the garlic and cook for another 5 minutes. Add the bay leaf and the chopped tomato. Let it cook for 20 minutes or until the tomato sauce reduces, sweetens, and thickens. Finish with the cold butter and salt and pepper to taste. Add the red pepper flakes, if desired.

Roughly chop the oregano and the parsley. In a 9-inch square baking pan, lay down half of the tomato sauce. Cover with an even layer of the zucchini, and then lay about half of the tomato rounds on top. Sprinkle with ½ cup of Parmesan and half of the herbs. Repeat the process, first laying down the sauce, then the zucchini, then the tomato rounds, then the cheese and herbs. Place in the oven for 40 minutes or until the gratin looks golden brown and most of the liquid has baked off. Remove from the oven and let set for 10 minutes. Slice into pieces and serve warm.

CORN SOUP
WITH SUMMER MUSHROOMS

Serves 6

August is undeniably corn season in Maine. You can't go to the market without seeing a big corn display, front and center, with a deal that makes the local harvest look too good to pass up. After all, the golden summer corn will soon be replaced by sad, old, imported ears that really have no business being on the shelf. This soup tastes intensely of the summer corn crop, using the cobs to make a corn stock, enriching the velvety corn puree. Not to mention the lovely foraged mushrooms, fried up in a bit of butter and set carefully at the center of each bowl.

FOR THE CORN STOCK

10 ears corn

2 carrots and their greens, unpeeled and roughly chopped

2 stalks celery and their leaves, roughly chopped

2 yellow onions, peeled and roughly chopped

2 sprigs parsley

2 sprigs thyme

2 sprigs rosemary

12 peppercorns

1 bay leaf

FOR THE SOUP

4 tablespoons butter

4 sweet onions, medium dice

Kosher salt

FOR THE MUSHROOMS

2 tablespoons butter

½ pound cleaned foraged mushrooms (chanterelle, black trumpet, lion's mane, oyster, lobster)

Sea salt

To make the stock: Husk the corn. Cut the kernels away from the cobs and reserve. Place the cobs in a large stockpot with all of the remaining stock ingredients. Cover with water. Bring to a boil and reduce to a simmer. Let the stock cook over medium heat for 45 minutes. Strain it, reserving all the liquid.

To make the soup: In a large heavy-bottomed pot, melt the butter over medium-low heat. Add the diced onions and a pinch of salt. Cover and let them sweat for 15 minutes, stirring from time to time. Once the onions are soft and translucent, add the corn kernels and another big pinch of salt. Let them cook for 15 to 20 minutes or until sweet and soft. Turn off the heat.

Move one-third of the corn and onion mixture to a blender. Season and add just enough corn stock to barely cover the corn and onions. Blend on high for 3 minutes, until smooth. Pour the corn soup through a fine-mesh sieve or a chinois, pushing the juice out of the sieve with a wooden spoon and catching it in a large bowl. You should be left with only a dry mash (the shells of the corn kernels) in the sieve. Prepare and season the remaining two batches of corn, onions, and stock in the same manner. Adjust the soup to your desired consistency with less or more stock. Taste for a final seasoning. Return the soup to the pot and let cook over low heat to warm for 5 to 10 minutes.

To prepare the mushrooms: Cut the mushrooms into bite-size pieces. In a cast-iron pan, heat the butter over medium-high heat. Season the mushrooms with salt. Brown the mushrooms in batches and set aside.

To plate, ladle the soup into a small soup bowls. Garnish with the mushrooms at the center of each bowl.

PORK CHOPS

WITH TOMATO, EGGPLANT, BASIL, AND ZUCCHINI

Serves 4

In August, we are always looking for opportunities to incorporate tomatoes, zucchini, and eggplant into dishes, and sometimes the simplest recipes are the best. There is not much to this dish, yet it is a meal fit for the queen. Make every effort to source well-fed, local pork and be sure not to overcook it.

1 medium eggplant

2 medium zucchini

Kosher salt

Extra virgin olive oil

2 or 3 bone-in pork chops, about 1½ inches thick

12 large cherry tomatoes

1 bunch basil, leaves picked from stems

Sea salt

Fresh ground pepper

Cut the eggplant and zucchini lengthwise into ¼-inch slices. The length makes them easier to grill. Now season them with salt and coat them lightly in olive oil.

Prepare the grill. I usually turn it to high to get it hot and then turn it down to medium heat. Lay down the vegetables on the grill, being careful not to crowd them. Grill the vegetables in two batches if necessary. Let the zucchini and eggplant acquire grill marks, about 6 to 7 minutes, before you flip them. Cook them on the other side for an additional 3 to 4 minutes, or until they are tender but not falling apart. Transfer them to a sheet pan and let them rest.

Cook the pork chops. Lay them down on the grill and let them cook for 8 to 10 minutes. Once they have grill marks and are ready to be released from the grill, flip them and cook for another 5 to 6 minutes, until the meat registers medium rare. If you haven't heard, there are new rules on cooking pork: pink is just fine. Remove the meat from the grill and let it rest for at least 5 minutes before cutting it up.

Slice the tomatoes in half and place them in a small mixing bowl. Sprinkle with sea salt and a little olive oil. Toss them with the basil. Cut the zucchini and eggplant into smaller portions if necessary. Cut the pork into slices against the grain and away from the bone. Plate the meat alongside the grilled vegetables and tomato salad.

MELON, HUSK CHERRY, PROSCIUTTO, AND SOFT CHEESE

Serves 4

This dish is a nod to a wonderful and simple appetizer that I had in Positano, Italy, on my honeymoon: unbelievably ripe melon, sweet and salty prosciutto, and a soft cheese reminiscent of a triple cream. The memory is only enhanced by the fact that my feet were bare and in the sand, and my glass of white wine was replenished every twenty minutes.

1 medium-ripe sweet melon, such as cantaloupe or honeydew

2 pickling cucumbers

1 pint husk cherries (optional)

⅓ pound thinly cut imported prosciutto

One 5-ounce round fresh or semi-aged soft cheese of your choosing

4 sprigs green basil, leaves picked from stems

4 sprigs purple basil, leaves picked from stems

1 handful arugula

1 lemon

Sea salt

Extra virgin olive oil (preferably good-quality Italian), to finish

Cut the melon in half and scoop out the seeds. Cut each half into long wedges. Cut the rind off each wedge and cut the wedges in half, to make them more manageable. Stripe the cucumber by peeling every other ½ inch. Cut the cucumbers in half lengthwise. Lay each half flat and cut again in three pieces lengthwise. Cut across the cucumber, in ½-inch pieces. Remove the husk cherries from their husks and cut them in half, if using.

On a big, beautiful platter, arrange the melon, cucumber, husk cherries, slices of prosciutto, and cheese. Sprinkle the green and purple basil and arugula on top. Squeeze a lemon through a sieve over all of the ingredients. Sprinkle with sea salt and drizzle with olive oil. Serve with a glass of Italian white wine.

SHOPPING FOR CHEESE Rarely do I go into the cheese shop with a fixed idea of what I want. I spent a number of years working at a cheese counter in Brooklyn, New York, and loved introducing customers to cheeses from around the world and picking our favorites. A good cheese counter will happily let you taste any of their selection and should entice you to try something new each time, rather than going with the familiar. Always ask, "What's good?" before checking out.

BUTTERMILK PANNA COTTA
WITH PEACHES

Serves 6 to 8

Peaches have a short and treasured season in Maine, as those with proliferating peach trees in their backyards know. (The long winters make it hard for adolescent peach trees to establish themselves and many die off.) This very basic panna cotta recipe offers a cool and gentle companion to a pile of sliced peaches, a sweet way to end a summer meal.

2 teaspoons gelatin	2 cups buttermilk
1½ cups heavy cream	4 ripe peaches
½ cup sugar	Honey, for drizzling
1 vanilla pod	

Dissolve the gelatin in about 2 tablespoons of water in a small bowl. In a medium saucepan, combine the heavy cream and sugar. On a cutting board, split the vanilla pod in half lengthwise and scrape out the seeds with the backside of a knife and add them to the cream with the pod. Set the saucepan over medium heat to dissolve the sugar in the cream. Once the cream is hot and the sugar has dissolved, turn off the heat. Whisk in the gelatin and the buttermilk. Let cool to room temperature, allowing the vanilla to steep in the cream.

Pour the cream base through a sieve into a glass bowl, discarding the vanilla pod. Divide the base among 6 to 8 ramekins or small decorative bowls. Let the panna cotta set in the refrigerator for at least 4 hours or until it has set. Just before you are ready to serve, slice the peaches and pile the slices on top of each panna cotta. Drizzle with honey and serve.

SEPTEMBER

I am particularly fond of the month of September. My daughter was born on August 25 and the month (or so) that followed seemed like a dream. In my hazy memory of the first few weeks of her life, it was warm and sunny every day and we lay on a blanket under the apple tree in our backyard cooing at our sweet new child, who mostly slept and nursed. Friends came by to visit with baskets of ripe peaches, bowls of heirloom tomatoes and fairytale eggplants, fresh cheeses from the farmer's market, beautiful breads made with local grains, and hearty greens tied up like bouquets. One neighbor delivered a gorgeous salade Niçoise with imported canned tuna, and another neighbor brought a chicken stew made with a host of late-season vegetables from their farm. A dear friend (in fact, the woman who married my husband and me) came over to cook an entire Peruvian feast for the two (well, three) of us, making us feel like new-parent royalty. The house was filled with vases of sunflowers and dahlias, and a warm breeze moved through the rooms from morning until evening. Dinnertime was a sacred time, when I cooked up all the beautiful ingredients that were delivered to our doorstep, with the baby bound to my chest, the two of us listening to summertime jazz or soulful blues.

When the procession of visitors with gifts began to slow, I spent afternoons pulling carrots and beets from our backyard garden for salads and to accompany roast chickens. I had planted the seeds in June, knowing how wonderful it would feel to be eating our own food during a time when we were so home-based. There were also plenty of greens, kale, and rainbow Swiss chard to sauté and mix into savory tarts. Back at the farm, blackberries ripened on brambles along the stone walls, begging to be picked for breakfast embellishment and sweet breads. Apple trees, old and new, stood in crowds across the fields and into the woods, bearing crisp, sweet, and complex-flavored fruit, some fit for a pie, others for cider, and a good many delicious for simply eating.

I remember the day we first brought our daughter to the farm, to introduce her to the place we hold so dear. The dogs awaited us, curious about this newest addition to the family, smelling her head and licking her cheeks. We meandered around the land, collecting fruits and vegetables that had ripened while I was in the hospital and recovering at home. One hot, late September afternoon, we walked down to the water's edge, passing the grassy landing on which we were married, and watched as eagles and osprey flew overhead, just as they did on our wedding day. The water was shimmering with a school of mackerel, an easy target for the birds of prey. We sat on the big, round rocks, warm from the afternoon sun, and scooped salt water with our hands, letting it run over the baby's head: nature's baptism. I felt grateful for all of it: my husband, our child, the farm, the sky, and the water.

When I felt able, I proudly took the little one to the farmer's market so she could meet the town. There we came across the most beautiful pink speckled bean pods, which would make their way into a homemade pasta dish, with stewed, super-ripe tomatoes. And just a few stands over, piles of foraged mushrooms of all earthly tones ended up in my basket and a few hours later in a buttery pan. The house was filled with the smells of onions sweating, bread baking, soup simmering, and fruit cooking down. It was a magical time, one I will never forget.

September has always been a month of abundance and comfort. At the cooking school, the gardens are flush with late-season herbs and vegetables and our fruit trees are delivering on the promises of their buds. Our tiered vegetable gardens are fully established, their tall greens moving with the sea breezes. The onions and carrots have grown to the perfect size for making stock, and with the summer chickens meeting their end, there is plenty of use for stock vegetables. A colorful row of Swiss chard flashes its rainbow ribs, and leaves and kale of all kinds (Russian red, cavolo nero, purple, and frilly) need constant harvesting.

While many of our students have returned to their homes, there are plenty of fall visitors and locals alike who join us for our autumnal curriculum. In September, we focus our attention on building flavor through soups, stocks, and sauces and commit to making the most of what's left in the garden. Resourcefulness is arguably one of the most important country-cooking skills and a welcome challenge for any accomplished home cook. During the harvest season, there is no reason to go to the store. With even a minimally stocked pantry and some late-season fruits and vegetables, there are so many directions in which a cook can head. I always tell the students in September that the gardens are their grocery store. If they see something they like, they can load it into their basket and we will always find a place for it in the meal.

With such a glut of produce, we maintain some flexibility in the day's recipes, making last-minute additions to a soup or a salad. One of the primary goals of our classes is for students to feel free to substitute or supplement a recipe without worrying that it won't come out right. In fact, many of the recipes at the school are a product of this journey in improvisation in our classes over the years. With so much nourishment at our fingertips, rules and restrictions seem superfluous in building a dish.

The recipes in this chapter take advantage of the September harvest, finding culinary applications for an assortment of vegetables and a plethora of fruit. The Chicken Guisado (page 186) is a late summer stew that uses up a variety of garden vegetables, made salty with capers and spicy with hot peppers. The Rustic Quiche with Fall Greens (page 189) conquers an arduous harvest of mature greens, packing their nutrients into a decadent cheese and egg base, set into a buttery piecrust. The handmade Pasta e Fagioli (page 192) swims in a slow-cooked tomato sauce, enriched with fresh borlotti beans. A Green Gazpacho (page 190) turns swollen zucchini and big bunches of herbs into a smooth and elegant chilled soup. And finally, a Blackberry Buckle (page 195) is laden with a basketful of the morning berry harvest and topped with a sweet crumble.

CHICKEN GUISADO

Serves 6

Our neighbors from across the street run a fairly expansive farm and each year they raise about fifty meat birds. On a crisp September afternoon, they brought over a quart of chicken guisado, made with a half dozen vegetables from the fields and chicken from the recent harvest. This dish has Puerto Rican origins and is halfway between a soup and a stew. The flavor is exceptionally well-balanced (for an adventurous palate), combining salt from the capers, heat from the peppers, and acid from the lime juice. We ate it along with a sourdough from the farmer's market that was made with corn stock and corn kernels. I was in heaven.

In a large, heavy-bottomed pot, warm the olive oil over medium heat. Add the onions, celery, and carrots along with a big pinch of salt and pepper. Cover and let them sweat for 10 minutes, stirring occasionally. Remove the top, give the vegetables a stir, and add the garlic. Stir to incorporate and cook for another 5 minutes. Add the tomato paste and massage it into the vegetables with a wooden spoon. Cook for 2 to 3 minutes. Add the chopped tomatoes, corn kernels, peppers, potatoes, and stock and bring it to a boil. Reduce to a simmer and let it cook for 20 minutes. Add the chicken and cook for 5 more minutes. Add the capers. Divide the stew among six bowls. Garnish each bowl with half a lime (encourage those eating to use the whole thing) and a big handful of cilantro. Serve with sourdough bread.

2 tablespoons extra virgin olive oil

1 medium yellow onion, medium dice

3 stalks celery, roughly chopped

3 medium carrots, lightly chopped

Kosher salt

Fresh ground pepper

6 cloves garlic, peeled and minced

1 tablespoon tomato paste

3 fat, juicy tomatoes, roughly chopped

2 ears corn, kernels removed from cob

2 sweet peppers, seeds removed and diced

8 small white potatoes, diced (any small potato variety will do)

2 quarts chicken stock

2 cups pulled cooked chicken

2 tablespoons capers

3 limes

½ bunch cilantro, roughly chopped (discard the stems)

1 loaf sourdough bread

RUSTIC QUICHE
WITH FALL GREENS

Serves 8

A late harvest of greens needs purpose in the kitchen. This quiche puts late-season greens to good use, making an otherwise decadent egg dish rich with vitamins. While I never considered myself a quiche advocate, this one breathes life into an old and too-familiar egg pie. It's also the perfect dish to bring to a brunch or to make in the morning and serve throughout the day. It holds up remarkably well.

FOR THE CRUST

1½ cups all-purpose flour

½ cup fine cornmeal

½ teaspoon salt

14 tablespoons butter

Ice cold water

FOR THE FILLING

2 tablespoons butter

1 yellow onion, thinly sliced

Kosher salt

1 bunch fall greens (Swiss chard or kale), ribs removed and cut into 1-inch strips

Apple cider vinegar

6 eggs

½ cup milk or cream

2 tablespoons crème fraîche (optional)

3 sprigs thyme, leaves picked from stems

Fresh ground pepper

1 pinch nutmeg

1 cup finely grated Gruyère

To make the dough: Combine the flour, cornmeal, and salt in a large bowl. Cut the butter into the mixture until no piece is bigger than a pea. Sprinkle with just enough ice water, about 3 tablespoons, so that the dough holds together. Form the dough into a ball, wrap it in plastic, and refrigerate for 20 minutes.

Preheat the oven to 350°F. Transfer the dough to a lightly floured surface and roll it out into a 10-inch round disk. (You can also do this between 2 pieces of parchment paper.) Ease the dough into an 8-inch tart pan, pressing it into place. Cut off the excess dough and pinch the crust around the edge. Place it in the refrigerator.

To make the filling: In a large skillet, warm the butter over medium-low heat. Add the onion and a pinch of salt and sweat with the cover on, stirring occasionally. Cook until the onions are translucent, about 10 minutes. Add greens and a splash of apple cider vinegar and cook down for 5 more minutes.

Meanwhile, whisk the eggs in a medium bowl with the milk (or cream), crème fraîche, thyme, a pinch of salt, a few twists of the pepper mill, nutmeg, and half of the Gruyère. Lay the greens in the crust in a single layer. Pour the egg mixture over top. Finish with the second half of the Gruyère sprinkled evenly on top. Place the quiche in the oven for 30 to 40 minutes, until golden brown. You may want to rotate it halfway through the cooking process for equal browning. Slice and serve warm or at room temperature.

GREEN GAZPACHO

Serves 8 to 10

For some, the rawness of gazpacho makes it enjoyable in smaller quantities, rather than a whole bowl. This recipe applies heat to half of the ingredients, giving the final product a bit of a charred flavor, which shifts the appeal of a cold soup. Pepitas offer a textural contrast and a spoonful of yogurt introduces welcome sour notes.

2 pounds tomatillos, husks removed

1 white onion, peeled and quartered

6 cloves garlic, in their skins

2 medium or 1 large zucchini

Kosher salt

2 tablespoons extra virgin olive oil

2 medium cucumbers, peeled and seeds removed if tough

2 tablespoons lemon juice

2 tablespoons red wine vinegar

1 bunch basil, roughly chopped

1 bunch chives, roughly chopped

1 bunch parsley, roughly chopped

Fresh ground pepper

Red pepper flakes, to taste

Greek yogurt, for garnish

Roasted and salted pepitas, for garnish

Preheat the oven to 400°F. Place the tomatillos, onions, and garlic on a baking sheet lined with aluminum foil. Place in the oven for 20 minutes, or until the tomatillos begin to gain color and soften. Remove the vegetables from the oven. Squeeze the garlic out of their skins or simply remove the skins from the cloves. The garlic should have softened and the onions should have gained color on the outsides and slightly softened within. Reserve the cooked tomatillos, onions, and garlic.

Preheat the grill to high. Slice the zucchini lengthwise into ⅓-inch-thick pieces and season with kosher salt and coat in olive oil. Place the zucchini on the hot grill using tongs. Turn the heat down to medium-high, close the lid, and sear the vegetables, about 5 minutes. When there are decisive grill marks, flip the zucchini. Turn the heat down to medium, cover, and grill until cooked through, about 5 more minutes. When cooked to your desired tenderness, set the zucchini aside. Slice the cucumbers in half lengthwise and cut across into ½-inch pieces.

Blend the tomatillos, onion, garlic, zucchini, cucumbers, lemon juice, vinegar, basil, chives, and parsley in two batches in a food processor until well blended. Season to taste as you go with salt, pepper, and red pepper flakes. Serve in bowls and garnish with a dollop of Greek yogurt, a sprinkle of pepitas, and a drizzle of good oil.

MARINATED PEPPERS, EGGPLANTS, AND ONIONS

Serves 6

In the lush backyard of a two-hundred-year-old ship captain's house, a friend celebrated her thirty-fifth birthday with thirty-five already-cooked and chilled rock crabs under a magically lit apple tree. Along the center of the table were a half dozen side dishes to accompany the crabs, one of which was marinated summer vegetables. I couldn't quite determine why they were so marvelous and so I asked the birthday girl. She said they had been roasted and then marinated days before, so the flavors had a chance to meld and fortify. Often time is the secret ingredient in a dish.

4 red bell peppers

2 medium eggplants

2 Vidalia onions, peeled

Kosher salt

8 tablespoons extra virgin olive oil

4 tablespoons balsamic vinegar

2 tablespoons honey

Preheat the grill to high. Cut the peppers in half, removing the seeds and veins with a paring knife. Cut the eggplants into ½-inch rounds, discarding the stem ends. Cut the onions into rounds, discarding the stems and root ends. Season all the vegetables with plenty of salt. Coat them with 2 tablespoons of olive oil, massaging it into all the vegetables. Lower the grill to medium, then grill the peppers, eggplants, and onions on both sides until they are tender. Remove them from the heat and place in a medium glass baking dish. While still hot, add the vinegar and honey and the remaining 6 tablespoons of olive oil. Gently toss the vegetables in the marinade to coat. Cover with plastic and let them stand in the fridge for at least one day and up to three. Serve cold or at room temperature.

PASTA E FAGIOLI

Serves 4

This meal was inspired by a pile of gorgeous speckled pink and white borlotti beans that I posted on Instagram, asking my followers, What should I do with these? My dear friend, who gave me an incredible tour of Rome while he was working at the American Academy, suggested pasta e fagioli. The garden was full of overripe tomatoes, and we had plenty of garlic still drying in the greenhouse, so it seemed like the perfect dish. And once it was on the table, it did indeed remind me of the time that we had spent together in Rome. If you're unable to source fresh borlotti beans, any fresh bean will do. In a pinch, you can use a dried bean, such as Jacob's Cattle Beans.

1 cup borlotti beans or other fresh bean, removed from pods

Kosher salt

4 tablespoons extra virgin olive oil

6 cloves garlic, peeled and minced

2 sprigs rosemary, leaves removed from stems and roughly chopped

3 cups ripe garden tomatoes, roughly chopped

Kosher salt

Fresh ground pepper

1 bay leaf

Red pepper flakes

1 pound fresh egg pasta

Grated Parmesan, for garnish

Extra virgin olive oil, for finishing

4 small sprigs oregano, for garnish

Cook the beans. Bring a small pot of water to a boil. Salt generously. Add the beans, and cook until tender, about 5 minutes. Drain the beans, reserving 1 cup of the bean liquid, and cool immediately with cold water to stop the cooking. (You do not want the beans to overcook, as they will turn to mush.)

To make the sauce: In a large, shallow, heavy-bottomed pan warm the olive oil over medium-low heat. Add the garlic and let soften, about 5 minutes. Add the chopped rosemary and cook until fragrant, about 2 minutes. Add the tomatoes, a pinch of salt, pepper, and the bay leaf. Bring to a simmer and let cook until the sauce thickens, about 20 minutes, stirring occasionally. Season to taste with salt, fresh ground pepper, and red pepper flakes.

To cook the pasta: Fill a large pot with water and salt generously. Bring it to a boil. Add the fresh pasta and cook until al dente, about 5 to 6 minutes. Warm the sauce over medium heat. Add the beans to it, along with 1 cup of bean water. Once cooked, transfer the pasta to the sauce with a set of tongs, bringing a bit of pasta water along with it. You want the sauce to be loose but not liquidy. Toss the pasta in the sauce with the beans for 1 or 2 minutes and then twist nests of pasta into individual bowls. Garnish with a little grated Parmesan, a small pour of good olive oil, and a sprig of oregano.

BLACKBERRY BUCKLE

Serves 6

For ten years at the cooking school, I have taught a class called Cobblers, Buckles, and Grunts. These are all funny New England terms for some combination of sugar, flour, butter, and berries. The class typically celebrates the berry of the moment: strawberries in June, raspberries in July, blueberries in August, and blackberries in September. This recipe is great for breakfast or with afternoon tea.

Preheat the oven to 350°F. Butter and flour six 6-ounce ramekins or one 9-inch springform pan lined with parchment paper.

To make the topping: In a medium bowl, stir together the butter, flour, sugar, salt, cinnamon, and nutmeg. The mixture should be crumbly in texture. Set aside.

To make the base: In a medium bowl, whisk the flour, salt, and baking powder. Set aside. In the bowl of a stand mixer, beat the butter and sugar on medium speed until pale and fluffy, about 1 minute. Add the vanilla and egg and beat until smooth. Scrape the sides of the bowl. Add the flour mixture and milk and mix for 1 minute. Using a rubber spatula, fold the blackberries into the batter. Pour the batter into the prepared ramekins or springform pan and sprinkle with the reserved topping. Bake until a toothpick inserted into center of the cake comes out clean, about 1 hour. Let cool before serving.

FOR THE TOPPING

4 tablespoons butter, softened

6 tablespoons all-purpose flour

½ cup sugar

¼ teaspoon salt

¾ teaspoon ground cinnamon

⅛ teaspoon freshly grated nutmeg

FOR THE BASE

1½ cups all-purpose flour, plus more for the pan

¾ teaspoon kosher salt

1½ tablespoons baking powder

8 tablespoons (1 stick) butter, softened, plus more for the pan

1 cup sugar

1 teaspoon vanilla extract

1 egg

¾ cup milk

1 pound blackberries

OCTOBER

In October, there is a visible change in the landscape. The forests of Maine fade from a deep green to a varied auburn, only to be left gray after a stiff wind and a hard rain as November approaches. Ocean harbors empty out their boats as hurricane season poses an imminent threat, leaving only buoys and the occasional year-round lobster boat. The water in the lake is so low that otherwise well-hidden rocks are exposed, cautioning navigators. At the farm, we mow the fields to maintain the brush, transforming the wild golden growth to a tamed, low-cut slope. The sun sets behind the hills at five o'clock, casting pink light over the islands in the bay.

It's time to shut and lock the windows at the cooking school that have been cracked for months, bringing in fresh air. Now the kitchen smells come entirely from within: woodsmoke from last night's fire, a savory stew that bubbles away in the oven, and chicken stock that has cooled overnight on the stovetop. In October, we dive into a curriculum that focuses on traditional cooking techniques practiced in colder months, with classes such as Braising on the Bone, Savory Pies, and Cooking Over Fire. I cherish these classes, because their menus provide comfort as we turn toward winter. With a fire roaring and a stew in the oven, there is little to protest.

Braising on the Bone was one of the first classes that I taught in 2009, when the school opened, and it was the first to fill. Who knew cooking meat on the bone had such widespread appeal? Clearly, many people see bone-in cuts of meat as a bonus rather than an obstacle to be dealt with. The bone is what prevents the meat from drying out. Any meat lover knows that the best bites are along the bone, where the meat is the most flavorful and tender. Every year on my birthday, since I was a child, my father makes a rack of pork ribs, which is my favorite meal on earth. While gnawing on the bone isn't exactly a vision of good manners, it is an indulgence that I will never pass up.

Our Savory Pies class is another favorite among our students, a slightly more challenging skill set that includes both braising and handling dough. After a memorable trip to London's Borough Market, it felt incumbent upon me to teach a savory pie class. A meat pie is a truly historic culinary pursuit, made for both the rich and the working class. Multi-tiered meat pies were concocted for the celebrations of the kings and queens of Europe (with birds flying out the top), while simpler versions were made for long transport by land and sea. The premise of a meat pie is that it contains a full meal in the confines of a thick and protective crust, made with enough fat to preserve whatever lies within. The English have meat pies down to a science and use machines to cut and fold the crusts, but in this chapter, we will lovingly mold them by hand.

Our final class, Cooking Over Fire, is taught by both my father and me. The menu is extensive, as we can never seem to settle on just a few dishes. (This is always what happens when the two of us cook together.) My father begins his lengthy monologue about how to properly build and maintain a fire in a cooking oven, and the class usually gets more than they bargained for, in terms of both a meal and knowledge. As a group, we prepare shellfish, meat, and vegetables for their foray into the fire. After many years experimenting with wood-fired cooking and a fairly extensive cookbook collection on the subject (not to mention all the cast-iron cooking implements we've acquired), this class is, in a way, a celebration of our mutual interests. Of course, we have a hard time not interrupting each other, but it's to be expected when working alongside a family member. It offers a bit of "authenticity."

After the classes are done for the season, we deep clean the kitchen and put all the gardens to sleep, harvesting the last of the greens, pulling the remaining carrots and beets from the cool earth, and digging up any herbs that won't overwinter. Perennials such as apples, pears, and quince need a once-over, making sure no fruit has been left behind. The cooler temperatures act as refrigeration, until the final harvest. Before the ground freezes, the garlic must be planted with a marker, reminding us in the spring not to reseed the bed.

The month of October includes many anticipated traditions, almost all of which include my father's participation. On October 21, we celebrate his birthday. As all of the women in my family are born in June, this is his month to be recognized. One of his favorite hobbies (of which the man has many) is cooking, and we typically spend his birthday preparing a feast for a table of my parents' closest friends. My father is a true lover of poetry and insists that each of his friends brings a poem to the table to be read aloud. Maine is known for its poets, and between the elements and the isolation, it is a wonderful place to reflect on the world.

As my father and I are the farm managers, it is our job to preserve the final harvests. Each year, we press apples and pears, boil down quince to make a paste, pickle mushrooms, and use a steam extractor to make the loveliest Aronia and beach plum juice. While many of these tasks are time-consuming and fairly repetitive, I enjoy the slower pace of the work, the quiet in the kitchen, and the time spent with my dad. These chores have become an annual tradition, a sort of reaping of the benefits of decades of investment in the land.

The recipes in this chapter are fairly simple, taking advantage of the final harvest. Pork and chicken are the featured meats in an attempt to make a dent in the densely packed freezer. For the Apple Cider Braised Chicken (page 200), the chicken is braised on the bone; and pork is stewed and packed into a savory Pork Pie (page 208). We tackle the application of quince in the Roast Quince and Brussels Sprouts recipe (page 207), which can be challenging due to its extreme tartness and firmness. The fruit must always be tamed, either pickled or cooked down, as in its raw form it's not even fit for the birds. A friend delivers an enormous maitake mushroom each October, and after my father and I have cooked as much of it as we can in a buttery pan (alongside eggs, dropped into soups, and to accompany pork chops), we pickle the rest for Pickled Hen of the Woods Mushrooms (page 203). It gives us the opportunity to nibble on the delectable annual gift from the woods for another couple of months. This chapter makes use of squash and specialty onions in a Salad "Agrodolce" (sour and sweet) (page 204), combining honey and balsamic vinegar to achieve the perfect harmony of flavors. And finally, a simple dessert of Honey and Butter Pears with Pear Brandy (page 209) commands our perfectly ripe pears, which we have patiently waited to harvest, cooking them over the fire with a little brandy in dramatic form.

APPLE CIDER BRAISED CHICKEN

Serves 4

This recipe is influenced by a wonderful vinegar-based chicken dish that originates in the Alsatian region of France. Like Maine, this area is known for its old orchards, magnificent apples, and products such as apple cider, fermented cider, and apple cider vinegar. I love the tartness of this dish. A touch of honey adds a welcome sweetness as well.

1 whole chicken, cut into 10 pieces (each breast in half, 2 legs, 2 thighs, 2 wings)

Kosher salt

2 tablespoons extra virgin olive oil

2 small yellow onions, large dice

4 carrots, peeled and cut into 1-inch pieces

2 shallots, thinly sliced

1 tablespoon tomato paste

⅓ cup apple cider vinegar

1 cup hard cider

1 tablespoon honey

2 small purple top turnips, cut into 8 wedges

1 sweet/tart apple (such as Honeycrisp, Braeburn, or Cortland), diced

3 cloves garlic, peeled, smashed, and left whole

2 cups chicken stock

1 savory herb bundle (2 sprigs oregano, 1 bay leaf, 2 sprigs rosemary, 2 sprigs thyme) tied up in kitchen string

6 sprigs parsley, leaves removed from stems and roughly chopped

Preheat the oven to 350°F. Lay the chicken out on a cutting board. Pat it dry with a paper towel for optimal browning. Salt generously on both sides. In a large, shallow, heavy-bottomed pan, heat the olive oil over medium-high heat. Brown the chicken in two batches, skin side down first, until golden and crispy. Once the chicken is browned, remove it to a plate and reserve.

Turn the heat down to medium-low. Add the onions, carrots, shallots, and a pinch of salt and cook for 10 minutes, or until the onions are translucent. Add the tomato paste and massage into the vegetables with a wooden spoon. Cook for 2 minutes, stirring constantly so as not to burn the tomato paste. Add the apple cider vinegar, turn the heat up, and let it reduce for 2 minutes. Add the hard cider and honey and let reduce for an additional 3 to 4 minutes. Add the turnips, apple, garlic, and 1 cup of stock, and continue to cook for 10 minutes. Nestle the chicken into the vegetables in a single layer and add the remaining 1 cup of stock (it should not cover the chicken). Tuck the bundle of herbs into the braise, making sure to submerge it in liquid for maximum flavor.

Place the pan in the oven for 55 minutes. The liquid should have reduced and the chicken should be crispy on top. Remove the herb bundle before serving. Garnish with a sprinkle of parsley.

MAKING HERB BUNDLES There's not much to making a bouquet garni. Traditionally, it's 2 sprigs thyme, 2 sprigs rosemary, 2 sprigs parsley, 12 peppercorns, and 1 fragrant bay leaf. It can be tied up in cheesecloth with kitchen string, or, if you intend to strain whatever it's flavoring, you can simply toss all the ingredients in the pot.

PICKLED HEN OF THE WOODS MUSHROOMS

Makes 1 quart

Each year, a dear friend offers us an enormous maitake mushroom (also known as hen of the woods), some of which we fry up with butter and eggs, the rest of which needs preserving. One of my favorite ways to preserve a mushroom is in pickling liquid, which allows you to enjoy it as a predinner snack along with some crackers and cheese throughout the fall and into the holiday season. The method of preservation involves a combination of oil, which becomes infused with the mushroom's earthy scents, and vinegar, which gives the mushroom a sharp flavor.

In a medium saucepan, combine the vinegar, white wine, peppercorns, thyme, bay leaf, red pepper flakes, and garlic. Bring it to a boil. Add the mushrooms, cook for 1 to 2 minutes, and turn off the heat. Let cool. Strain the mushroom mixture. Place it in a 16-ounce mason jar along with the orange peel. It should just about reach the top of the jar. Fill the jar with olive oil to preserve. Cover and keep it on the counter. The mushrooms will last for 2 to 3 months if submerged in oil. Snack on the mushrooms along with cured meats, cheeses, and crackers before meals.

2 cups rice wine vinegar

1 cup white wine

12 peppercorns

4 sprigs thyme

1 bay leaf

½ teaspoon red pepper flakes

3 cloves garlic, peeled

1 pound cleaned mushrooms, cut into bite-size pieces

2 strips orange peel

Extra virgin olive oil, to cover

SALAD AGRODOLCE

Serves 6

In the fall, I'm always looking for a hearty salad that can accompany a roast chicken. The beauty of this dish is the marriage of roasted vegetables accented in a sweet-and-sour glaze and fresh and crunchy elements like apple, spinach, and crushed hazelnuts. I've named it Salad Agrodolce because of the balsamic vinegar and honey that lend the dish most of its flavor. If you're looking to bulk up the salad for a complete lunch, throw in a handful of cooked grains, such as barley, farro, or wheatberries.

1 buttercup squash, peeled and seeds removed

4 cipollini onions, peeled and quartered

6 cloves garlic, peeled

3 tablespoons extra virgin olive oil

4 sprigs thyme

2 tablespoons honey

2 tablespoons balsamic vinegar

½ teaspoon salt

FOR THE DRESSING

Juice of 1 lemon

1 teaspoon mustard

2 tablespoons apple cider vinegar

4 tablespoons extra virgin olive oil

FOR THE SALAD

1 bunch spinach

Sea salt

1 sweet/tart apple (such as Honeycrisp, Braeburn, or Cortland)

¼ cup roasted and lightly crushed hazelnuts

Preheat the oven to 400°F. Chop the squash into bite-size pieces. In a big bowl, toss the squash, onions, and garlic with the olive oil, thyme, honey, vinegar, and salt. Lay out the vegetables on a sheet pan lined with aluminum foil (or two if it's crowded). Place it in the oven and roast for 25 minutes, moving the vegetables so that they don't stick halfway through cooking. You want the vegetables to be fully cooked and crisp around the edges, without burning. If they start to burn, just pour a tablespoon or two of water onto the pan to release them. Once they are finished cooking, remove them from the oven and let cool.

To make the dressing: Combine all of the ingredients in a mason jar, cover it, and give it a good shake.

To make the salad: Place the spinach in a big wooden bowl and add a pinch of salt. Thinly slice the apple and toss it in a tablespoon of dressing to prevent browning. Add the apples to the salad. Add the roasted vegetables once they have cooked a bit. Toss the salad with the remaining dressing and finish with the hazelnuts.

AGRODOLCE These Italian words translate to "sour sweet," and there are very few palates that don't take pleasure in this combination. When I was a child, I watched my father slowly cook small yellow onions (cipollini) on the stovetop, bathing them in butter, honey, and balsamic vinegar until they were soft throughout, sweet from caramelization and still acid from the vinegar. It was such a revelation to me, a savory treat to be served alongside a roast bird or a pork chop. To this day, Thanksgiving is never complete without a side of these onions.

ROAST QUINCE AND BRUSSELS SPROUTS

Serves 4

Quince can be a tricky fruit, as it needs to be "treated" in a way that apples and pears do not. The flesh of a raw quince is rock-hard, tannic, and tart. In order to make it palatable, it needs to be cooked down and typically sweetened. It's worth the effort, as it has a truly unique floral quality and pairs beautifully with contrasting flavors, such as brussels sprouts. I love to go out into the garden after the first frost to harvest the sprouts, as they are the only plant still green and standing tall and proud.

To make the dressing: Combine the shallot, lemon, and mustard in a small bowl. Whisk to combine. Add the olive oil. Whisk again. Let sit to meld flavors.

Preheat the oven to 425°F. Clean the brussels sprouts and cut them in half. Slice the quince around the core. Line two sheet pans with foil. Salt the brussels sprouts and coat in 2 tablespoons of olive oil. Pour them onto a sheet pan, their interior side down, evenly dispersed. Place them in the oven for 25 minutes. Remove from oven when they begin to brown on the bottom. Now salt the quince and coat it with the remaining 2 tablespoons of olive oil and the honey. Pour the quince onto the other sheet pan and evenly disperse. Place them in the oven for 20 minutes, watching carefully, so as not to burn them. Turn the sheet pan if necessary to promote even caramelization. Remove from oven once they are crispy around the edges. Toss the brussels sprouts and quince together in a large bowl with half the dressing. Taste, and dress further if necessary. Garnish with candied walnuts.

FOR THE DRESSING

1 shallot, minced

Juice of 1 lemon

1 teaspoon Dijon mustard

4 tablespoons extra virgin olive oil

2 pounds brussels sprouts

1 pound quince

Kosher salt

4 tablespoons extra virgin olive oil

1 tablespoon honey

½ cup candied walnuts

PORK PIE

Serves 6

Many shops in the United Kingdom specialize in meat pies and have been using the same recipe for centuries. While I can't boast the same history of savory pie making, I can stand by this recipe as hands-down delicious. In an effort to cut calories, we are applying a piecrust top rather than a fully encased pie. The dish must be served with pickles and a good-quality mustard to offset the richness of this decadent endeavor.

FOR THE CRUST

7 tablespoons butter

½ cup water

2¼ cups all-purpose flour

¾ teaspoon salt

1 medium egg, beaten, for the dough

1 egg, lightly beaten, for brushing

FOR THE FILLING

2 tablespoons extra virgin olive oil

2 pounds ground pork

Kosher salt

Fresh ground pepper

2 large yellow onions, small dice

4 stalks celery, small dice

4 carrots, small dice

2 tablespoons minced rosemary leaves

3 cloves garlic, peeled and roughly chopped

2 tablespoons all-purpose flour

One 12-ounce bottle pale ale

2 cups water

2 teaspoons Dijon mustard, plus more to serve

1 tablespoon Worcestershire sauce

1 pinch mace (optional)

1 bay leaf

Pickles, to serve

To make the crust: Put the butter and water in a saucepan and heat gently until melted; do not let it boil. Put the flour and salt in a mixing bowl. Make a well in the center, add the egg, and stir gently until half mixed. Pour in the melted butter and water and mix to form a soft dough. Add extra water if the mixture is too dry. Gently knead, adding more flour if the dough is too sticky. Wrap it in plastic and chill for 30 minutes.

To make the filling: Heat the oil in a large skillet set over medium-high heat. Season the pork with salt and pepper, add to the skillet, and cook until browned and cooked through, 10 to 12 minutes. Transfer the meat to a bowl with a slotted spoon. Reduce the heat to medium and add the onions, celery, carrots, rosemary, and a pinch of salt to the pan and cook until soft, about 10 minutes. Add the garlic and cook for an additional 5 minutes. Add the flour and cook, stirring until evenly dispersed. Add the beer and let it reduce, another 10 minutes. Return the pork to the pan along with the water, mustard, Worcestershire sauce, mace, and bay leaf and bring to a simmer over medium-low heat. Cook, partially covered, about 1 hour, until the pork is tender and the liquid has reduced significantly. The filling should be thick and moist but not soupy.

Preheat the oven to 375°F. Divide the pork mixture among six ceramic crocks or small ovenproof vessels. Roll out the dough into a ¼-inch-thick sheet. Punch out six circles in the dough to fit the top of each ceramic bowl or crock. Place the dough over the crocks (or pie dish) and press to seal. Brush the pastry with the egg wash. Bake until browned, about 40 minutes. Remove from oven and let set. Serve warm with pickles and mustard.

HONEY AND BUTTER PEARS

WITH PEAR BRANDY

Serves 4

When the pears in our orchard have reached full ripeness, I like to prepare them simply in their whole (or near whole) form. This recipe calls for a bit of honey, butter, and booze to amplify the flavor of the pear. We often do the first step over the fire rather than on the stovetop, just for fun.

4 tablespoons butter

4 crisp pears, cut in half and cored

Kosher salt

2 sprigs thyme

2 tablespoons pear brandy (or cognac)

2 tablespoons honey

Cold cream, to serve

Preheat the oven to 400°F. In a large oven-safe frying pan, melt the butter over medium-low heat. Lay the pears flesh side down in the pan and sprinkle with salt. Nestle the thyme beside the pears and into the butter. Cook for 15 minutes or until the pears begin to brown. If the pan looks too dry and the pears are gaining color too quickly, add a few tablespoons of water. Once they are golden on the flesh side, turn each of the pears. Turn the heat off and add the brandy to the pan. Turn the heat up to medium and cook until the brandy evaporates. (Careful, as the brandy may ignite.) Add the honey and shake the pan to distribute. Place the pan in the oven and let cook for an additional 15 minutes or until the pears are soft throughout. To check, use a small, sharp knife to push through one of them. Remove the pears from the oven and let cool slightly. Place them in a beautiful bowl and pass around the table, followed by a small pitcher of cold cream.

NOVEMBER

While some begrudge this quiet and somber month, artists appreciate it for the unique blue light that passes through the trees and across bodies of water. People in northern climates tend to turn inward during this time of year, waiting to come out again around the holidays when there is more to celebrate. I find November to be the perfect stretch of downtime, when I spend entire days in the kitchen, trying new recipes and reading recently purchased cookbooks from the fall release. The first snow typically falls in November, tracing trees with a layer of white. The smell of woodsmoke permeates my clothes and hair, a sort of winter perfume. My pack of two Australian shepherds love the cold—they are built for it, their coats thick and warm.

There is infinite pleasure in the simplest of routines at home. I wake to cooing in the nursey, put on my slippers and robe, and let my daughter's sounds guide me to her, my head still groggy with sleep (or lack thereof). As I peek over the edge of her crib, we meet eyes, bringing an instant smile to her face, and then mine, like a reflex. This is the best part of the day. I have always loved the morning, the first light, a gentle fog of the mind and soft eyes opening to another day. It is still quiet in the house, save the creaks and moans of a two-hundred-year-old cape and a heating system that ticks and thumps. I fill the kettle and light the woodstove. Coffee and smoke are the pillars of our morning order. The baby patiently waits to be fed, now old enough to understand that there are others that need tending first. The dogs stand by their breakfast bowls and the chickens line up in the henhouse, anticipating their release from the coop.

In November, the lake begins to freeze, leaving large patches of open water. There are a few coveted saunas on the lake's perimeter, and there is nothing more refreshing than jumping in the ice-cold water after a roast. In the Scandinavian tradition, after a sauna and a swim, we put out a Maine-style smorgasbord in the late morning, complete with rye bread and smoked fish, soft mashed potatoes with roast garlic, and scrambled eggs. The adrenaline from the morning's activities leaves a hunger in the belly that is best met with this deeply comforting meal, consumed while still wrapped in a towel.

The long dark nights of early winter encourage a chef to take dinner a bit more seriously. Not a simple, two-step meal but rather a cooking process that develops flavor over time. A dish such as the Cassoulet in this chapter (page 223) is made in various stages: the beans simmering for hours on the stovetop with bay and aromatics, the sausages fried, the duck rendered in its own fat, and the bread crumbs baked to perfection for the finished presentation. This is a meal that deserves applause. Beans are a frugal winter protein. Historically, pork and beans got many a Mainer through the barren winter months, stretching food for the family. I've always considered cassoulet an elevated pork and beans to be enjoyed with many friends beside a fire.

A well-stocked pantry is a critical consideration as we drift into the winter months. Ingredients or condiments that add flavor to simple dishes can turn a lackluster dinner into a deeply satisfying meal. In this chapter, we learn how to make a mostarda (a fruit compote with mustard seed and spices) to serve with a Hot Pot of Sausages with Onions (page 215), or smothered on a pork chop or spread on a sandwich. A salsa verde, aioli, garlic confit, preserved lemons, pickled mushrooms, romesco, or anchovy butter are just a few examples of pantry jewels that can bring a meal to life. You will find several of these recipes in the pages of this book. Consider homemade condiments as the ingredients that can drive a dish.

November is a wonderful time to practice dishes for the great American meal: Thanksgiving. There is nothing more familiar, more red, white, and blue than stuffing. We save this dish for the holidays, but I've never totally understood why. A stuffing is a lovely accompaniment to a roast chicken or duck any night of the week—it's inexpensive, resourceful in its use of day-old bread, and calls for the most basic of ingredients, most of which are likely in your refrigerator. The Sourdough, Sausage, Apple, Sage, and Sherry Stuffing recipe in this chapter (page 219) combines Italian sausage, chestnuts, sherry, mirepoix, and buttered bread, an ensemble of flavors that sing and dance of the holiday season.

As Thanksgiving nears, I begin to contemplate an unanticipated contribution to the table, a dish that is a bit out of the ordinary. (I spent years in New York City as a personal chef making traditional Thanksgiving dinners for a number of families, so these days, I like to think a little outside the box.) Many years ago, a friend made me a spectacular dish, not only in taste but in color too! It was a beet and beet-green gratin with a cheddar béchamel and a hazelnut crumble. I was determined to re-create the dish to the best of my ability. The result: Beet Gratin with Oat Crumble (page 220). Guests are always amazed as the beet-red sauce draws across their plate and pleasantly surprised by the combination of earthy root vegetables, their greens, a decadent sauce, and a crunchy nutty topping.

After the holidays, a simple, meat-free meal can be just what the doctor ordered. Soup making is a wonderful practice to balance the decadence of all the celebratory feasting. A bowl of soup is great for digestion and offers the body much-needed hydration during this sweet and salty season. Classic combinations are my go-to, restoring order to my kitchen and my mind. This chapter features Potato Leek Soup with Celery Root Puree (page 216), which uses celery root for flavor and thickening. When soup making, it always behooves you to double the recipe and freeze the excess, so that the next time you are looking for a restorative meal, you simply turn on the burner.

These November meals are a means of building up to the holidays, leaning on both culinary tradition and resourcefulness in the kitchen. Take some time to yourself, mulling over recipes and imagining a long, candlelit table, dressed up with beautiful dishes of food and surrounded by friends and family. A well-planned and well-orchestrated meal is much appreciated by those lucky enough to be guests at the table.

SMOKED HADDOCK

WITH SOFT POTATOES, RYE TOASTS, AND SCRAMBLED EGGS

Serves 4

A pillowy mix of potatoes, fish, roast garlic, and parsley called a brandade is the inspiration for this dish. While traditionally brandade is served as an appetizer, baked off and spread on coarse, toasted bread, I found that it is deeply satisfying on a cold morning with scrambled eggs, chives, and crème fraîche. The rye toasts are a nice, hearty vessel for consumption and lean on their long and mutually beneficial relationship with smoked fish. This is surely a meal to be shared among many friends and served hot.

FOR THE FISH AND POTATOES

1 pound smoked haddock (or ½ pound smoked trout or smoked mackerel)

3½ cups milk

1 bay leaf

6 cloves garlic

1 tablespoon extra virgin olive oil

2 Idaho potatoes

Kosher salt

6 sprigs Italian flat-leaf parsley, leaves picked from stems

Fresh ground pepper

FOR THE TOAST AND EGGS

10 eggs, well whisked

Kosher salt

Fresh ground pepper

4 tablespoons butter

⅓ cup crème fraîche

1 small bunch chives, minced

4 slices rye bread

If using trout or mackerel, simply flake the fish into pieces. If using smoked haddock, place the fish, 2 cups of milk, and the bay leaf in a large rondeau pan set over medium heat. Cook for 10 minutes. Pour off the milk and flake the fish into small pieces, discarding the skin and any tough bits. Set aside.

Preheat the oven to 375°F. Coat the garlic in the olive oil and place it in a small ovenproof dish. Cover it with foil. Roast for 20 to 25 minutes, until the garlic cloves are soft and fragrant but not burnt. Remove from oven, let cool, and peel. Cut away the roots and reserve the roast cloves.

Peel the potatoes, cut them into sixths, place them in a medium pot, and cover them with water. Salt generously and bring to a boil. Let the potatoes cook until tender, about 15 to 20 minutes. Drain and let cool slightly.

In the bowl of a food processor, combine the potatoes, garlic, parsley, fish, and the remaining 1½ cups of milk. Run on low until the ingredients are thoroughly combined. Taste and season with salt and pepper.

Season the eggs with salt and pepper. In a large cast-iron skillet, melt 2 tablespoons of butter. Pour the eggs into the pan and run the edge of a soft spatula along the outside of the skillet and the base continuously, making sure that no part of the eggs gains any color. Once the eggs are beginning to set but are still loose, add the crème fraîche and chives. Turn the heat off and cover, allowing the residual heat to finish the cooking process.

Pop the rye bread into a toaster or the oven. Serve the eggs alongside the potatoes and shovel both onto toasts.

HOT POT OF SAUSAGES
WITH ONIONS AND MOSTARDA

Serves 4

While some would consider sausage to be a pedestrian food, I find these scrumptious links not only an elevated culinary art but the best meat money can buy. There is great skill involved in sausage making. It requires the perfect ratio of fat to meat and a powerful spice mixture that is evenly incorporated into the grind. Temperature is critical in the production of a good sausage; if the meat or fat gets too warm, the finished product will be mushy rather than coarse. Stuffing the ground pork into casing at just the right speed and tying each link off with the perfect amount of pressure are what make a sausage juicy. An excellent sausage is no miracle. It is the product of a good butcher who has logged a thousand hours mixing, grinding, and stuffing so that your sausages cook up just right.

To make the mostarda: Chop the apples into small dice. In a small saucepan, warm the olive oil over medium heat. Add the rosemary, apples, and a pinch of salt. Let it cook for 15 to 20 minutes, until the apples cook down and begin to brown slightly. Place the Dijon mustard, grain mustard, lemon juice, and brown sugar in a blender. Once the apples are fully cooked, add them to the blender. Blend the contents until the mostarda is thick and smooth. Season to taste with salt and pepper.

To make the sausages: In a large, heavy-bottomed pot, warm the olive oil over medium-high heat. Brown the sausages on both sides. Remove from the pot, lower the heat to medium-low, and add the onion and a pinch of salt. Cover and cook until the onion is translucent, stirring occasionally, for about 20 minutes. Remove the cover and let the onions begin to caramelize. Add the apple cider and the sausages and bring it to a boil over high heat. Then reduce to a simmer and cook until the apple cider dries up and the sausages are cooked through, about 10 minutes. Serve hot with a spoonful of mostarda on each plate.

FOR THE MOSTARDA (MAKES 1 CUP)

2 crisp, tart apples, peeled and cored

1 tablespoon extra virgin olive oil

2 sprigs rosemary, leaves removed from stems and roughly chopped

Kosher salt

2 tablespoons Dijon mustard

2 tablespoons grain mustard

Juice of 1 lemon

1 tablespoon brown sugar

Fresh ground pepper

FOR THE SAUSAGES

1 tablespoon extra virgin olive oil

4 excellent sausages (to your liking)

1 large Vidalia onion, peeled and sliced

Kosher salt

1½ cups apple cider

POTATO LEEK SOUP

WITH CELERY ROOT PUREE

Serves 4

The first cold snap of the year calls for a no-fuss soup to warm the bones. I find that a potato, which holds heat better than just about any root vegetable and whose starches leave a comforting mouthfeel, makes for the perfect introductory winter soup. It's confirmation that food can combat the cold. No potato soup is balanced without a companion onion or leek, cooked slow and long to develop the utmost favor. I often double this recipe so that I can freeze a pint or two, a kind of insurance for the next stretch of cold weather.

1 large or 2 small celery roots, peeled and diced

1 teaspoon kosher salt

1 cup heavy cream

4 tablespoons unsalted butter

4 thick slices sourdough bread

Fresh ground pepper

4 leeks, white and light green parts thinly sliced

1 cup apple cider

4 cups vegetable stock

2 Idaho potatoes, peeled and diced

Juice of ½ lemon

4 sprigs parsley, leaves removed from stems and roughly chopped

Place the diced celery root in a medium pot and cover with water. Add the salt and bring to a boil. Let it cook until the celery root is tender, about 15 to 20 minutes. Drain and place the celery root in a blender. Add the cream and blend to a puree. Move it to a small bowl and reserve.

Preheat the oven to 375°F. Melt 2 tablespoons of butter over the stovetop. Cut or tear the bread roughly into ¾-inch cubes and place them on a sheet tray. Pour the butter over the bread and salt and pepper generously. Toss with your hands to coat and massage the butter into the bread. Place it in the oven for 10 to 15 minutes or until the bread is golden brown on the edges. Depending on your oven, you may have to turn the tray or shake up the croutons to turn them. Once they are golden, move them to a big mixing bowl.

In a heavy-bottomed soup pot, melt the remaining 2 tablespoons of butter over medium heat. Add the leeks and a pinch of salt and cover. Let them sweat for 10 to 15 minutes, until the leeks are soft and tender. Then add the apple cider and stock and bring it to a boil. Reduce it to a simmer and add the diced potatoes. Cook until the potatoes are fork tender. Add the celery root puree and stir to achieve an even texture. Add the lemon juice. Taste the soup for seasoning. Distribute it among bowls while still hot. Garnish with homemade croutons and parsley.

SOURDOUGH, SAUSAGE, APPLE, SAGE, AND SHERRY STUFFING

Serves 4

There is no good reason to have stuffing only on the holiday table. It's a wonderful accompaniment to a roast chicken, with a little pan sauce and a sprinkle of chopped parsley. Stuffing can be made of many things, but typically it includes fruit, bread, aromatics, spices, a binder such as stock, wine, or eggs, and fresh herbs. This particular recipe calls on many of my favorite flavors, and it is no mistake that sherry has found its way into the dressing. It's an excellent excuse to buy a decent sipping sherry and nurse a small glass as the stuffing bakes.

6 tablespoons butter

4 thick slices sourdough bread

Kosher salt

Fresh ground pepper

3 sausages, meat pulled from casings and broken up into small pieces

1 yellow onion, medium dice

3 stalks celery, medium dice

1 sweet/tart apple (such as Honeycrisp, Braeburn, or Cortland), medium dice

1 teaspoon chopped fresh rosemary leaves

1 teaspoon fresh thyme leaves

4 sage leaves, roughly chopped

½ cup golden raisins

1 pinch nutmeg

½ cup sherry

¼ cup roughly chopped Italian flat-leaf parsley

2 cups chicken stock

Preheat the oven to 375°F. Melt 2 tablespoons of butter over the stove top. Cut the bread into ¾-inch cubes and place them on a sheet tray. Pour the butter over the bread and salt and pepper generously. Toss with your hands to coat and massage the butter into the bread. Place it in the oven for 10 to 15 minutes, until the bread is golden brown on the edges. Depending on your oven, you may have to turn the tray or shake up the croutons to turn them. Once they are golden, move them to a big mixing bowl.

In a large, heavy-bottomed pot, melt the remaining 4 tablespoons of butter over medium heat. Add the sausage meat to the butter and cook through. Add the onions, celery, and a pinch of salt and continue to cook over medium-low heat for 10 minutes with the cover on. Add the apple to the pot and cook, uncovered, for an additional 5 minutes. Add the rosemary, thyme, sage, raisins, and nutmeg and continue to cook for 1 to 2 minutes. Turn the heat off, so as not to ignite the sherry, and add the sherry to the pot. Turn the heat up to medium-high and let some of the alcohol burn off, about 3 to 4 minutes. Remove the pan from the heat and add the stuffing ingredients to the croutons. Add half of the parsley. Ladle 1 cup of stock over the stuffing and gently fold the ingredients to mix. The bread will slowly absorb the stock. Once it does, add the remaining 1 cup of stock and continue to fold until the stock is fully absorbed. The stuffing should be moist and a little spongy but not wet.

Move the stuffing to a baking dish. Place it in the oven for 30 minutes. The top should be crisp and golden when done. Sprinkle with the other half of the parsley. Serve family style alongside a roast chicken.

BEET GRATIN
WITH OAT CRUMBLE

Serves 6

You know when you eat something that is so delicious that it seems impossible it was made on a whim? It probably wasn't. Several years back, a chef interviewing to run the kitchen at my restaurant made this dish for me, and let's just say, it got him the job. Five years later, I recalled the dish and typed the ingredients I could remember into Google. Sure enough, it was a Melissa Clark recipe from the *New York Times*. This is an adaptation of that recipe, too good not to make and share once more.

FOR THE GRATIN

1 bunch beets with their greens

Kosher salt

6 tablespoons unsalted butter, plus more for greasing the pan

⅔ cup all-purpose flour

2 cups milk

1 tablespoon Worcestershire sauce

1 teaspoon Tabasco sauce

1 tablespoon Dijon mustard

2 cups finely grated cheddar cheese

Fresh ground pepper

FOR THE OAT TOPPING

1 cup walnuts

⅔ cup oats

½ cup all-purpose flour

½ teaspoon kosher salt

¼ teaspoon nutmeg

6 tablespoons cold butter

Bring a large pot of generously salted water to a boil. Cut the beets from their greens. Cut the greens into 2-inch pieces. Cook the greens for 2 minutes. Remove them with a set of tongs, shake off the water, and set them on a plate. Add the beets to the water and let them cook for 25 minutes or until tender. Drain the pot and let the beets cool. Peel, slice with a mandoline into ⅛-inch-thick rounds, and reserve them piled up in a bowl.

In a large sauté pan, melt the butter over medium-low heat. Whisk in the flour, creating a roux. Let it cook for 1 to 2 minutes, continuing to whisk. Gradually add the milk to thin out the roux, making a béchamel. Add the Worcestershire sauce, Tabasco sauce, and Dijon mustard. Whisk the grated cheddar into the sauce. Continue whisking and cook until the texture is uniform, another 2 to 3 minutes. Season to taste with salt and pepper.

To make the topping: Roughly chop the walnuts. In a medium mixing bowl, combine the walnuts, oats, flour, salt, and nutmeg. Cut the butter into small pieces, then cut it into the topping mixture until you have the texture of coarse meal.

Build your gratin. Preheat the oven to 350°F. Butter a 9-inch square baking pan. Spoon half of the béchamel into the base and spread it out evenly, coating the bottom of the pan. Spread half of the beets and beet greens across the béchamel. Sprinkle a little salt across the beets. Now add a second layer of béchamel, coating the beets. Again, place a layer of beets and beet greens across the sauce. Finish with a heavy layer of the crumble. Place the gratin on a sheet pan in the oven for 40 to 45 minutes. Remove and let rest for 5 to 10 minutes. Serve hot.

CASSOULET

Serves 8

With roots in the southwest of France, this dish is named for the vessel in which it is made, a *cassoule*, which is nothing more than a deep earthenware pot. Slowly simmered Great Northern white beans stand up to the richness of both the pork and duck fat, and a thin layer of homemade bread crumbs (made from day-old bread pulsed in a food processor until fine) soaks up a depth of flavor while crisping on top. I suggest buying the duck legs already as confit, which simply means cooked very slowly in their own fat (typically the fat rendered from the breasts). Think of it as a dressed-up pork and beans, suitable for a dinner party served alongside a nice bottle of red wine from southwestern France.

4 cups dried Great Northern white beans, soaked overnight

⅓ pound slab bacon, cut into ¼-inch pieces

2 medium yellow onions, peeled and diced

3 carrots, peeled and diced

3 leeks, white and light green parts, diced

2 cloves garlic, peeled and minced

Kosher salt

Fresh ground pepper

1 tablespoon tomato paste

¼ teaspoon nutmeg

2 cloves

1 bay leaf

2 sprigs thyme

6 cups duck or chicken stock

2 duck legs confit, including the fat

2 tablespoons duck fat or butter

1½ cups homemade bread crumbs

6 sprigs parsley, roughly chopped

Rinse the beans thoroughly in cold water. Cook the bacon in a large, heavy earthenware pot (about 4 inches high) set over medium heat until the fat is rendered and the bacon starts to brown. Add the onions, carrots, leeks, garlic, and a pinch of salt and cover. Cook over medium-low heat until the onions are translucent, about 10 to 15 minutes. Add the tomato paste and massage it into the vegetables with a wooden spoon. Cook for 2 minutes, stirring constantly. Add the beans, nutmeg, cloves, bay leaf, thyme, and enough duck or chicken stock to cover and simmer for 1½ hours. If the beans dry up, add more stock.

In a large sauté pan, heat the duck legs over medium heat until the fat melts. Remove the duck legs from the pan and reserve. Pour off the fat into a measuring cup.

Nestle the duck legs into the beans. Add the stock to almost cover. Bake, uncovered, about 1 hour, until the cassoulet comes to a simmer and a crust begins to form. About 30 minutes into cooking, sprinkle the bread crumbs on top and spoon about 2 tablespoons melted duck fat over the bread crumbs. When finished, garnish with parsley and serve hot.

HAZELNUT CAKE
WITH CREAM

Serves 8 to 10

I love a good nut cake, especially when the nuts are fresh and of good quality. I almost always toast them, as the heat of the oven draws out their oils, making them fragrant and bringing out their flavor essence. It's up to you how finely ground you want them. Nuts ground into a flour will result in a lighter cake and a finer crumb, whereas a coarser grind will offer a texture that is more reminiscent of the nut itself.

2 cups hazelnuts

1 cup (2 sticks) unsalted butter, softened, plus 1 tablespoon for greasing the pan

1 cup brown sugar

3 eggs

1 teaspoon vanilla

½ cup all-purpose flour, plus more for flouring the pan

1 tablespoon baking powder

½ teaspoon salt

FOR THE WHIPPED CREAM

2 cups heavy cream

1 tablespoon sugar

½ teaspoon hazelnut extract (optional)

Preheat the oven to 375°F. Arrange the hazelnuts on a sheet pan and place them in the oven on the middle rack. Set a timer for 10 minutes. Check them. They ought to be golden and fragrant. They may need an additional 2 minutes. Don't walk away from the oven, as they easily burn. Once they are done, transfer them from the pan to a bowl and let cool. If the hazelnuts aren't skinned, follow the method outlined on page 132. Add the hazelnuts to a food processor and pulse until they are coarsely chopped. Move them to a bowl.

In a stand mixer, beat the butter and brown sugar on medium for 3 minutes. Scrape the sides of the bowl. Add the eggs, one at a time, and beat until fully incorporated. Scrape the sides once more. Add the vanilla. Put the flour, baking powder, and salt in a small mixing bowl. Whisk to combine. Add to the batter and continue beating on low for 1 minute. Remove the bowl from the mixer and, using a whisk, incorporate the hazelnuts fully.

Turn down the oven to 350°F. Line a 9-inch round baking pan with parchment paper. Butter and flour the sides of the pan. Pour the batter into the pan and knock it a few times on the counter to get rid of any bubbles. Place the cake pan on a sheet pan and put it in the oven. Bake for 40 to 45 minutes. Test for doneness by inserting a toothpick and removing it. If it is dry, the cake is done. Remove from oven, unmold, and let rest on a rack.

To make the whipped cream: In a stand mixer, beat the heavy cream along with the sugar and hazelnut extract, if using, until you have soft, voluminous peaks. Serve the sliced hazelnut cake with the whipped cream.

A QUALITY NUT We don't think of nuts as seasonal, but they absolutely are. It is very common in European countries to harvest nuts as they fall from the trees in the late fall and to keep a bowl of them, unshelled, alongside a nutcracker for snacking. While living in New York City and routinely shopping at some of the finest specialty food shops in the country, I came to appreciate the difference between an old nut from the bag at a grocery store and a freshly cracked nut, its oils, textures, and scents still intact. There is a world of difference between a fresh nut and a stale nut. An old nut is typically dried out and sticks to crevices in your molars. It tastes rancid and is not worth purchasing. A fresh nut should have an interesting texture and a flavor that lingers in the back of your palate, making you want another. Find a good source. I buy them from our local (and most excellent) bakeshop, already skinned.

DECEMBER

Maine loses so much daylight in the month of December as we near the winter solstice. If you look at a map, you'll see that the coast stretches easterly into the Atlantic, causing the sun to set before four o'clock. It is pitch-black well before dinnertime. Luckily, our home looks over a forty-acre field with big sky and the mountains behind it. The evening light is cast across the rolling, snow-white hills and floods into our kitchen windows in deep shades of orange and yellow. Sometimes it feels as though we are the last to see the sun each night as it falls behind the mountain ridge. A barred owl joins us for the show, perched on a telephone wire across the street. Propped up on the couch, the dogs watch him intently as he scans the field for mice and other small, delectable creatures. As my husband and I work from home in the winter months, we take a moment each afternoon to watch the magnificence of this moment and bathe in the final warm light of the day.

Come morning (some fourteen hours later), the yard and fence surrounding the house are lain with a fresh coat of snow and frost coats the northern-facing windows of our home like a crystallized art installation. A bird feeder sits fastened to the window above the kitchen sink, and blue jays, red robins, and little gray finches rotate feeding, waiting for their turn. Often, the red squirrels, even the gray ones twice their size, will camp out in the feeder not two feet away from our kitchen sink, looking me straight in the eye, almost as if to ask, "Could you top off my coffee?" The crows dive into the compost pile and scatter last night's dinner scraps across the lawn for the dogs to drag back into the house. I love watching the creatures of the yard, especially the birds with their brilliant reds and blues against the backdrop of winter white.

With a cup of coffee in hand, my mind turns to the day's kitchen projects. A few bone-cold days call for comfort food, and I open the freezer door to inventory what types of pork remain from our autumn pork share. I am eager to pull meat from the freezer, thaw it for a day or two, and embark on a culinary journey that honors the well-raised pigs from our neighbor's farm. I always end up with the cuts that require a bit more culinary know-how, and the chops go to those customers interested in quick-cooking techniques. The beauty of the off cuts are their particular uses for special dishes. Ham hocks (or the feet), for instance, are wonderful for making pork stock and ultimately a cassoulet. The cheeks (*guanciale*) are the traditional meat used in pasta carbonara, which you will find in this chapter. Lard is wonderful for making piecrusts and richening a pot of greens, such as collards. And ground pork finds its way into little tortellini, which are presented in *brodo*, a rich Italian broth. The pig is truly a magical animal with infinite culinary application.

The first of the big snowstorms often hits in December and the grocery store is a madhouse. Everyone is afraid of losing power and the community prepares for two to three days of staying indoors and keeping the woodstove roaring. Inventory begins to empty out and a cook must start to figure out how to make do. One of my favorite dishes on a cold, snowy evening is French onion soup, made with homemade beef stock, slow-cooked onions, sourdough, and heaps of melted Gruyère cheese. It requires only onions and parsley from the produce department, a means of bypassing insipid greens and vegetables. The only hazard of this dish is burning the roof of your mouth, as it is nearly impossible not to dig your spoon into the bubbling cheese and beef-soaked bread the minute it arrives at the table. It's a small price to pay for divinity.

While comfort food features largely in the month of December, there is also good cause to put on your finest dress, light some tall, elegant candles, and flood the house with holiday song. A traditional holiday meal in our home draws inspiration from Italy, as historically, we spent Christmas with my Italian grandparents and celebrate our heritage through food. No holiday feast is complete without a generous antipasto platter: a colorful assortment of meats, cheeses, olives, pickles, and peppers—little salty bites of heaven that beg for a glass of wine or an aperitif. It's nearly impossible not to gorge on these delectable imported Italian treats, alongside torn crusty bread dipped in good olive oil with a sprinkle of sea salt. In keeping with Italian tradition, the *primi piatti* (first course) is made of pasta and broth, a means of cleansing. The broth is slightly decadent, calling for marrow bones and prosciutto, making a very special bath for the ricotta and Swiss chard–filled pasta. This is followed by a tricolored salad of roast cauliflower, radicchio, and parsley, and, for the main course, we make a traditional osso buco, a dish that never tires.

More often than not, I host a New Year's Eve party at Salt Water Farm, as the space allows for large gatherings, games, and dancing. When the guests arrive, there is a big, beautiful batched cocktail, often in a punch bowl, waiting for them to ease into the evening. My go-to cocktail recipe is featured in this chapter: Bourbon, Italian Lemonade, Bitters, and Champagne (page 230). New Year's Eve is an opportunity to draw out the evening with a number of fun and delicious appetizers as the clock inches toward midnight. Dinner is something simple and lovely that's easy to make and serve, so the host can enjoy the company of the guests into the evening hours. At 11:30, dessert is served—something that delights the eye, is plenty sweet to keep the spirits high, and has an air of celebration. The Chestnut, Chocolate, and Orange Tart (page 241) does just that. At 11:55, we queue up "Auld Lang Syne" and get out the bells and air horns to welcome in the new year. There is truly no better way to celebrate this turn of time than with the people you love the most. It assures you that despite all that is grim in the world, you will always have each other.

BOURBON, ITALIAN LEMONADE, BITTERS, AND CHAMPAGNE

Makes 8 drinks

Typically, I recommend exact measurements for cocktails, as you need the right balance of sweet, sour, acid, and booze. This recipe, however, is pretty forgiving. If your guests like a sweeter drink, you can pour in a little extra lemonade; if they like it stiffer, a little more bourbon. Just make sure it's nice and cold and effervescent when it enters your guest's hand.

Fill a pitcher to the top with ice. Add the bourbon, champagne or prosecco, lemonade, bitters, and lemon rounds. Stir for 30 seconds. Serve immediately in punch glasses or short cocktail glasses alongside a beautiful antipasto spread.

Ice, to fill a pitcher

12 ounces bourbon

12 ounces midlevel champagne or prosecco

12 ounces sparkling lemonade (Italian or quite sweet)

4 shakes Angostura bitters

1 lemon, cut into rounds

FRENCH ONION SOUP

WITH BEEF BONES AND CIDER

Serves 4

In my early twenties, I was living in Paris and on a budget. A restaurant called Au Pied de le Cochon continually tempted my appetite but not my pocketbook. I was determined to have the experience of eating there and, finally, still pickled from the previous night's Beaujolais Nouveau release, I marched into this legendary restaurant and requested a seat. I watched as gloved servers brought out classically composed salads, chocolate soufflés standing taut and tall, and their signature dish, a pig's foot stuffed with foie gras. There was only one dish that was within my price range, an old classic: French onion soup. It came out in a traditional white bowl (intended for exactly this dish) marked with a lion's head on each protruding side, Gruyère cheese melted to golden perfection, and a sprinkling of parsley on top. And the smell, my god, the smell! It instantly made my hangover a thing of the past. Here is my more modest, homemade version of the dish.

FOR THE BEEF STOCK

5 pounds beef bones (ask your butcher ahead of time)

2 yellow onions, peeled and quartered

4 carrots, peeled and chopped into 1-inch pieces

4 stalks celery, cut into 1-inch pieces

1 head garlic, skin on, cut in half widthwise

3 sprigs thyme

3 sprigs rosemary

3 sprigs parsley

1 bay leaf

12 peppercorns

12 cups water

FOR THE SOUP

4 tablespoons unsalted butter

4 large yellow onions, sliced

Kosher salt

4 cloves garlic, peeled and minced

1½ tablespoons all-purpose flour

4 sprigs thyme, leaves picked from stems

2 tablespoons Worcestershire sauce

1 cup apple cider

10 cups beef stock

Kosher salt

Fresh ground pepper

FOR THE TOASTS

4 thick slices sourdough

2 cups grated Gruyère cheese

6 sprigs parsley, leaves picked from stems and roughly chopped

To make the beef stock: Preheat the oven to 400°F. Lay the beef bones on a sheet pan and place them in the oven for 25 minutes, shaking them every so often so that they don't stick. Add the onions, carrots, celery, and garlic to the pan and roast for another 25 minutes, or until the vegetables are crisp around the edges and soft at the center. With a set of tongs, move all of the ingredients into a large stockpot. Pour off the grease from the pan and discard. Place a cup of water in the pan and place it back in the oven for 5 minutes to deglaze. Pour the remnants into the stockpot, scraping off any loose bits. Add the thyme, rosemary, parsley, bay leaf, and peppercorns to the stockpot. Fill it with the water to cover and bring it to a boil. Skim any scum that rises to the top with a slotted spoon and discard. (These are the impurities from the bones and dirt in the vegetables.) Reduce the stock to a simmer and cook over low heat for a minimum of 3 hours. Strain through a chinois or a fine-mesh strainer, pushing the vegetables against the mesh to a pulp to get the most flavor possible (and the most juice). Compost the pulp and discard the bones. Save the stock for the soup.

To make the soup: In a large, heavy-bottomed pot, melt the butter over medium heat. Add the onions to the pan and sweat with a big pinch of salt, covered, for about 20 minutes, stirring every 5 minutes or so. Once the onions are broken down and translucent, add the garlic. Cook for an additional 5 minutes. Sprinkle the flour over the onions and massage it into them with a wooden spoon. Let the flour toast in the pan for a minute or two. Now add the thyme and Worcestershire sauce. Cook down until the pan is dry and you see golden marks around the edges from the onions sticking. This helps to promote flavor. Now add the cider and cook it down until it dries up. Add the beef stock and bring it to a simmer. Season to taste with salt and plenty of fresh ground pepper.

To make the toasts: Toast the sourdough in a toaster or the oven until it is golden around the edges. Divide the soup among four ovenproof bowls, topping each with a toast. Distribute the cheese among the four bowls, piling it high on top of the toasts. Place the soup bowls on a sheet pan and move into the oven. Let them cook until the cheese is melted and begins to brown, about 15 minutes. Sprinkle with parsley and serve immediately.

PASTA CARBONARA

Serves 4 to 6

There is a reason that pasta tastes better in Italy than anywhere else. It's the way in which they make it, which for some reason hasn't translated very well into American cookbooks. The pasta is cooked al dente, then moved to its sauce (usually in a large frying pan, the sauce simmering away) with traces of salty, starchy pasta water, which helps to lubricate the dish. The pasta continues cooking in the sauce and is often finished with a cube of cold butter or a little pour of good olive oil. Carbonara is unique in that it is best made with raw eggs, cooked entirely from the residual heat of the pasta water. Also, don't skimp on the cheese. (You're not doing yourself any favors.)

½ pound bacon or guanciale (ask your butcher), chopped into small pieces

6 cloves garlic, peeled and minced

4 sprigs thyme, leaves removed from stems

1 egg, plus 3 egg yolks

1½ cups finely grated pecorino

1½ cups finely grated Parmesan

Kosher salt

½ teaspoon fresh ground pepper

1 pound good-quality spaghetti (imported)

6 sprigs parsley, leaves removed from stems, cleaned, and roughly chopped

In a large frying pan, render the fat from the bacon or guanciale over medium-low heat, about 20 minutes. Once the bacon begins to crisp, remove it with a slotted spoon and put it into a large mixing bowl. Add the garlic and thyme to the bacon fat and cook for 3 to 4 minutes, until the fat becomes fragrant, making sure not to burn the garlic. Turn off the heat and remove the pan from the burner to prevent further cooking.

In a small bowl, whisk the egg and egg yolks. Add the eggs to the bowl with the bacon. Add the pecorino and Parmesan. Add a pinch of salt and lots of fresh ground pepper. Pepper is one of the main components of the dish.

Bring a large pot of water to a boil. Salt generously. Add the pasta and stir frequently to prevent sticking. Place the pan with the fat, garlic, and thyme over medium heat for 1 minute. Add 1½ cups of pasta water and bring it to a boil to deglaze the pan. Turn off the heat. Cook the pasta until al dente, about 8 to 10 minutes. Drain the pasta and add it to the mixing bowl with the eggs and bacon, and pour the contents of the frying pan over the pasta. Toss with a set of tongs. Serve hot, using the tongs to twist the pasta into each bowl. Sprinkle with parsley.

ROASTED CAULIFLOWER
WITH RADICCHIO, CAPERS, AND PARSLEY

Serves 6

Bitter greens have always had a place in Italian cuisine, as they are good for digestion. This partially cooked salad combines red, white, and green ingredients to make the perfect Christmas salad.

FOR THE SALAD

1 small head cauliflower

2 tablespoons extra virgin olive oil

Kosher salt

1 head radicchio

½ bunch parsley, leaves picked from stems

FOR THE DRESSING

Zest and juice of 1 lemon

1 tablespoon white wine vinegar

1 tablespoon Dijon mustard

1 tablespoon capers

1 tablespoon honey

4 tablespoons extra virgin olive oil

Kosher salt

Fresh ground pepper

Preheat the oven to 400°F. Cut the florets away from the stem of the cauliflower, making them small enough to fit on a spoon. Toss with olive oil. Line a sheet pan with parchment paper, and place the cauliflower on the sheet and spread it out evenly. Place into the oven and cook for 20 to 25 minutes, until the cauliflower begins to brown on the edges. Remove from oven, sprinkle with salt, and let cool on the sheet pan.

Cut the radicchio in half. Cut away the stem. Then cut each half into quarters and break up the leaves into a big bowl. Add the cauliflower and parsley to the bowl.

To make the dressing: In a small bowl, combine the lemon zest and juice, vinegar, mustard, capers, honey, and olive oil. Season to taste with salt and pepper.

Toss the salad with the dressing. Pour it onto a medium-size platter and serve family style at room temperature.

OSSO BUCO

Serves 4 to 6

This is a deeply pleasurable dish, fit for a Sunday evening at home or a holiday feast. It takes time to prepare, but those consuming it will reap the benefits of every minute it spends bubbling away on the stovetop. Your entire home and your clothes will smell of this wonderfully savory classic. A note: you can substitute lamb for the veal if you choose.

FOR THE SHANKS

2 tablespoons extra virgin olive oil

4 pounds veal shanks, beef shanks, or oxtail

Fresh ground pepper

2 medium yellow onions, medium dice

3 carrots, peeled and dice

4 stalks celery, peeled and diced

Kosher salt

3 cloves garlic, peeled and minced

1 tablespoon tomato paste

1 cup red wine

One 28-ounce can whole plum tomatoes, roughly crushed with your hand

1 herb bundle (1 sprig thyme, 1 sprig rosemary, 1 sprig parsley, 1 bay leaf, and 8 peppercorns)

4 cups beef stock

2 tablespoons cold butter

Zest from 1 lemon

10 sprigs parsley, leaves picked from stems and roughly chopped

FOR THE POLENTA

Kosher salt

2½ cups coarse polenta

1 cup heavy cream

4 tablespoons cold butter

½ cup grated Parmesan

Fresh ground pepper

In a large, heavy pot, heat the olive oil over medium-high heat. Brown the veal shanks on all sides and set aside. Pour off the extra grease and add the onions, carrots, celery, and a pinch of salt. Reduce the heat to medium and cover. After 8 to 10 minutes, add the garlic and cover for another 2 minutes. Once the vegetables are translucent and begin to brown, massage the tomato paste into the vegetables with a wooden spoon until evenly distributed. Move the vegetables continuously for 1 minute, allowing the paste to cook. Add the red wine and reduce by half. Reintroduce the shanks, then add the tomatoes, the herb bundle, and enough stock to almost cover the shanks. Bring it to a boil, reduce to a simmer, and cover, leaving room for air to escape. Leave it over low heat for 2½ hours or in a 325°F oven for 3 hours.

To make the polenta: Bring 10 cups of water to a boil. Salt the water generously. Slowly whisk in the polenta. Continue whisking until the polenta begins to thicken. Turn the heat down to medium and cook for 20 minutes, stirring constantly. Add in the cream and butter. Grate the Parmesan over top. Salt and pepper to taste.

Once the osso buco has thickened, remove the shanks from the sauce. At this point you can strain the sauce for a finer presentation, making sure to push all the vegetables through a sieve to get as much flavor as possible. The vegetable pulp left behind can be composted. Swirl the butter into the sauce. If the sauce is too thin, reduce it in the pan over high heat until you have rendered about 2 cups of sauce. Add the meat back to the sauce and place it over medium heat. Serve the osso buco over soft polenta and sprinkle with lemon zest and chopped parsley.

TORTELLINI IN BRODO

Makes 24 tortellini

Filling pasta is sort of the level two of pasta making. It's a bit more complicated, and it requires a couple of extra steps and a small measure of confidence and commitment. *But*, if you decide to tackle a culinary project such as this, my recommendation is that you make enough for several meals and freeze what you don't use, which will render the project time well spent. The recipe here will make enough tortellini for two meals. Each filled pasta requires only ⅛ of a teaspoon of filling, so a little filling goes a long way. Make sure the filling is nicely seasoned, because once it's sealed in the pasta, you can't alter it. While there are many tools for pasta making such as rollers and presses, the truth is the whole thing can be done with your own two hands, if the spirit moves you.

FOR THE BRODO

1 yellow onion, roughly chopped

2 carrots with their greens

3 stalks celery, roughly chopped

¼ pound prosciutto ends

1 pound marrow bones

12 peppercorns

4 sprigs parsley

2 sprigs thyme

2 sprigs rosemary

1 fresh bay leaf

FOR THE PASTA

2 batches homemade Pasta Dough (page 47), rolled out into four 12 x 8-inch sheets

FOR THE FILLING

2 tablespoons extra virgin olive oil

1 small yellow onion, small dice

2 carrots, peeled and finely diced

2 bunches Swiss chard, ribs and leaves separated and finely chopped

Kosher salt

1 pound ground pork

2 eggs

½ cup finely grated Parmesan

1 pinch nutmeg

½ cup ricotta

Fresh ground pepper

FOR ASSEMBLY

1 egg, beaten

Cornmeal or flour, for the pan

TO FINISH

Lemon juice

Fresh ground pepper

Freshly grated Parmesan

(recipe continues)

To make the brodo: In a large pot, add all of the brodo ingredients. Cover with water and bring it to a boil. Reduce to a simmer, skim any foam that rises to the top, and let cook for 1½ hours. Place a fine-mesh sieve or a chinois over a large pot. Pour the brodo through the sieve, collecting the broth in the pot. Using a wooden spoon, push the juice out of the vegetables to the best of your ability. Discard the contents of the sieve and place the brodo in the pot back on the stovetop and cover. Reserve.

To make the filling: In a sauté pan, warm the olive oil over medium heat. Add the onions, carrots, chard, and a pinch of salt. Let them cook for 6 to 8 minutes, until they soften. Add the ground pork and sauté until it is cooked through and begins to gain color, about 10 minutes. Add the chard leaves and cook until they wilt, stirring them into the pork. Move the contents of the pot into a bowl and let cool. Add the eggs, Parmesan, nutmeg, ricotta, and salt and pepper to taste. Stir to fully incorporate.

To assemble the tortellini: Make sure you have access to a large work space. Lay out the pasta sheets side by side, lengthwise. Cut each sheet in half from top to bottom (lengthwise) so that you have eight 4 x 12-inch sheets. Cut each sheet side to side (widthwise) every 3 inches. You will be left with twenty-four 4 x 4-inch sheets of pasta. Place a small spoonful of pork filling at the center of each sheet. Brush the outside edges of the sheet with the egg wash. Fold each sheet over the pork filling on a diagonal and press to seal. Bring the opposing ends together to form a tortellini and press to seal again. Line a sheet pan with cornmeal or flour. Let the tortellini rest on the sheet pan until you are ready to cook them.

Bring a large pot of water to a boil. Salt generously. Add the tortellini and cook for 7 to 8 minutes, until al dente. With a slotted spoon move them to a large bowl to rest.

Turn the heat on to medium under the brodo pot to bring it to a simmer. When ready to serve, place three tortellini in each of the four bowls. Ladle the brodo over top. Finish with a squeeze of lemon, fresh ground pepper, and a little freshly grated Parmesan.

CHESTNUT, CHOCOLATE, AND ORANGE TART

Serves 8 to 10

You are in for a treat. I came across this divine chocolate tart almost by accident, when I sort of "winged it" for an impromptu dinner party. Little did I know it would make it into the vault of crowd-pleasers. It takes on an entirely different character after a few hours spent in the fridge, becoming almost fudgelike. I prefer it slightly warm but fully set. You must serve it with a little whipped cream.

FOR THE CRUST

¾ cup chestnut flour

1 cup all-purpose flour

½ teaspoon kosher salt

1 tablespoon sugar

12 tablespoons cold unsalted butter

2 to 3 tablespoons heavy cream

FOR THE FILLING

1 cup heavy cream

½ cup milk

10 ounces bittersweet chocolate

3 eggs

⅔ cup sugar

1 teaspoon vanilla

½ teaspoon salt

Zest of ¼ orange

FOR THE CREAM

2 cups heavy cream

½ teaspoon vanilla extract

1 tablespoon sugar

To make the crust: Combine the chestnut flour, all-purpose flour, salt, and sugar in a mixing bowl. Whisk to incorporate. Cut the butter into small pieces and add it to the mixing bowl. Cut the butter into the flours until it resembles coarse meal. Pour 2 tablespoons of cream into the bowl and bring the dough together in your hands quickly with a bit of force. Wrap it in a dish towel and let it rest in the refrigerator for 20 minutes.

To make the filling: Preheat the oven to 350°F. In a medium saucepan, combine the cream and milk. Bring it to a simmer and turn off the heat. Whisk the chocolate into the saucepan, melting it fully. In a medium mixing bowl, whisk the eggs and sugar vigorously until they become light and frothy. After the chocolate and cream has cooled slightly, slowly whisk it into the mixing bowl. Add the vanilla, salt, and orange zest. Mix until the filling has an even texture.

In the bowl of a stand mixer, combine the heavy cream, vanilla, and sugar. Whip the cream to soft peaks and chill.

Remove the dough from the fridge and roll it out between two pieces of parchment paper. Lay the dough over a 9-inch shallow pie dish (a French fluted pie dish with a removable bottom is best). Set it into the dish, allowing the excess to come up over the edges. If using a fluted pie dish, cut away the edges. If using a traditional pie dish, crimp the edges around the outside of the crust with your hands or a fork. Pour the chocolate filling into the pie dish. It shouldn't be full to the brim but should have at least a half inch to rise. Place it in the oven for 55 minutes, or until set. Remove and let cool for 45 minutes. Serve slightly warm with a little whipped cream.

ACKNOWLEDGMENTS

As with anything, it's always easier to write a cookbook the second time around. The team at Roost Books made my first book, *Full Moon Suppers at Salt Water Farm*, such a pleasure to create that I knew *Modern Country Cooking* would be a wonderful next step. I am forever grateful for my photographer, Kristin Teig, who came all the way from Los Angeles to Maine on several occasions to shoot this book. In a decade of working together, we have built not only a fantastic friendship but also an incredible archive of imagery that tells the story of Salt Water Farm so beautifully. And thanks to Frances Bateman and Emily Seymour for their much-needed support on our photoshoot days (and hand modeling). Good writing is largely a product of good editing. My generous editor, Jennifer Brown, helped to shape this book into a useful tool and allowed me to keep my authentic voice throughout the chapters. All books begin with a good idea, a concept that is the first of its kind and genuinely appealing to the market. Sara Bercholz, publisher of Roost, helped me to find a compelling angle for the book, effectively turning hundreds of cooking-school lectures into instructive lessons and complementary recipes. Truthfully, I couldn't have created this book without my students, who, unbeknownst to them, acted as my recipe testers, their eager hands and minds helping me to tweak measurements and directions. Finally, thanks to my husband for minding our baby and vacuuming the house, which allowed me to spend more time in the kitchen.

Roost Books
An imprint of Shambhala Publications, Inc.
4720 Walnut Street
Boulder, Colorado 80301
roostbooks.com

© 2020 by Annemarie Ahearn
Photographs by Kristin Teig

9 8 7 6 5 4 3 2 1

First Edition
Printed in China

♾ This edition is printed on acid-free paper that
meets the American National Standards Institute
Z39.48 Standard.
♻ Shambhala Publications makes every effort to
print on recycled paper. For more information
please visit www.shambhala.com.
Roost Books is distributed worldwide by Penguin
Random House, Inc., and its subsidiaries.

Designed by Ian Dingman

Library of Congress Cataloging-in-Publication
Data
Names: Ahearn, Annemarie, author. | Teig,
Kristin, photographer.
Title: Modern country cooking: kitchen skills and
seasonal recipes from salt water farm / Annemarie
Ahearn; photographs by Kristin Teig.
Description: Boulder: Roost Books, 2020. |
Includes index.
Identifiers: LCCN 2019007675 | ISBN
9781611806540 (hardcover: alk. paper)
Subjects: LCSH: Cooking, American. | LCGFT:
Cookbooks.
Classification: LCC TX715 .A253 2020 | DDC
641.5973—dc23
LC record available at https://lccn.loc.
gov/2019007675